THE SENIOR'S QUICK AND EASY GUIDEBOOK TO USING COMPUTERS, SMARTPHONES, AND THE INTERNET

You Don't Have to Be a Rocket Scientist!

Publisher's Note

This book is intended for general information only. It does not constitute medical, legal, or financial advice or practice. The editors of FC&A have taken careful measures to ensure the accuracy and usefulness of the information in this book. While every attempt has been made to assure accuracy, errors may occur. Some websites, addresses, and telephone numbers may have changed since printing. We cannot guarantee the safety or effectiveness of any advice or treatments mentioned. Readers are urged to consult with their professional financial advisors, lawyers, and health care professionals before making any changes.

Any health information in this book is for information only and is not intended to be a medical guide for self-treatment. It does not constitute medical advice and should not be construed as such or used in place of your doctor's medical advice. Readers are urged to consult with their health care professionals before undertaking therapies suggested by the information in this book, keeping in mind that errors in the text may occur as in all publications and that new findings may supersede older information.

The publisher and editors disclaim all liability (including any injuries, damages, or losses) resulting from the use of the information in this book.

The Lord bless you and keep you; the Lord make his face shine on you and be gracious to you; the Lord turn his face toward you and give you peace.

Numbers 6: 24-26 (NIV)

FC&A Publishing®
103 Clover Green
Peachtree City, GA 30269

Produced by the staff of FC&A

ISBN 978-1935574842

Table of Contents

Search smarter, better, and faster with Google 210

Email — an easy way to stay in touch. 221

Top tips to navigate social media 234

Know your system to compute like a pro

Get to know your operating system

The computer industry is not only one of the most widely used around the world, it also has a dazzling array of jargon and acronyms. From RAM to iOS, to cloud computing and streaming services, it is easy to feel swamped by the terminology that is part of using digital devices and services.

But help is at hand. This chapter looks at the terms for the software used to power computing devices — aka the operating system (OS) — and the apps you use on them, so that you're ready to fully embrace the digital world.

What is an operating system? It's the software that gets your computing devices up and running and enables the apps to run on them properly. All computing devices have an operating system and the ones used in the book are:

- Windows 10 for Windows desktop computers, also known as Personal Computers (PCs), and laptops.

- macOS Catalina for Mac computers such as the iMac desktop and MacBook laptops.

- iPadOS 13 for the iPad tablet.

- iOS 13 for the iPhone smartphone.

- Android for tablets and smartphones, other than the iPad and the iPhone. The Android operating system is unique in that it has several versions being used at any given time. This is because manufacturers can put whichever version of Android they want on their devices. The latest version is Android 10, but versions 7 and 8 are the most widely used. The good news is that there is little difference in the main functions of the different versions of Android.

The top systems you need to know. Here's a basic rundown of the various operating systems you should be familiar with.

- Windows. Created by Microsoft, Windows has powered most of the world's desktop and laptop computers since its introduction in 1985. They've created numerous versions over the years, and Windows 10 is the successor to Windows 8 (there was no Windows 9). It was Microsoft's first attempt to produce an operating system that could be used for both PCs and mobile devices.

  Unfortunately, Windows 8 was an awkward combination of two functions that failed to fully satisfy either of the groups it was looking to impress. Windows 10 was released with some of the traditional features of Windows reinstated, and it is a much more familiar environment for the desktop computer and laptop user.

  One of the features of Windows 10 is that it is updated online in incremental updates rather than as a whole new operating system. This is why there are no plans for a Windows 11 version. This method enables Microsoft to keep Windows 10 as up to date as possible.

- macOS. This operating system is used on Apple's desktop and laptop computers. These include the iMac desktop, the Mac Mini, which does not include a monitor, and the MacBook range of laptops. macOS is the successor to the OS X (pronounced 10) operating system and is based on the UNIX system, which is renowned for its stability.

- iPadOS. If you have an iPad tablet, then iPadOS is the operating system you're using. Previously, the iPad used the same operating system as the iPhone, but it now has its own unique option, although it remains very similar to iOS. The latest version of the iPad operating system is iPadOS 13.

- iOS. This is the operating system that is used by the Apple iPhone. Each new version of the operating system has a sequential number, and the latest version is iOS 13.

- Android. Google owns this operating system. It is similar to iPadOS and iOS in that it is used widely on tablets and smartphones. But it has one very important difference. Android is what is known as an open-source operating system, which means manufacturers can customize it, to a certain extent, on their own devices.

  This results in dozens of different varieties of Android, meaning Android on a Samsung smartphone will look different than Android on an HTC tablet. Not only can manufacturers customize the way Android looks, they can also add their own apps to the standard ones produced by Google.

A closer look

Trying out new things and making mistakes is how you'll discover new tips and learn more about your devices. But if you make a mistake you absolutely have to fix, don't despair. You actually have a special "undo" key on your computer. It will correct all sorts of "oops" moments — from bringing something out of the trash to reopening a closed browser tab. Removed some text by mistake? Just press Ctrl+Z (Command+Z on a Mac) and the damage is repaired. Keep doing this to go back multiple steps. It's that easy.

┌─ **Money-saver** ─────────────────────────────────────┐

New versions of smartphones and tablets are usually released
once a year, and these are inevitably the most expensive. To
avoid paying top dollar, look at models that are a year or two
older than the newest releases. These will still be extremely
powerful and sophisticated, and you may be able to snap up
some bargains, particularly if you buy them around the time
the latest models are released.

└───┘

Updates — the key to good performance

The most important thing to remember about your operating system
is to keep it up to date.

Computer companies issue regular updates to their devices' operating systems. A new version is released approximately once every
year and other, smaller, updates are issued as required. (Although,
for Windows, the annual update still goes by the name of Windows
10, even though it may have an additional reference name.)

The smaller updates are usually to fix any bugs that have been
identified or security issues that have arisen. It is best to keep your
devices as up to date as possible in terms of the operating system,
to keep them as secure as possible and running smoothly. To look
for operating system updates on different devices:

- On a Windows desktop or laptop, look in Settings > Update
  & Security. It is also possible to schedule a time for automatic
  updates in this section.

- On a Mac computer, look in System Preferences >
  Software Update.

- On an iPad or iPhone, look in Settings > General >
  Software Update.

- On an Android tablet or smartphone, look in Settings > Advanced > System Update. This can vary between Android devices, and updates sometimes appear in Settings > About device.

7 tips to get up and running in the digital world

Does the thought of learning new computer skills seem daunting — even a little scary? Fear not. The information throughout this book will help you understand a range of computing devices, including desktop computers, laptops, tablets, and smartphones. But first, here are some basic steps to follow to help you get up and running in the digital world.

Take your time. Computing devices can be frustrating at times. However, if you try and rush what you are doing, or get annoyed, this will only slow you down in the long run.

Expect things to go wrong. It is a fact of life that computers don't always behave as they should. While this can be another source of frustration, if you accept this is going to happen at times, then you can get on with trying to fix the problem.

Learn the settings. All computers have a selection of settings that can be used to manage and customize them. If you become familiar with these at the start then you will have an excellent foundation for taking control of your computing world.

Be organized. Just as in the real world, it is usually easier to work in the digital world if everything is neat and tidy. Keep your devices clean and free from dust, and make sure you use a folder structure on a desktop computer or laptop to keep everything in a logical place. This will make it much easier to find something when you are looking for it in the future.

Experiment. Trying new things is how you will discover new functions on your computing devices, and a few tips and tricks, too.

An easy way to teach yourself to use the computer in the privacy of your home is through websites like *linkedinlearning.com* and *Youtube.com*. They have plenty of tutorials that will walk you through anything you'd like to learn.

Save everything as you work on it. One of the worst computer experiences you can have is losing what you are working on. Don't worry — everyone has experienced this at one time or another.

The first step to avoiding this is to make sure you save everything as you go along. Don't wait until you have finished working on your document to save it. Do it at regular intervals, using the File > Save command from the menu bar, or the keyboard shortcut Ctrl+S (Command+S on a Mac).

Back up your documents. In addition to saving everything as you go along, backing it up is equally important, if not more so. This involves copying files from your computer onto an external device that is kept away from the computer. If something happens to the computer then you will still have a copy of your precious photos and documents.

Caution

Some apps have an option called "in-app purchases." The app may be free to download, but if you want to use additional features, you'll need to pay for them. Manufacturers are hoping you'll enjoy using the app enough to pony up the cash.

A lot of apps with in-app purchases are games apps, but more and more other types of apps are offering this, too. Make sure you understand exactly what you're getting when you download the app.

Understanding apps — the lifeblood of your system

App, short for application, is just a modern name for what was traditionally called a computer program. Apps are essential for performing all of the common tasks on desktop computers, laptops, tablets, and smartphones. They can be used for organization, entertainment, communication, research, photography, and much, much more.

In terms of your devices, there are three main types of apps to consider.

Pre-installed apps. These will be installed on your device when you buy it. They provide the type of options you would expect — address book, calendar, note-taking app, email app, and a browser for accessing the internet. (Web browsers are apps in the same way as any others.)

In addition you'll find entertainment apps for listening to music or watching movies, a messaging app for sending text messages, an app for making video calls, and a phone app on smartphones for making calls.

Pre-installed apps will provide more than enough options for getting started with your device and, in a lot of cases, these may be all that you require for your day-to-day computing needs.

Apps from an app store. Apps are huge business in the computing world and all of the main players — Apple, Microsoft, and Google — have their own stores for downloading more apps to your devices. You'll find thousands of apps available, covering a huge range of topics. If you can't find an app for one of your hobbies or interests, then it will be a very niche topic.

All devices have a related app store. The Apple app store serves Apple devices, the Microsoft store handles Windows 10 devices, and the Google Play Store is your pick if you own an Android device. In each case, you will require a free account with the relevant service, but this can be created when you first start using your device.

Once you have a user account, you can access the relevant app store, browse the store to see what is available (either by looking through the separate categories of apps or by using a search box to look for specific topics) and download any apps that you want to use on your device.

Third-party apps. Beware of downloading apps that are not pre-installed or come from your device's linked app store. You'll find many out there, but they can be a security risk.

If you use an app from a non-verified source there is more chance it could contain a virus or malware (malicious software) that could do great harm to your device. Of course, apps from recognized app stores are not immune from viruses, but there is less of a risk than from a third-party site.

Money-saver

Many apps in the app stores are free, so if you are looking for an app for a particular task, such as note-taking, don't be afraid to download several to see which you like best. Once you have made your choice, you can remove the apps you don't want.

Some free apps also have a premium version, which is a paid-for version with added features. In most cases the free version should have enough features for what you want to do.

Put your newfound knowledge to work

Once you've become familiar with your computer system, you're ready to put it to work. And what better way to use it than to help you save money? Here are 12 ways to do that.

Take advantage of comparison websites. When you want to buy anything online, have a look at a comparison website so that you can get the best price. Two to check out are Shopzilla at *shopzilla.com* and PriceGrabber at *pricegrabber.com*.

Use auction sites. Websites such as eBay will get you bargains on a huge range of goods, and also allow you to sell your own items to make a bit more money.

Find daily bargains. Go to DealNews at *dealnews.com* for hundreds of bargains on items such as clothing, computers, furniture, and garden supplies.

Collect coupons. If you like the idea of collecting coupons to save money on your grocery shopping, have a look at *coupons.com* for printable and digital coupons. You'll also find coupon codes and an option to add receipts to your online coupon account.

Money-saver

If you want to find money-off bargains and deals at your local supermarkets and stores, apps can help. Here's how to pay the rock-bottom price on everything you buy. It's easier than you think.

- The Slickdeals app finds the best daily bargains, based on users posting details about a range of money-saving deals. If you register with the app, which is free, you can customize the offers to ones in your own area, or specific products. Check out the website at *slickdeals.net*.

- The RetailMeNot app offers money-off coupons and other bargains for a range of stores. Look for it at *RetailMeNot.com*.

- The Flipp app enables you to select stores in your area to view the latest special offers. Its website is *flipp.com*.

Locate secret deals on Amazon. For the best bargains on Amazon, take a look in the Amazon Warehouse section. This contains good value products, usually from independent sellers.

Enter "Amazon Warehouse" into the search box at the top of the Amazon home page to locate the Warehouse. When buying items here, check their condition before you make a purchase. This will include New, Like New, Very Good, and Acceptable.

Another option on Amazon is the Amazon Outlet section, where there are thousands of bargains on overstocked items. Enter "Amazon Outlet" into the search box to find it.

Download free software. Access a huge range of free software at the website *softpedia.com*.

Make the most of email. Use email whenever you can instead of spending money on postage. Most companies or organizations have an email address, which can usually be found on their website.

Print greeting cards and invitations. Instead of paying for expensive cards or invitations, you can print your own on a home printer for a fraction of the cost.

Use live chat when negotiating. When you are looking for a new deal for your cable, phone, or internet, try the live chat option on a company's website instead of calling them. You may feel more confident about asking for a better rate if you're not dealing with someone directly over the phone.

Also, when options are written down, it gives you more time to assess them, rather than having to make a quick decision when you are talking to someone.

Take advantage of free movies. In addition to the major online streaming services for movies, such as Netflix and Amazon Prime Video, there are also some companies that offer free options.

Understandably, these are not as extensive as the subscription services, but they're free. Two to have a look at are Crackle at *crackle.com*, and Popcornflix at *popcornflix.com*.

Enjoy free music. Most subscription services offer a free trial, usually up to three months. If you use this, remember to cancel before the end of the free trial if you do not want to continue. Otherwise you will start being charged.

Also, several sites offer free music, but make sure they are legitimate. If you use an illegal site, not only will you break the law, you will also run the risk of viruses infecting your computer. Enter "legal free music" into Google to see some of the options.

Read books for free. Reading provides a rich vein of free content on the internet. Several companies offer a large range of free material, such as Manybooks at *manybooks.net* and Free-eBooks at *free-ebooks.net*.

Another excellent option is Project Gutenberg at *gutenberg.org*, which has over 60,000 free titles, including a large collection of classic literature for which the copyright has expired, so they can be read for free.

You can read more about your free entertainment choices in the chapter *Entertainment magic — stream movies, music, and more.*

A closer look

Save your fingers and stop typing "www" at the beginning of every web address. Gone are the days of typing long URLs (which stands for unique resource locator). Just enter the name of the site in the address bar of a web browser — for example, *fca.com* — and it will identify the page. How easy is that?

7 top websites seniors need to bookmark

Whatever device or app you use, the web remains one of the best resources for information on almost anything you're interested in. For most topics, you'll find sites tailored specifically to seniors. Search for a topic online and add "for seniors" to view the options.

In the meantime, here are seven websites that every senior should have in their "bookmarks" or "favorites." They can save you money and perhaps even save your life.

- AARP (formerly the American Association of Retired Persons) at *aarp.org*. This site contains a wide range of content relating to seniors. It includes topics such as health, work, volunteering, retirement, travel, money, entertainment, food, and fraud issues to avoid. It charges a subscription fee, but a lot of the content on the site can be viewed without a membership.

- Social Security Administration at *ssa.gov*. The official U.S. government website covering social security, including information on retirement and Medicare.

- National Institute on Aging at *nia.nih.gov*. Another official government site that provides a wealth of information about health issues. Type a keyword into the Search box on the home page to see all the related content.

- SeniorCitizenDiscountlist at *seniorcitizendiscountlist.org*. This lists a wide range of shopping discounts for seniors, which can be accessed for individual states.

- Workforce 50 at *workforce50.com*. Aimed at the 50+ workforce, this site has a directory of available positions that can be searched for using the range of search tools, including a Quick Job Search by State option.

- Senior Planet at *seniorplanet.org*. A site that promotes Aging with Attitude, with articles and resources covering subjects including news, health, dating, senior style, travel, and entertainment.

- RetiredBrains at *retiredbrains.com*. This is a multipurpose site for seniors, covering topics from travel and entertainment, to money and health.

A closer look

It can be frustrating to repeatedly access the same menu commands for simple, repetitive tasks. Instead, try these six basic Windows keyboard shortcuts everyone should use but few even know about. On a Mac, use the Cmd key rather than the Ctrl key.

- Save a document — Ctrl+S

- Copy an item — Ctrl+C

- Cut an item — Ctrl+X

- Paste an item — Ctrl+V

- Undo the previous action — Ctrl+Z

- Close a document — Ctrl+W

The expert's guide to understanding your device

Quick fix for hardware problems

Hardware devices include desktop computers, laptops, tablets, and smartphones, which all have screens so you can see what is being produced by the computer. Other hardware devices include printers and a range of computing accessories. Anything that you can hold and contributes to your daily computing activities is considered computing hardware.

If a hardware device is acting up and not working properly, be it a desktop computer, laptop, tablet, or smartphone, there is one simple trick you should do first that may fix the problem right away — turn it off and turn it back on again.

This is a cliché of the computing world, but a lot of times it does work, and it just might save you time, money, and hassle. Computers are complex devices, and sometimes they just need a chance to reorder everything and start again.

Another option is to press the Esc key on the keyboard twice in quick succession. This can sometimes remove a blockage that prevents an app from working properly on a desktop or laptop computer.

7 computer tech terms you need to know

As with every other area of computing, hardware devices are not short of their own jargon and terminology. However, once you understand it, you can make more informed decisions about which hardware is best for your needs. This is particularly important if you are looking to buy a new one. Here are some of the terms you need to know.

Processor. This determines the speed at which operations are performed on the device. The quicker the processor, the faster the device should work. The speed of processors is usually measured in gigahertz (GHz) and the higher the number, the faster the processor. Look for a minimum of 2GHz.

Memory. Also known as Random Access Memory (RAM), it determines how quickly operations can be performed on a device by managing the operating system and any apps that are being used. RAM is not the same as the storage capacity of a device, which is sometimes also called memory.

In some ways RAM can affect the speed of the device more than the processor. Having several apps open at the same time can slow down the device if it does not have enough memory, as it's trying to perform too many operations at once. RAM is usually measured in gigabytes (GB) — look for a minimum of 8GB.

A closer look

If you are going to spend money on upgrading one item on a desktop computer or laptop, make it the RAM. This will improve the overall performance and operation of the device. When you buy a new computing device, including tablets and smartphones, try and get one with as much RAM as you can afford.

Storage. This relates to the physical storage capacity on your device, in terms of how much content can be saved onto it. This is measured in gigabytes or terabytes (TB).

The storage capacity of computers is one area which has expanded at a great rate in recent years, partly to deal with the increase in the size of files such as videos, photos, and music that are now increasingly stored on computers. Look for a minimum of 512GB of storage for a desktop computer or laptop.

Graphics card. Also known as a video card or display card, this is a piece of hardware that manages and displays graphical elements on a computer, from photos to animations for playing games.

Ports and slots. Desktop computers and laptops have a range of ports and slots around the body of the device, which can be used to connect external devices, also known as peripherals.

These include USB slots for connecting devices with a USB cable, such as a USB flash drive for storing files; an Ethernet slot for connecting to the internet with an Ethernet cable; and a DVD/CD player and/or writer for playing media DVDs and CDs and also copying information onto them.

Battery. For laptops, tablets, and smartphones, battery life is an important issue. Every computer user wants a battery that lasts as long as possible, but the time it takes to charge a battery is also critical.

Look at the spec for battery life for talk time (on a smartphone); standby, when the device is on but not being used; surfing the web; and playing videos and music. If possible, try and use mobile computing devices while they are connected to main power, to save battery usage.

Caution

The latest version of USB is USB 3.2. If you have the updated port, you will still be able to use devices with earlier USB versions. There is also a USB-C version, which is significantly faster at transferring data than USB 3.2, but it uses a different type of port. You'll need an adapter for non USB-C devices.

Connectivity. This refers to the method for connecting to other networks or devices. The two main ones to look for are Wi-Fi, for connecting to the internet, and Bluetooth.

The latest version of the Wi-Fi standard is known as 802.11ac (the "ac" is the part that changes when a new standard is available). The latest version of Bluetooth is Bluetooth 5.0, and this can be used to share data over short distances, and connect compatible devices.

A closer look

Data on computing devices is measured in bits (binary digits). This is the smallest unit of digital data and has a value of either 1 or 0. Larger units of data are multiples of bits as follows:

- Byte = 8 bits

- Kilobyte (KB) = 1,024 bytes

- Megabyte (MB) = 1,024 kilobytes

- Gigabyte (GB) = 1,024 megabytes

- Terabyte (TB) = 1,024 gigabytes

To translate that into the real world of computing: a plain text email would consist of approximately 2KB, while a one-hour movie, with suitable compression, would be about 4GB.

Tablets and smartphones — a whole new learning curve

Although tablets and smartphones are relative newcomers in the world of computer technology, they have quickly become established and developed a language all their own. If you buy a tablet or smartphone, here are some terms you need to be familiar with.

Touch screen. This is both the screen for viewing content on tablets and smartphones, and also the way in which commands are relayed to the devices. Instead of using an input device, such as a mouse or keyboard, you perform commands by tapping, swiping, and pinching on the screen. The touch screen also displays a virtual keyboard, which appears at the bottom of the screen when you need to enter text or data.

Home screen. This is the screen that first appears when you turn on the device. It is where all the device's apps are initially located. As you add more apps and the home screen fills up, another one can be accessed.

Home button. A button on tablets and smartphones that can be used to return to the Home screen, usually by clicking it once. It can also perform other functions depending on how many times it is clicked. Some smartphones have now removed the Home button, and its functions have been replaced by a range of gestures on the screen.

Fingerprint sensor. As a security feature, tablets and smartphones have a Lock screen, which can be used to prevent unauthorized access to the device. In some cases you need to create a passcode to unlock the screen. Another option is to unlock a device with a fingerprint sensor, which is incorporated into the Home button. Once a fingerprint has been recorded, it is used as authorization for unlocking the device.

A closer look

When buying a smartphone, look to see if it has a fast-charging function, for example, the time it takes for up to 50% of the battery to be charged. This can be invaluable if you have to charge your smartphone when you are away from home and you only have a limited amount of time.

Face recognition. Used mainly on smartphones, it is similar to fingerprint recognition, except that face recognition enables unlocking of a smartphone simply by looking at the camera at the top of the device's Home screen. This is generally only available on the most recent smartphones, but it is a highly effective way to secure your device.

Tapping. This is the method you use to access items on a tablet or smartphone. You open apps by tapping on them, and buttons, such as a Save button, are also activated by tapping. Some functions can be performed by double-tapping rather than a single tap.

Swiping. This is how you move up and down the screen when there is more content than can be displayed on a single screen. You'll use it a lot when viewing web pages or long text documents.

Spreading and pinching. Do you want to zoom in or out on a web page or photo, or view it in more detail? To do this, hold your thumb and forefinger together on the screen and then spread them diagonally, towards opposite corners on the screen. To zoom back in, hold your thumb and forefinger apart, at diagonal corners, and pinch them together towards the center.

Text speak. Text messaging is a popular use for smartphones, and this has created a whole language of abbreviations and shortcuts, known as text speak. If you've seen abbreviations like LOL for Laugh Out Loud or FOMO for Fear of Missing Out, that's an example of text speak.

Emojis. Another aspect of text messaging is the inclusion of emojis. These are small graphical symbols that are usually used for humorous effect in text messages. They are also used to convey the emotions of the sender, which can sometimes be unclear in a plain text message.

Selfies. One of the functions that has advanced the use of smartphones is their ability to take selfies. These are self portraits, usually taken with a sense of humor rather than as a serious photographic portrait.

Taking selfies on a smartphone is easy because the phone has two cameras, both front-facing and back-facing. When you want to take a picture of yourself, you use the back-facing camera, which you get to by tapping the camera icon. You'll see yourself on the screen once the camera has opened.

Selfie stick. This serves as an extension to the smartphone, so you can take a selfie with a greater amount of background. It's especially useful if you want to include a landmark in the background of the photo, or for larger groups of people.

A closer look

Before buying a computer or tablet, it's helpful to look at the specifications (specs) to learn how fast they process information, their storage capacity, and their methods for connecting to the internet.

Your best bet is to check the manufacturers' websites for all the technical details. Also, websites such as *cnet.com*, *pcmag.com*, *zdnet.com*, and *pcworld.com* regularly review new devices and can help you compare similar models.

The world of computer accessories

Every industry has its own range of gadgets and accessories, and the digital industry is no different. Here are a few computer accessories you may find essential.

USB flash drive. A flash drive, also called a thumb drive, has become an indispensable accessory for many computer users. It is about the size of a packet of gum, is inexpensive, and can hold large amounts of data.

A flash drive is an excellent option for backing up your photos and documents, and it can give you additional peace of mind to know it's stored separately from your computer. Also, because it's so small, it's easy to take with you.

You can buy a 32GB flash drive on *Amazon.com* for $6, and a 128GB for $14. That should be more than enough to back up or transfer your important photos and documents. If not, just buy a larger one.

External hard drive. This is a step up from a USB flash drive in terms of storage. Like a flash drive it connects via a USB port and can hold huge amounts of data. An external hard drive on Amazon costs in the range of $50 for 2 terabytes (TB).

The main advantage to an external drive is it can be used to back up your whole operating system for Windows or macOS. For Windows this is done through Settings > Update & Security > Backup; for macOS it is done with the Time Machine backup app.

Wireless mouse and keyboard. Without a wire attached to your mouse and keyboard, you can position yourself where you like and, most importantly, where you are most comfortable.

These devices generally connect via Bluetooth and have to be "paired," that is the computer has to recognize the accessory so that it can work properly. Ensure that Bluetooth is turned on before you start using your wireless mouse or keyboard.

A handy guide to printers

A printer is an important addition to your digital hardware, whether you want to print out family photos, a page from the web, or a hard copy of a letter. As with most things in the digital world, there are different types to consider.

- Inkjet printers. They can be used for black and white documents, color documents, and also photos, for which photo-quality paper is the best option. The ink is placed onto the paper using nozzles connected to the ink cartridges.

- Wireless printers. These printers connect to your Wi-Fi network so they don't have to be physically connected to your computing device. The printer can then be accessed from a computer that is connected to the same Wi-Fi network. Some wireless printers are also designed to work with mobile devices, so you can print to them directly from your tablet or smartphone.

- Laser printers. These are generally for printing in black and white. Color laser printers are available but are expensive. Lasers are fast and print documents at a high quality. You may want to consider one if you do a lot of black and white printing.

First things first — connect your driver. When you connect your printer to a desktop computer or laptop, the computer may recognize the printer automatically and install the elements required for them to communicate with each other, known as drivers.

If this does not happen, the printer can be installed manually. On a Windows 10 device, go to Settings > Devices > Printers & scanners, and click on the *Add a printer or scanner* button. On a Mac computer with macOS Catalina, go to System Preferences > Printers & Scanners, and click on the + button at the bottom of the *Printers* panel.

Ink — get it cheap and make it last. The most expensive part of the printing process is undoubtedly the ink. In fact, ink for your printer can cost more than vintage champagne at the store, so it pays to look for discounted ink online. Just make sure the cartridges are compatible with your printer. Here are some more great ink-saving tips.

- Only print what you need.

- For inkjet printers, use separate color cartridges for each color. If one color runs out, you only have to replace one cartridge.

- Use a bookmarklet app when printing web pages. This will allow you to print the info you want from a website without wasting expensive ink and paper on stuff you don't want, like ads and banner content. The different apps can be downloaded for free from their respective websites. Once they are downloaded they reside on your browser, displaying a button for printing web content. Two bookmarklet apps to look at are *printwhatyoulike.com* and *printfriendly.com*.

- Ignore your printer if it says it is out of ink. Just keep printing until it actually runs out — you could save up to 40% of your ink. Sometimes a gentle shake can free up more ink, too. In some cases a sensor on the side of the printer cartridge will claim the printer is out of ink. Cover this with a small piece of black tape to disable it, and keep using your printer. That's a simple way to get more life out of your ink cartridges.

Money-saver

The nozzles in inkjet printers can get blocked, which results in poor performance in terms of streaks and faintness. Try to solve this, and extend the life of your cartridges, by running the head cleaner function. Check your printer's manual (or online help) for how to access it. It should be through the printer's own control panel, or through the printer's app on your computer.

Learn how to use your printer to its best advantage

Having a home printer is not just a great way to print out text documents like letters and forms, you can also use it to print a whole range of interesting stationery items, such as invitations, greeting cards, business cards — even photos. Here's how to print invitations to your next get-together.

1. Buy the required size of paper or card. Or cut a larger piece of paper or card to size.

2. Place the paper in your printer, using the paper tray guides to hold it in place.

3. Open a new document in your word processing app on your desktop computer or laptop.

4. For Word, access Page Layout > Size from the menu bar.

5. In the *Width* and *Height* boxes, enter the dimensions of the paper.

6. Select Page Layout > Margins and enter a margin size as required.

7. Enter the text for the item as required.

8. Access the Print dialog box using the File > Print command from the menu bar.

9. In the Print dialog box, select a *Paper Type* and *Paper Size* that matches the item you are printing (depending on the type of printer, these options may be available from the *Properties* button).

10. Click on the *OK* button to print the item.

If you want to print photos, use a color inkjet printer and photo-quality paper. This is a thick, glossy paper that is similar to the paper used in commercial photo printing.

Have a look at the website LCI Paper at *lcipaper.com* for a wide range of specialty papers, envelopes, and cards that you can use to print your own items.

Money-saver

Some printers have a function for scanning and copying documents, but these printers are more expensive than standard ones. Save yourself some money by using the scanner you already have, in the form of your tablet or smartphone.

You can find several scanning apps to use with iPad OS/iOS or Android devices to scan documents and save them as PDF (Portable Document Format) files. A PDF retains the original formatting of a document and is designed to be compatible with different devices and operating systems. Have a look at the scanning apps Scanbot or Tiny Scanner from either the Apple App Store or the Google Play Store.

Master the 10 most useful computer skills

Let's face it — the computer has become a common household appliance. You can use it for just about anything once you get comfortable with it. Here are 10 invaluable computer skills that will have you working like an expert once you've mastered them.

Selecting text or files. Once text or files have been selected, you can perform many different actions. But how do you select them in the first place? For text, hold down the mouse button and drag the cursor over the text. For files, click on them in your file management software (File Explorer for Windows, and Finder for Mac). That's it, the item will be selected.

Cut, Copy, Paste. Three of the most useful actions for selected text or files are Cut, Copy, or Paste. These can be accessed from the menu bar, usually from the Edit menu, or keyboard shortcuts can be used: Ctrl+X to cut an item; Ctrl+C to copy an item; and Ctrl+V to paste an item. (On a Mac, use the Command key instead of the Ctrl key.)

Printing. Use the print command to print the current document. This is done with File > Print from the menu bar, or the keyboard shortcut Ctrl+P (Windows), or Command+P (Mac). Within the Print dialog window, click on the *Properties* or *Preferences* button to access options for managing the printer, such as selecting the paper size, the orientation, and the print quality.

Backing up an address book. If you want your address book of contacts to always be backed up and available, use an online cloud service. Windows backs up content to its OneDrive cloud service, Apple uses the iCloud service, and Android devices can use the Google Account backup service. Once you set this up, your address book and a range of other content will automatically be backed up and saved in this way.

Uninstalling unwanted apps. What was previously called a computer program now generally goes by the generic name of an app. If you want to get rid of any apps from your computer, click on the Start button, right-click on an app on the Start menu and click on *Uninstall* (Windows). Or for Mac, drag an app from the Applications folder in the Finder over the Trash icon on the Dock.

Copying files to an external device. If you want to copy files from your computer, use a USB flash drive. These are inexpensive, convenient, and can store large amounts of data.

Plug the flash drive into an available USB port on your computer, and copy the files from the File Explorer (Windows) or Finder (Mac). Another option is to burn (copy) files onto a CD, although this method has been largely overtaken by the USB flash drive.

Searching the internet. Google is still the first port of call for many people for searching for content on the internet. In addition to text searches, Google can also do so much more — voice searches, translations, flight tracking, and identifying song lyrics, to name a few.

Downloading files from the internet. If you see a link on a web page to download a file, click on it to load it to your computer. Look in the *Downloads* folder in either File Explorer (Windows) or Finder (Mac) to access the item.

Attaching files to email. You can do more with email than just send text. You can attach longer documents as well as photos and videos. When you are composing an email, click on the paperclip icon to attach a file to the email.

And if you want to be doubly sure you don't forget to attach your file, do it before you write the text. Numerous emails have been sent saying "Have a look at this attachment" when no attachment is included.

Using Windows Administrative Tools. It always pays dividends to try and keep your computer working as efficiently as possible. With Windows, you can access some of these options from the *Windows Administrative Tools* button on the Start menu. Two to look at are *Disk Cleanup* and *Defragment and Optimize Drives*.

Set yourself up for computing success

Settings — what they are and why you need them

Although they are not the most exciting aspect of the digital world, settings are one of the first things you should investigate when you start using any new device. Think of the settings as a multipurpose tool that can be used to fix some of the problems your computing devices may have. They can also redesign certain elements of its appearance so you can customize it exactly as you want.

The best way to find out about the settings on your devices, and what they can do, is to access them and explore the various categories and options.

Where to find settings. Each type of computing device will have its own unique settings, but they are accessed in a similar way regardless of the device being used.

The icon for accessing settings on desktop computers, laptops, tablets, and smartphones is the gear symbol. The design can vary slightly between devices and manufacturers, but it is the most widely used icon for settings.

On different devices the settings icon is accessed as follows:

- Windows 10 desktops and laptops. Click on the gear icon on the Taskbar at the bottom of any screen within Windows. Also, click on the Start menu icon in the bottom, left-hand corner of the screen, ⊞ and click on the *Settings* tile on the Start menu.

- Mac computers and MacBooks. On Mac devices, using macOS Catalina, the settings are known as System Preferences and are accessed from this icon on the Dock at the bottom of the screen.

- iPad and iPhone. Tap on this icon on the home screen of an iPad or an iPhone.

- Android tablets and smartphones. For Android devices, tap on this icon on the home screen.

How to make them your own. While settings can be used to apply important functions, they are also a great way to customize your devices. Here are some of the ways you can do it.

- On a Windows device, use the *Personalization* setting to change the appearance of certain elements of Windows including a background image for the Desktop, an image for the lock screen, and the overall color scheme used by Windows.

- On a Mac device, use the *General* option in System Preferences to change the overall appearance of the operating system including colors for buttons, menus, scroll bars, and windows.

- On an iPad or iPhone, use the *Wallpaper* setting to change the background image for the home screen and also the lock screen (these can be the same image for both, or different ones).

- On an Android tablet or smartphone, use the *Wallpaper* setting in the same way as an iPad or iPhone, and use the *Display* setting to change the brightness of the screen and also the size of text.

Personalize your Windows settings

The Windows settings contain a wealth of options for taking control over how your version of Windows looks and operates. To investigate the available settings:

1. Access the main *Settings* page from the icon on the Taskbar, or on the Start menu.

2. Click in the *Find a setting* box to look for a specific setting or topic.

3. Click on one of the main categories to view the options.

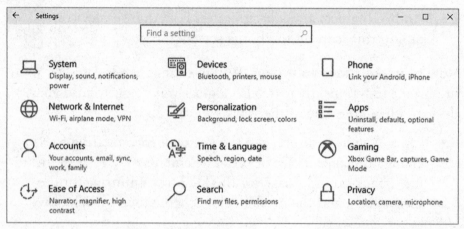

4. Check the options within each category listed in the left-hand panel.

5. Click on one of the items in the left-hand panel, for example *Display*, to view the options for it in the main window.

6. Click on the *Home* button from any category to return to the main settings window.

Here are some of the main Windows settings you should be familiar with, and how you can use them.

System — edit a range of options for how the computer operates, including the display, sounds used by the computer, how notifications are managed when an alert sounds, and options for when the computer is turned off or put into sleep mode.

Devices — add more devices to increase the functionality of the computer, such as adding the required elements when a printer is connected.

Phone — link a Windows computer to a smartphone so that content can be shared between the two.

Network & Internet — connect to a Wi-Fi network so your Windows 10 computer can connect to the internet.

Personalization — fully customize the appearance of Windows 10 on your computer, including the overall color theme, the way text is displayed, and options for customizing the Start menu and the Taskbar, which appears along the bottom of the Windows screen.

Staying secure

For added security, use an app or browser that blocks web tracking to stop websites from gathering information about you. Try Ghostery at *ghostery.com* to download it to your desktop or laptop browser. For iPadOS/iOS or Android, download the Ghostery Privacy Browser app from the App Store or the Google Play Store respectively.

Apps — manage the apps on your computer, including setting default apps for specific operations; for example, which app to use when playing music or sending an email.

Account — add more users to the computer so that other family members can use it with their own unique account.

Time & Language — set the time and date and also the default language used throughout your version of Windows.

Gaming — for options when playing games on your Windows computer.

Ease of Access — apply a range of accessibility settings for any users who have issues with vision, hearing, or motor skills when using a computer.

Search — specify options when searching the web, such as restricting certain types of content.

Privacy — define how apps can interact with your computer, and how much access they can have in terms of communicating with other elements of the computer.

Staying secure

The Privacy settings also deal with online advertising and how it follows you on the web. Windows 10 users can manage the types of advertising seen, to a certain extent. Select Settings > Privacy, and click on the *General* option in the left-hand panel. The page contains options for managing the types of advertising displayed by apps and websites. There is also a link to learn more about your privacy options.

Learn how to use your Mac settings

The settings on a Mac computer or MacBook laptop are accessed from the System Preferences icon. Here's how to use them.

1. Access the *System Preferences* from the icon on the Dock.

2. Click on one of the main categories in the System Preferences window, as shown below.

3. Click in the *Search* box to look for a specific setting or topic.

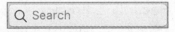

These are some of the main Mac System Preferences available and what they're used for.

General — to customize the appearance and colors of the macOS operating system on the Mac. It also has an option for showing or hiding scroll bars when you scroll around pages in apps and also on the web.

Desktop & Screen Saver — to apply background images for the Desktop, and also apply a Screen Saver for when the screen is inactive.

Dock — to apply settings for the way the Dock operates. This is the collection of app icons that, by default, is located at the bottom of the Mac screen.

Notifications — to specify how you receive notifications from your apps. This occurs when you receive new messages from email or messaging apps, and also when certain apps have updated information. It is possible to turn notifications On or Off for specific apps.

Internet Accounts — to link to online services, such as Apple's online backup and sharing service iCloud. It can also be used to link to other online services, such as Gmail, so you can receive these emails on your Mac.

Users & Groups — to add more users to the Mac so that other family members can use it with their own unique account.

Accessibility — to apply a range of accessibility settings, for any users who have issues with vision, hearing, or motor skills when using the Mac.

Screen Time — to report on, and limit, how much the Mac is being used. It is particularly useful if grandchildren are using the device, as it enables you to put time limits on how long it can be used, and also block certain types of apps or inappropriate content.

Security & Privacy — to apply a range of security settings, such as requiring a password to be entered to unlock a Mac once it has experienced a period of inactivity. There is also an option to turn on a firewall to try and prevent unwanted viruses from infecting your Mac.

Software Update — to determine how updates to the operating system are handled. They can be installed automatically whenever they are available, or you can select to view available updates and install them manually as required.

Network — to link to an available Wi-Fi network so you can access the internet.

Printers & Scanners — to add a new printer or scanner to the Mac. If any additional software is required for the device, the Mac will try and install this automatically.

Energy Saver — for MacBooks, these can be used to specify what happens when the device is not being used. For example, it can put the screen and the Mac to sleep after a specified period of time to preserve the battery.

Staying secure

In addition to all the other amazing things it does, your iPhone could also save your life. One of the settings on the iPhone is for automatically connecting to emergency services.

To do this, open the *Health* app and enter the required details in the *Set Up Your Medical ID* section. Then, go to Settings > Emergency SOS and drag the *Call with Side Button* option to *On*. Once you do this, you can make an emergency call by quickly pressing the side button (also the On/Off button) five times in a row.

Successfully set up your iPad and iPhone

iPads and iPhones have very similar settings, except for the Call options for the iPhone. To use these settings:

1. Access the *Settings* from the icon on the Home screen.

2. Swipe up and down on the screen to view the full range of settings.

3. Tap in the *Search* box to look for a specific setting or topic.

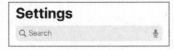

4. Tap on a category to view the options.

5. If an item has an arrow next to it, tap on this to view the additional options.

6. If an option has a button next to it, tap on the button to turn it On or Off, to activate or deactivate the setting. (If the button is green, this indicates that it is On.)

These are the main iPad and iPhone settings you'll want to check out.

Apple ID. You use this setting to create a free Apple ID with an email address and a password. Once it has been set up, it provides access to a range of Apple services including iCloud, the backup and sharing service, and apps such as the App Store, for downloading new apps.

Airplane Mode. Turn this On when you are on a flight, and it will disable network communications, in case they interfere with any of the aircraft's own communications.

Wi-Fi. Use this to connect to a Wi-Fi network and get access to the internet.

Bluetooth. This is used to link your iPad or iPhone to Bluetooth devices, such as speakers or earphones. Bluetooth is a wireless technology that works over short distances. Linking to a Bluetooth device is known as "pairing."

Cellular (for iPhones). This can be used to apply settings for the company that provides your cellular phone service, and also data usage options.

Notifications. Access this setting to specify how you receive notifications from your apps. This occurs when you receive new messages from email or messaging apps, and also when certain apps have updated information. It is possible to turn notifications On or Off for specific apps.

A closer look

Now that you're finally comfortable with your device and its apps, do you hesitate to try anything new? Don't. It can pay great dividends if you leave your comfort zone and dive into some of the unknown features on your gadgets.

The good news is that it is genuinely hard to permanently erase items from modern computing devices. Short of physically harming the device, you can undo most things in a couple of steps.

So go ahead, click or tap on those buttons or icons that you haven't used before, just to see what happens. Experimenting with the settings is an excellent first step to gaining a better understanding of your device.

Sounds & Haptics. These can be used to edit the sounds on your iPad and iPhone, such as when you receive messages, the ringtone when you receive a call, or the sounds when you use the keyboard. The haptic settings refer to the vibration that can be applied when you press items on the touch screen, to indicate that the item has been accessed or activated.

Do Not Disturb. Use this setting to mute calls and messages during certain times, such as in the evening.

Screen Time. These can be used to report on, and limit, how much the iPad or iPhone is being used. It is particularly useful if grandchildren use the device as it lets you put time limits on how long it can be used, and also block certain apps or inappropriate content.

General. This includes a wide range of settings, including checking to see if an update is available for the operating system software, setting the date and time, checking the amount of storage on the device, and applying settings for using the device's virtual keyboard.

Display & Brightness. Here, you can alter the screen brightness and also apply the Night Shift option, which reduces the amount of blue light emitted from the screen. That helps improve your sleep.

Caution

Getting a good night's sleep can be one of the most beneficial things for your overall health and well-being. But if you regularly use your computing device at night, you may be jeopardizing that sleep.

The light emitted from mobile devices such as tablets and smartphones is known as "blue light." This type of light instructs your body that it is time to be awake and alert. If your device has an option for reducing the amount of blue light being emitted, such as the *Night Shift* option, make sure you turn it On in the evening.

Accessibility. You can adjust these settings if you have issues with vision, hearing, or motor skills while using an iPad or an iPhone.

Siri & Search. These can be used to set up Siri, the digital voice assistant on the iPad and the iPhone, so you can perform voice searches.

Battery. This setting can put the iPad or iPhone into Low Power mode to make the battery last longer so that you can get more use from the device.

Privacy. These can be used to turn Location Services On or Off. If it is turned Off then it will, in effect, hide the location of your iPad or iPhone. However, for a lot of apps, such as the Maps app, it is beneficial to have Location Services turned On.

If Location Services is turned On for the device, individual apps can also have it turned On or Off, as required. You can also set the apps to only use Location Services when they are being used, rather than all the time.

Learn Android settings in a snap

Android settings can vary slightly between different devices, but the process for accessing them is generally the same.

1. Access the *Settings* from the icon on the Home screen.

2. Swipe up and down on the screen to view the full range of settings.

3. Tap on the Search icon to access the Search box to look for a specific setting or topic.

4. Tap on a category to view the options.

Different manufacturers of Android tablets and smartphones can customize the settings on their devices, to a certain extent. In a lot of cases this involves adding some of their own settings to the standard ones that appear on most devices.

For instance, on a Samsung Android smartphone you may have settings that are specific to Samsung. But the settings below will be consistent across all Android devices.

Wi-Fi. Connect to a Wi-Fi network and get access to the internet.

Bluetooth. Link your Android tablet or smartphone to Bluetooth devices, such as Bluetooth speakers or Bluetooth earphones.

Data Usage. It will show how much data is being used on an Android smartphone, in terms of browsing the web, or download-ing music or movies. Pay attention to this if you have a limited data plan from your cellphone provider because you will be charged if you go over the data limit.

Sounds & Notifications. Edit the sounds used on your Android device and specify how you receive notifications from your apps.

Display. Change the screen brightness and the size of text on the device. You'll also have an option to lock or unlock the screen rota-tion. This means you can change whether the content on the screen moves, or not, when you rotate the device vertically or horizontally.

Wallpaper. Set a wallpaper image for the Home screen, or the Lock screen, of an Android device.

Power Saving. Activate Power Saving mode to save battery power for an Android tablet or smartphone.

Accounts. Link to services which require an online account, such as the file backup and sharing service Dropbox.

Backup & Reset. Back up all the content on the device to a selected account. This is usually the Google Account that is first created when you start using an Android device.

You'll also have an option for resetting the device to its factory set-tings, which wipes all the data from the device and puts it back to its original state. This can be used if the device is not running properly, but it should only be performed if everything on the device has been backed up.

Security. Used for a range of security options, such as encrypting the data on the device so it is protected from unwanted access.

Applications Manager. Allows you to manage the apps on the device.

About Device. Display information about the device, including details of the version of Android being used, and options for updating Android if a newer version is available.

┌─ A *closer* look ─────────────────────────────

Android devices have a Quick Settings option, which is a panel at the top of the screen that contains the most frequently used settings. The Quick Settings can be customized so you can put your favorite settings in this panel.

What you need to know about app settings

Individual apps on desktop computers, laptops, tablets, and smartphones also have their own settings in most cases. If they do, these will frequently be accessed from the app's main menu button.

The settings icon will usually be in the form of three dots, either horizontally or vertically, or this icon, ▤ which is also sometimes know as a "hamburger" icon because of its design.

Once the menu button has been clicked or tapped on, the *Settings* button will be available on the menu options that appear.

Click or tap on a *Settings* button to view the options for the app. These will be unique to the app you are using.

For instance, these examples show the Settings menu for the Amazon Alexa home smart speaker app and the Settings menu for the Edge web browser on a Windows computer.

Caution

Computer manufacturers have obviously been unable to agree on a common charging standard for smartphones and tablets, which puts consumers at a disadvantage.

Apple has always had its own type of charging cable, which only works with the iPad and iPhone. Its plug is unique to Apple devices and doesn't fit any other devices. Manufacturers of Android tablets and smartphones have also developed their own versions of chargers.

So if you buy products from different manufacturers, be aware that you can't mix and match chargers.

Strategies for dealing with unresponsive apps

If an app is unresponsive or "frozen," explore these helpful options to try and get out of the problem.

- On a Windows computer press Ctrl+Alt+Delete and click on the *Task Manager* option. This displays the currently open apps and background processes that are taking place on your computer. If an app has a *Not responding* message next to it, click on the *End task* button. If in doubt, do this for all open apps that you think may be causing a problem.

- On a Mac, select Apple Menu > Force Quit, select an app, and click on the *Force Quit* button to force it to close.

- On an iPad or iPhone, access the App Switcher window, and swipe the app to the top of the screen (iPad), or from left or right (iPhone).

- On an Android device, tap on the *Recents* button to access the *Recents* window, and swipe the app to the left or right of the screen.

- Uninstall the app, and then reinstall it from its related app store.

- Turn off the device and turn it back on again. Make sure you have saved all of your work before you do this, and close down any other open apps first.

A closer look

Wondering how to delete an app from your device? Here's the quick and easy answer.

- To uninstall a Windows app, click on the *Start* button, right-click on the app on the Start menu and select *Uninstall*.

- To uninstall a macOS Catalina app, drag it over the *Trash* icon on the Dock. To uninstall an iPad or iPhone app, press on the app until a small cross appears on it, and tap on the cross.

- To uninstall an Android app, drag it to the top of the screen and release it over the *Remove* icon.

Windows — an old favorite with new features

Choose the best Windows computer for your needs

The Windows operating system can justifiably claim to be the product that helped bring home computing to a global audience, together with desktop computers, also known as Personal Computers (PCs). Here's what you need to know to buy — and install — a Windows system.

Desktops — a longtime favorite. Traditionally, the desktop computer has been the go-to device for most people. It has a separate monitor to view what is on the computer, and a hard drive, which is where the computing power is housed, usually in a rectangular box.

However, desktop computers have become a victim of the relentless march of digital technology, and they have largely been replaced in the home by more portable devices, such as laptops and tablets.

Laptops — for those who want to move around. Laptops have grown in popularity as people want their computing to be more mobile, and they are now a genuine option as a replacement for a desktop computer.

One of the main differences between a desktop computer and a laptop is that a laptop uses a trackpad for moving the cursor on the screen, rather than a mouse (although a mouse can still be attached to a laptop, either with a USB cable, or wirelessly).

Before you buy a Windows laptop, try to use it first, as this will give you a chance to assess its size, and also the feel of the keyboard and the trackpad.

Four easy ways to load Windows. You can download the Windows operating system online as well as buy a disk from software retailers. Here are four options for obtaining Windows 10.

- Pre-installed. Buy a new desktop computer or laptop with the Windows 10 already installed.

- Use *Windows Update*. Replace an older version of Windows 10, retaining the installed applications and settings. This can be done through the Settings app (select Update & Security > Windows Update, and click on the *Check for updates* button).

- Use the *Windows 10 Update Assistant* app. This can be accessed from the Start menu and takes you through the process of updating Windows.

- Microsoft website. Visit the software download page on the Microsoft website *(microsoft.com/en-us/software-download/ windows10)* and click on the *Update now* button to start the *Update Assistant* and download Windows 10.

A closer look

When you first start using a Windows 10 computer you will have the option to create a Microsoft Account. This will give you your own unique details for logging in to your computer. It will also allow you to access a range of items, such as the Microsoft Store for downloading new apps, and OneDrive, Microsoft's online backup and sharing service. A Microsoft Account is free and can be created with an email address and a password.

10 maintenance tasks for the fastest, healthiest computer

Computers benefit from a rigorous maintenance regime, and Windows 10 is no different in this regard. These 10 habits should ensure your computer keeps working for many trouble-free years ahead.

Run anti-virus software (daily). Viruses are one of the most destructive enemies of a computer, so it's important you install anti-virus software on your Windows 10 device, and make sure it runs everyday. In most cases, anti-virus software can be set to run automatically at a specific time.

Keep your firewall up (daily). As with anti-virus software, make sure you have a firewall installed to protect your computer from unwanted software entering over the internet.

Shut down properly (daily). When you shut down a computer properly, it goes through a process that resets certain elements within the computer, ready for the next time it is turned on. If you do something else, for example press the On/Off button to turn it off, the shutdown process may not be performed properly, which could harm the computer's performance, particularly over time.

Back it up (daily/monthly). Whenever you create new items, you should back them up on the same day, either to an external device, such as a USB flash drive, or an external hard drive or online cloud backup service. Uploading photos is a good example.

Also, the whole system should be backed up every month to an external device, so that you have a copy of everything if your computer becomes inoperable for any reason. On a Windows 10 computer this can be done in Settings > Update & Security > Backup.

Declutter your desktop (weekly). Saving files to your computer's desktop can slow it down over time, particularly if there are a large number of items. A better option is to create folders for specific topics in File Explorer and store the relevant files there.

Update software (weekly). Check to see if there are any updates to Windows 10, including security patches. Have a look in Settings > Update & Security > Windows Update to view details about any available updates.

Delete old files (monthly). The more items stored on your computer, the more work it will have to do. If you have files, or apps, that you do not use anymore, delete them to free up more space. Think of it as spring cleaning for your computer.

Clear the web browser's cache (monthly). When a web browser is used, it stores a lot of information relating to the websites you've visited, known as the cache. Over time this can slow down your computer. To overcome this, the cache can be emptied — usually from the settings section of the browser.

Defragment the hard drive (monthly). This involves reassembling files that have been fragmented during use on your computer. See *Free tools to make Windows run like new* later in this chapter for details on how to defragment the hard drive.

Keep it clean (monthly). Dust is one of the great enemies of any computing device, so physically cleaning it will make it last longer. Just be careful not to use any type of cleaning products that could harm the computer's surface.

And here's a great keyboard tip — simply turn it upside down and tap gently to get rid of any dust or crumbs that have accumulated.

Get familiar with the Windows desktop

When you turn on a
Windows 10 desktop
or laptop, it opens at
the Desktop. Here's
an example of what
you'll see.

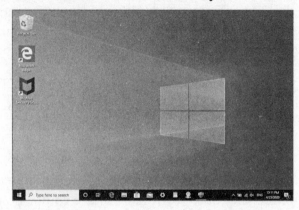

Desktop background.
This is the main area
of the Desktop. The
background image
can be customized
in Setting >

Personalization. Click on one of the *Choose your picture* options,
or click on the *Browse* button to look for photos on your own
computer to use as the Desktop background.

Shortcut icons. These can be added to the
Desktop for quick access to items. Click on
a shortcut icon to open the item. Shortcuts
can be used for files and apps, and can be
created in File Explorer by right-clicking
on an item and clicking on the *Create
shortcut* button.

Start button. You'll see a tiny window in the bottom left-
hand corner of the screen. Use it to access the Start menu.

Search box/Cortana. This is located to the right of the Start button and can be used to perform text and voice searches.

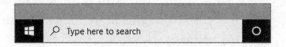

Taskbar. This collection of icons at the bottom of your screen houses shortcuts to some of the most frequently used apps on your computer. Click on an icon on the Taskbar to open the app.

Notifications area. It's located at the right-hand side of the Taskbar and has icons for speakers, network, and other system tools. Click on one to see more information about that item.

A closer look

Do you want to know the secret to keyboard shortcuts in Windows? Once you know this nifty trick, you'll be able to do just about anything — without using your mouse at all.

Simply use the Alt key and the number pad on the keyboard. You can hold down the Alt key and press combinations on the number pad to insert text characters, scientific symbols, and special characters. For instance, type Alt+0151 to enter a dash symbol, if you want to use this instead of a hyphen.

To find a full list of keyboard shortcuts that can be used with the Alt key, open Google in a web browser and enter "Alt key shortcuts."

Options for shutting down Windows

Time to shut down your computer? You have several ways to close Windows that you'll access from the Start menu. Here's how to shut down, sleep, and restart.

1. Click on the *Start* button.

2. On the Start menu, right-click on the *Power* button.

3. Click on either the *Sleep, Shut down,* or *Restart* buttons.

You can also do it this way.

1. Right-click on the *Start* button, and click on the *Shut down or sign out* button.

2. Select either *Sign out, Sleep, Shut down,* or *Restart.*

How to navigate the Start menu

The Start menu in Windows 10 is where you can view areas within your computer and also access your apps. There are two main sections of the Start menu — a list of the apps on your computer in alphabetical order; and larger tiles, also for accessing apps. To access the Start menu:

1. Click on the *Start* button.

2. The Start menu is displayed above the Start button. The left-hand side of the Start menu contains links to the most-used apps, a list of quick links to items such as the Power button, and an alphabetical list of all the apps on the computer. The right-hand side displays the colored tiles, giving access to the named apps.

3. Your most frequently used apps are displayed at the top of the left-hand panel. Click on one to open it (these items will change as you use different apps).

4. Click on the tiny person icon to access your own account settings or sign out from your account.

5. Click on these buttons in the left-hand panel to access, from top to bottom, your Documents folder, Pictures folder, and the Windows 10 Settings. The items on the Start menu can be customized in Settings > Personalization > Start. Click on the *Choose which folders appear on Start* link in the main window.

6. If you see a down-pointing arrow next to an app, this means you can access additional items. Click on the arrow to view these. It will look like this when it's opened.

A closer look

Some of the colored tiles on the Start menu are known as Live Tiles. This means that they display real-time content for certain types of apps. This is content that is updated automatically as it changes, such as for the News and Sports apps. To see if a tile has this functionality, right-click on a tile and look for More > Turn Live Tile on.

Easy way to pin apps to the taskbar

Move the cursor over items on the Taskbar to see open windows for that item. Click on a window to make that the active one.

You can pin apps to the Taskbar and the Start menu so that they are always visible. To do this, locate an app in the Start menu and right-click on it. Select either *Pin to Start*, or More > Pin to taskbar to pin it to one of these locations, or both. If an item is pinned to the Start menu, it appears there as one of the colored tiles.

Keep your device secure with a pin or password

It's essential to keep any computing device secure, and this is certainly true for a Windows 10 desktop or laptop.

When you first start with Windows 10, you will be asked to set up a method for signing in to your user account. This can be done in a variety of ways, such as a four-digit PIN (Personal Identification Number) or a longer password.

This means of verification will be required whenever you log on to your Windows 10 device, and also if the computer has been locked. You can change the method of verification as follows:

1. Access Settings > Accounts, and click on the *Sign-in options* button in the left-hand panel.

2. Select one of the *Sign-in options.*

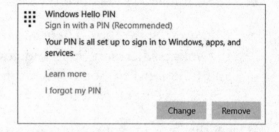

3. Click on the *Change* button to enter a new option for the selected item.

To lock a Windows 10 desktop or laptop, press the Windows key and the L key on the keyboard simultaneously (Win Key+L).

Staying secure

For added security, look for an option to specify that a sign-in is required if the device goes to sleep. To do this, access Settings > Accounts, and click on the *Sign-in options* button. Under the *Require sign-in* heading in the main window, click in the box and select *When PC wakes up from sleep*.

To specify when the computer goes to sleep, access Settings > System, and click on the *Power & sleep* button. Under the *Sleep* heading in the main window, click in one of the boxes and select a time period of inactivity after which the device will go to sleep.

Get going with Windows 10 apps

When it comes to your computer, apps are where the action is. Windows 10 uses three types of apps you need to be familiar with.

- Windows 10 apps. These are the pre-installed apps that you access from the Start menu. They cover the areas of communication, entertainment, information, and productivity. In Windows 10, they open in their own window on the Desktop, in the same way as the old-style, classic Windows apps.

- Windows classic apps. These are the older-style Windows apps that people may be familiar with from previous versions of Windows. These open on the Desktop.

- Microsoft Store apps. These apps can be downloaded from the online Microsoft Store and cover a wide range of subjects and functionality. Some Microsoft Store apps are free, while others have to be paid for.

To view the apps on your Windows 10 desktop or laptop:

1. Click on the *Start* button.

2. All of the apps are displayed. Use the scroll bar at the right-hand side to move through all the apps, which are listed alphabetically.

3. Click on a letter heading to view an alphabetic grid for finding apps. Click on a letter to move to that section.

The different types of apps in Windows 10 have been designed to function in similar ways to make it easy for you to work with them. Here are some of the things you can do.

- Click and drag on the top toolbar to move the app's window around the Desktop.

- Click and drag on the bottom or right-hand border to resize the height or width of the app's window (or drag on the bottom right-hand corner to resize the height and width simultaneously).

- Click on the X button on the top toolbar to close the app.

- Click on the square button on the top toolbar to maximize the app's window.

- Click on the minus sign button on the top toolbar to minimize the app's window (it will be minimized onto the Taskbar).

Step into the Microsoft store

Apps from the Microsoft Store cover a wide range of topics, and they provide an excellent way to add functionality to Windows 10. To use the Microsoft Store:

1. Click on the *Microsoft Store* tile on the Start menu, or on the Taskbar, to open the Microsoft Store. The currently featured apps are displayed on the Home screen.

2. Scroll up and down to see additional items and categories.

3. Scroll down the Home screen, and click on the *Show all* button next to a category, for example Top free apps.

4. The full range of apps for the selected category is displayed. Swipe up and down the page to view them.

5. Click on an app to preview it and see more details.

6. Click on the *Get* button to download the app to your Windows desktop or laptop.

Managing files in Windows — your key to organization

File management is an important part of working with a computer. As you create more and more content, it's good to know where to find it and organize it.

With Windows 10, file management is done with File Explorer. To open File Explorer, click on this button on the Taskbar.

Here's an example of what you'll see.

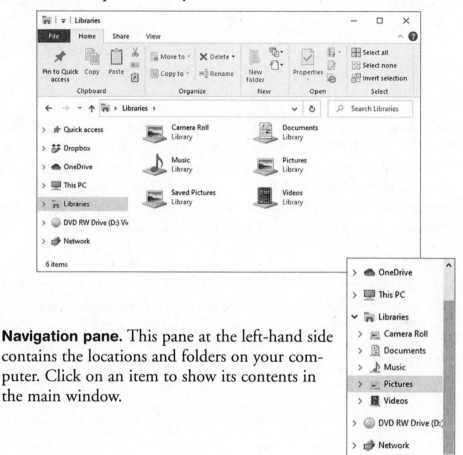

Navigation pane. This pane at the left-hand side contains the locations and folders on your computer. Click on an item to show its contents in the main window.

Address bar. This bar at the top of File Explorer displays the actual location of the item that is currently selected, or the location being viewed, such as Libraries > Pictures.

Ribbon (also known as the Scenic Ribbon). You can use this bar of controls at the top of the File Explorer window to apply a range of commands to the selected item or content being viewed.

Main window. This displays the contents of the selected item in the Navigation pane. For instance, if you select the *Libraries* location in the Navigation pane, it will be displayed in the main window. If it contains more folders (sub-folders), these will be in the main window and can be investigated by double-clicking on them. You can investigate numerous levels of folders in this way.

Caution

Oops! You deleted a file by accident. This sometimes happens when working with File Explorer. But is it really gone? Thankfully not. Click on the *Recycle Bin* icon located on the Desktop, and the file should be in there. Click on the file to select it, then click on the *Restore the selected item* button. Voila, it's back as if nothing happened.

---

5 file explorer locations to check out

The items in the Navigation pane are links to different locations within your computer. These include the following.

Quick Access. This is a collection of the most recent files and folders that you've created or edited on your computer. You can also add folders to Quick Access so you can see the latest items in specific folders. Try it with your Pictures folder to see your most recent photos.

To add a folder to Quick Access, navigate to the folder within the Navigation pane, right-click on it, and select *Pin to Quick access*.

OneDrive. This is an example of a cloud service, and files can be saved here and then accessed from another device if you are signed in with your Microsoft Account. You can also access OneDrive online from *onedrive.live.com* (again, log in with your Microsoft Account).

Have a look at the chapter *Save, protect, and share with the cloud* to see details about using cloud services, including OneDrive.

This PC. This contains links to all of the areas on your computer.

Libraries. This location collates relevant content from different places on your computer. It is not a physical folder like those under This PC, but it displays items that are in those locations.

Network. This displays any network connections that have been set up on your computer.

Surf the web with the Edge browser

Windows 10 uses the Edge browser for viewing web pages. It replaced Internet Explorer, which you may remember from years past. To start using the Edge browser:

1. Click on the *Edge* icon on the Taskbar.

2. The Edge browser opens as a new window on the Desktop.

3. The web address of the page currently being viewed is displayed in the Address Bar at the top of the window. This is

known as a Smart Address Bar, as it can search for specific web addresses and also individual words or phrases.

4. Enter a word or phrase into the Smart Address Bar. As you type, alternatives will appear. Click on an item to go to a page of search results based on the options displayed in the Smart Address Bar.

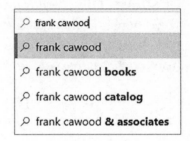

5. Click on the star icon at the right-hand side of the Smart Address Bar to add the current page as a Favorite. Once this is done, the star will appear solid.

6. Click on this icon, to the right of the Smart Address Bar, to open the Hub, which is a collection of options for working with the Edge browser.

7. The Hub contains the *Favorites* section, where items added in Step 5 are displayed; the *Reading list* section, where you can store web pages to read offline (these are added from the same button as in Step 5); the *Books* section for reading eBooks; the *History* section, where you can view a history of the web pages you have visited; and the *Downloads* section, where you can view any content you have downloaded with the Edge browser.

8. Click on this *Menu* button at the top, right-hand side, of the Edge window to access the main menu. This provides access to a variety of items for managing the browser, such as the *Settings* option. You can use Settings to customize the browser in a number of ways, including setting a unique home page that appears whenever you open the browser.

A+ security protection for Windows

Viruses are the scourge of computing devices. Unfortunately, hackers take a perverse and persistent delight in trying to attack Windows devices. That means anti-virus software should be your No. 1 priority.

In addition to using third-party virus programs, you'll get some protection against viruses and malicious software from pre-installed security features within Windows 10. The Windows Security app is a good starting point. Here's how to use it.

1. Select Settings > Update & Security, and click on the *Windows Security* option in the left-hand panel. Or click on the Start button and select *Windows Security* from the Start menu.

2. The Windows Security options are listed in the window under the *Protection areas* heading.

3. Click on one of the Protection areas categories to view its options.

4. Click on the *Open Windows Security* button to open the Windows Security app.

5. Click on each item to view its options. Use the left-hand toolbar to move between the sections.

6. Click on the *Home* button (the little house) to return to the main page after viewing a section.

You can use the Windows Security center to scan for any potential viruses or threats. To do this:

1. On the Windows Security home page click on the *Virus & threat protection* option.

2. Click on the *Quick scan* button to scan your system for viruses.

3. As the scan progresses, it will note any threats and list options for dealing with them. For example, it may recommend removing them from your computer or quarantining the items so that they are isolated and not able to cause any harm.

Top 10 reasons your computer runs slow

Computing devices don't always work as they should. At times they will appear to run slowly and take forever to perform simple tasks.

Here are some reasons you may be having problems and how to get back the lightning speed you crave.

Too many Startup items. If your computer has to open several apps when it first starts then this will contribute to a slower performance. See *5 simple tips to speed up your Windows computer* later in this chapter for details about removing Startup items.

Old hard drive. Like anything else, hard drives deteriorate over time, and the older it is the slower it will become. The only realistic remedy for this is to buy a new hard drive.

Hard drive is filling up. If the hard drive is nearly full it will take longer for the computer to find space to store and manage new items. Clear out any documents or apps that are not needed to help speed up the hard drive.

Too many browser windows open. If you have several windows open in your web browser, using different tabs, this can use up valuable processing power. Close any windows you're not using to help the computer get back up to speed.

Your computer has a virus. If a virus has infected your computer, this could be a major reason for it running slowly. Make sure you have anti-virus software running daily to protect against viruses.

A rogue app. Sometimes an app does not work as it should, and this can slow down the whole computer. If you suspect this is the case, delete the app and see if this fixes the problem. To do this, right-click on the app on the Start menu, and click on the *Uninstall* button.

Old hard drive, new operating system. If you have an old hard drive, it may struggle to run the latest versions of Windows 10 effectively. This is a long-standing issue with hardware and software — the older the hardware gets, the more difficult it is to run the latest software on it.

Not enough RAM memory. Insufficient RAM memory (the memory that manages the operations being performed by a computer) is one of the main reasons for a computer running slowly. Upgrade the RAM to get some of the original speed back. If you're not sure how to do this, take your hard drive to a computer store to have it done by a professional.

Slow processor. As with RAM memory, an upgrade to the computer's processor can make a considerable difference to the overall speed.

Restart needed. If your computer recognizes that a restart is required, for example to install a software update, this could restrict the speed until it performs the restart. If you are prompted to restart your Windows 10 computer you should do so, but only after you save what you are doing.

Free tools to make Windows run like new

You know how your car's performance deteriorates as the engine gets older? Your computer reacts the same way.

Luckily, Windows 10 includes some free tools that will have it working like new again. Speed up your slow computer by cleaning and defragmenting your hard drive. You can access these options from the *Windows Administrative Tools* button on the Start menu, and even have the computer do it automatically.

Clean up your disk. Windows will look through your files and identify ones that can safely be deleted to free up disk space and improve performance. To do this, click on the *Disk Cleanup* button from the *Windows Administrative Tools* option on the Start menu.

The files Windows 10 recommends for removal are checked in the *Files to delete* box, with the total amount of space that will be saved noted underneath.

Click on the *OK* button to remove the files. This clears the cobwebs from your computer's memory and file system. Watch it work like new again.

Defragment your hard drive. Also known as "defragging," this process puts tiny bits of data back together on your hard drive. Whenever files are modified and saved, bits of the file (which is just a collection of digital data) become detached, and saved in different parts of the hard drive. When you next access the file, all of the pieces are reassembled, so that you see the full file.

However, the more the file is fragmented, the longer it takes to reassemble the pieces. This is usually only a very small amount of time, but as files become more fragmented it can slow down your computer. This is where defragging comes in — it gathers together all of the pieces of data and puts them back where they should be.

To do this, click on the *Defragment and Optimize Drives* button from the *Windows Administrative Tools* option on the Start menu, and click on the *Analyze* button to see how fragmented the drive is, for example 12%.

Click on the *Optimize* button to defragment the drive.

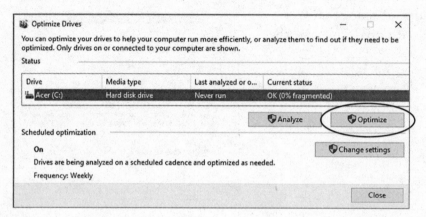

This could take several hours, depending on how fragmented the drive is. Once this is completed your computer should run faster again.

Speed up your computer automatically. Don't want to worry about remembering all these tasks? You can set the computer to defrag itself by setting up a regular schedule. It's simple when you know how.

Click on the *Change settings* button in the *Optimize Drives* window (for defragmenting the hard drive). Click in the *Frequency* box, and select how frequently you would like the operation to be performed automatically. That's all there is to it.

5 simple tips to speed up your computer

Your computer used to run like the wind — now it's as slow as molasses. Here are some options for returning a Windows computer to its former (speedier) glory.

Scan for viruses. Viruses on any computing device can slow it down, and this is certainly true for Windows 10. Check out *A+ security protection for Windows* in this chapter to learn how to regularly scan for viruses.

Remove apps from the Startup process. When Windows 10 boots up (starts) it opens a number of apps to get them ready for use. This can take a lot of processing power and make the Startup process longer than you would like.

You can disable items in the Startup process that you don't need. Right-click on the *Start* button, and click on the *Task Manager* button. Click on the *More details* button in the bottom left-hand corner, and click on the *Startup* tab to view all the items that are included in this process, as shown below. If an app has *Enabled* next to it, click on it to disable the app.

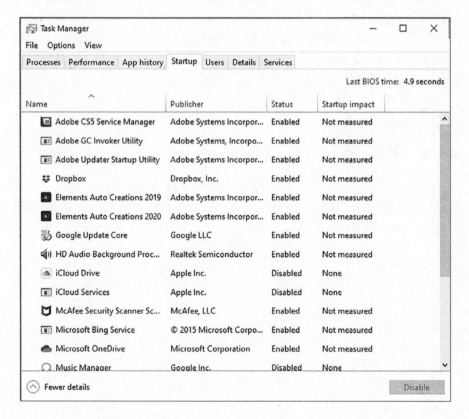

Empty the Recycle Bin. When you delete something on your Windows computer, it doesn't really go anywhere, except into the Recycle Bin, which is another folder on the hard drive.

This can be useful if you want to restore it at a later date. But it can also cause your computer to run slowly, particularly if you keep a large number of files in the Recycle Bin.

To solve this, empty it by right-clicking on the *Recycle Bin* icon on the Desktop, and click on the *Empty Recycle Bin* button. Take a quick look first to make sure there is nothing in it you want to keep.

Update Windows 10. Keeping Windows 10 as up to date as possible ensures that you have the latest version of the operating system, which should also be the most efficient.

To check for updates to Windows 10, go to Settings > Update & Security, and click on the *Windows Update* option in the left-hand panel. In the main window, under the *Update status* heading, click on the *Check for updates* button to see if any Windows updates are waiting to be downloaded and installed.

Turn off OneDrive syncing. Windows cloud service, OneDrive, can slow down your computer, since it regularly looks to synchronize the OneDrive folder on your computer with the online service.

To turn it off, right-click on the *OneDrive* cloud icon on the Taskbar, and click on the *Pause syncing* option. Select the length of time for pausing the syncing process.

Amazing tips to master your Mac

Apple gives you a variety of choices

Microsoft and Apple have entertained a long rivalry, and they each have devoted fans of their products. They both provide excellent options for anyone interested in entering the digital world. In terms of desktop and laptop computers, your favorite may be the system you're most familiar with, or which you consider to be the most cost effective.

Although both companies produce desktop and laptop computers, Apple has probably become better known for their mobile devices, such as the iPad and iPhone. But their range of computers is still very popular, as is the operating system that powers them — currently macOS Catalina.

iMac. The iMac is Apple's flagship desktop computer, and it has been known for its stylish design over the years. The iMac is an all-in-one desktop computer — essentially a monitor that also contains the hard drive. The latest models of iMacs feature 21.5-inch and 27-inch screens (measured diagonally) with high-quality displays.

The main drawback of the iMac compared to a Windows 10 desktop computer is the price, with the 21.5-inch model starting at $1,099 on the Apple website.

Mac mini. Another desktop option for a Mac computer is the Mac mini. This is just a hard drive, with no monitor, mouse, or keyboard. It can be attached to an Apple or a third-party monitor and, starting at $799, is an excellent option for a first venture into the world of Apple desktops.

MacBook. The Apple range of laptop computers is known as MacBooks and, in keeping with the usual Apple design ethos, they are sleek and stylish. The currently available MacBooks are:

- MacBook Pro. This is the main MacBook range and has two models, one with a 13-inch screen and one with a 16-inch screen.

- MacBook Air. The thinnest of the MacBook range (and one of the thinnest laptops on the market at a maximum height of 0.63 inch), this model has a 13.3-inch screen.

A closer look

The naming convention for the Mac operating system has changed over the years. Previously, it was known as OS X (pronounced 10) until it was changed to the current macOS. This is updated each year, and each version is identified by an area of natural beauty in California where Apple is based, such as Yosemite, High Sierra, and now Catalina.

Mac menus — the key to easy navigation

Your first step in navigating your new Mac is to get familiar with the menus. These appear at the top of the screen.

These menus relate mainly to the Finder management system since this is always open. That means the menu bar is available even if you haven't opened any apps.

- Apple menu — accessed from the Apple symbol. It contains access to System Preferences (Apple's version of settings), the App Store for updating software, and options for turning off or sleeping your Mac.

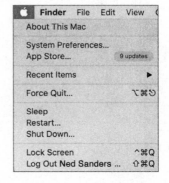

  A useful feature on the Apple menu is the *About This Mac* option. This displays a range of details about your Mac, including the version of the operating system, information about the display being used, and details about the amount of storage and memory in your Mac.

- Finder menu — for customizing the appearance and operation of the Finder.

- File menu — for applying actions to individual files that have been selected in the Finder.

- Edit menu — for applying a range of editing functions to selected files in the Finder. These include the standard Cut, Copy, and Paste options.

- View menu — for specifying how the windows, folders, and files appear in the Finder.

- Go menu — use it to move to different areas of the Finder and also different sections of your Mac.

- Window menu — for organizing the appearance of the currently open apps.

- Help — contains help files and links to online help resources.

┌─ Staying secure ─────────────────────────────┐

When you begin using your Mac, you'll go through a setup
process that includes items such as selecting a language, setting the time and date, and connecting to a Wi-Fi network.

During the setup process you will be asked to create a
password to use with your Mac. Don't ignore this as it's an
important security feature. You can use the password to
unlock the Lock screen or to change some of the settings
within System Preferences.

└──┘

A critical task you need to learn

An important part of using your computer is learning how to turn
it off. Don't laugh — it's not as simple as it seems since different
computing devices have their own methods of doing it. With
macOS Catalina you'll perform this task from the Apple menu.

1. Click on the Apple menu icon in the upper left corner of
   the screen.

2. The options are at the bottom of the menu.

3. Click on *Sleep, Restart,* or *Shut Down.* If you're finished for
   the day, you'll want to choose *Shut Down.*

Lock your device with a secure password

As with any computing device, it's important to ensure your Mac
computer requires a password when you log in, and also that it
locks itself after a period of inactivity, so no one else can gain
access. After you create your Mac account login password, you can
manage it in System Preferences.

1. Access System Preferences > Users & Groups.

2. Click on your own name in the *Current User* panel.

3. Click on the *Login Options* button.

4. Click on the padlock icon to make changes to your security settings.

5. Enter your Mac account login password to enable changes to be made. Click on the Unlock button.

6. Click in the *Automatic login* box and select *Off*. This will ensure that a password is required when you log in.

7. Click on the padlock icon to close it and apply the changes.

To specify that the screen locks if the Mac has been put to sleep, or the screen saver has been activated, and a password is required to unlock it:

1. Access System Preferences > Security & Privacy.

2. Click on the *General* tab.

3. Click on the padlock icon to make changes to your security settings.

4. Enter your Mac account login password to enable changes to be made. Click on the Unlock button.

5. Click in the *Require password* checkbox, so it is blue with a white check mark.

6. Click in the box next to *Require password,* and select a time period to wait until the screen locks. It's best if you set it for a few minutes at the most. If the screen remains available for too long, someone could access it before the password kicks in.

A closer look

You can easily add folders and individual files to the Sidebar so you won't have to search for them. To do this, access the folder in the main window, click and hold on it, and then drag it onto the Sidebar. Items can also be reordered on the Sidebar in the same way. Simply click and hold on them, and drag them into a new position.

Organize your files with the Finder

File management systems on computers are not necessarily the most exciting elements, but they are essential to finding your way around the folders, documents, and apps on your computer.

The macOS Catalina file management system is known as the Finder, and this is equivalent to File Explorer on a Windows desktop computer or laptop.

Get to know the Finder and you will always be able to navigate around your Mac. Click on this icon on the Dock to open it.

The elements of the Finder are:

Sidebar, which contains links to items on the Mac.

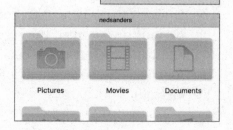

Main window, which displays the content of the item selected in the Sidebar.

View options buttons, which are the options for how the items in the main window are displayed. These include (from left to right) Icon view, List view, Column view, or Gallery view.

Search box, which can be used to look for items in the Finder.

The folders in the Sidebar are links to the relevant folders on your Mac. These include the following.

Recents. This contains the most recently created, opened, or modified files. The items here will change as you use the files on your Mac.

Home folder. This folder will contain the username you created during the setup process for your Mac, and it includes folders for all the content you create or use, such as Documents, Downloads, Movies, and Music. Some of these folders are also available on the Sidebar.

Applications. This contains all of the apps on your Mac. They can be opened from here, and also added to the Dock by dragging them onto it. Simply click and hold on an app's icon in the Applications folder, and drag it onto the Dock at the bottom of the screen.

iCloud Drive. This can be used for copying documents to Apple's cloud service, where they will be backed up and can be shared with other people.

A closer look

Want to create a new folder within an existing folder? Open the first folder, and select File > New Folder from the Menu bar (or Shift+Command+N on the keyboard). Type a name for the new folder and press the **Return** button on the keyboard.

The Dock — your shortcut to simplicity

The Dock is one of the most useful items you will use on your Mac. It acts as a shortcut bar for opening and accessing apps, and also for open items, such as a web page that is open in the Safari app.

By default, the Dock is located along the bottom of the screen, but you can change it if you prefer it in another location. It will remain where you place it regardless of which apps are open and being used.

The Dock has a narrow dividing line towards the right-hand side. Items to the left of the line are apps that can be opened by clicking on them. On the right you'll see the Trash icon as well as open documents that have been minimized. It also contains Stacks, which are folders you've dragged onto the Dock from the Finder.

The Dock can be customized in various ways. To do this, go to System Preferences > Dock. The options include changing the size of the Dock, enabling the icons to be magnified when the cursor is moved over them, and positioning the Dock at different locations around the screen.

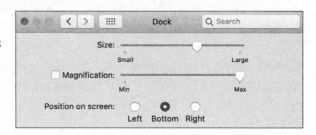

Quick access with the Launchpad

Apps on a Mac computer are located in the Applications folder within the Finder. You can open them from there by double-clicking on them. But if you want to do it more quickly, use the Launchpad.

1. Click on the *Launchpad* icon on the Dock.

2. All of the apps are displayed. Click on the dots at the bottom of the window (or swipe from right to left with a trackpad) to view all the apps on your Mac. Click on an app to open it.

3. Drag one app over another in the Launchpad window to create a folder and help organize your apps. The folder name is based on the category of the apps. Click on the folder name and overtype it to give it a new name.

To remove a macOS Catalina app, click and hold on it in the Launchpad window. When it starts to wobble, click on the cross in the top left-hand corner to remove it. Alternatively, drag an app over the *Trash* icon on the Dock, and drop it in there to remove it.

Discover the 'app'eal of apps

You have a whole range of apps pre-installed on your Mac. But if you want to expand your horizons, check out the huge number in Apple's online App Store. Here's how to download the ones you're interested in.

1. Click on the *App Store* icon on the Dock or within the Launchpad.

2. The App Store opens at the *Discover* page, which contains the current top-featured and best new apps.

3. Quick links to other areas of the App Store are listed in the left-hand panel. You can use these to view apps for specific categories like Work or Play. The Categories button can be used to view all the main topics within the App Store. Use the Search box above the quick links to search for specific keywords or phrases.

4. Scroll up the Discover window to see the range of apps that are available. Click on the *See All* button next to a category to view all of the apps within it.

5. Once you've found an app you're interested in, click on it to view a detailed description about it.

6. To start downloading an app, click on the button next to the app icon to download it. If the app is free the button will say *Get*. If there is a charge for the app, the button will say *Buy App* once the price is clicked.

7. Click on the *Get* or *Buy App* button, and click on the *Install* button.

8. You have to enter your Apple ID account details to continue downloading the app. An Apple ID can be created when you set up your Mac, or you will be prompted to create one when you first access the App Store. Click on the *Get* button to complete downloading the app.

9. Once you download the app, it will be available within the Launchpad, and it will also appear in the Applications folder in the Finder.

A closer look

Some apps on a Mac computer have a Full Screen mode. This enables them to use the entire available screen area so it is easier to view the contents of the app. These are generally the pre-installed Apple apps, such as Safari and Photos.

Full Screen mode is activated by clicking on the green button in the top left-hand corner of the app's window, or moving the cursor over it and clicking on *Enter Full Screen*.

When Full Screen mode is activated, the top toolbar is hidden and can be displayed by moving the cursor over the top of the screen. Full Screen mode is exited by clicking on the green button, or by moving the cursor over it and clicking on *Exit Full Screen*.

Secrets to getting the most out of Safari

Safari is the web browser that comes pre-installed with macOS, and it is designed specifically to be used with Apple devices (there are also versions of Safari for the iPad and iPhone). Here's how to get started with Safari.

1. Click on the *Safari* icon on the Dock.

2. All of the controls are at the top of the browser. These include the Toolbar, the Address Bar/Search Box, the Favorites bar, and the Tabs button (the plus sign), for adding more windows within the browser.

Address Bar/Search Box. In Safari, the Address Bar/Search Box is combined, and can be used for entering a specific website address to access it. It can also be used to search for topics using a keyword or phrase. To find websites using Safari:

1. Click in the Address Bar/Search Box.

2. Type a website address or a keyword. As you type, suggestions appear below the Address Bar/Search box. Click on the *Top Hit* option to go to that website.

Safari Sidebar. This useful feature is a panel where you can view items you have bookmarked so you can access them quickly. It also contains items you have added to the Reading List, which is a function that lets you view web pages when your Mac is offline, meaning it's not connected to the internet. Here's how to use the Sidebar.

1. Select View > Show Sidebar from the Safari menu bar, or click on this button.

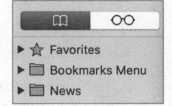

2. The Sidebar contains the Bookmarks and Reading List sections.

3. Click on the *Bookmarks button* (the one that looks like a book) to view all the items that you've bookmarked.

4. Click on the *Reading List* button (the glasses) to view all the items you've added to your Reading List to read later, even offline.

A *closer* look

Remember how you customized your Mac settings in System Preferences? You can modify Safari in the same way.

In the top menu bar of the Safari window, click on Safari > Preferences. You'll see a number of tabs, including General, for specifying how new windows and tabs are opened and for setting a homepage; Tabs, for managing new tabs; Search, for selecting a default search engine to use with Safari; and Security, where you can select an option to display a warning when Safari detects a fraudulent website.

Adding Bookmarks. If you visit several websites regularly, it can be frustrating having to enter the full website address every time you want to view them. This is where bookmarks come to the rescue. They create quick links to your favorite web pages, or the ones you visit most frequently.

1. Open the web page you want to bookmark, and click on the Share button in the top right-hand side of the Safari window.

2. Click on the *Add Bookmark* button.

3. Enter a name for the bookmark, and click on the *Add* button. It is also possible to select a specific folder for the bookmark.

Once bookmarks have been added, you can view and access them from the Sidebar in Safari's Bookmarks tab.

┌─ **A closer look** ────────────────────────

You can add Reading List items to the Sidebar in the same way as creating a bookmark. Access the required web page, select the Share button, and click on *Add to Reading List.*

└──

Tabs. Tabs on web browsers are an elegant feature that allows you to open multiple sites within the same browser window. To work with tabs in Safari:

1. Click on the plus sign on the far right of the Safari window to open a new tab.

2. Click on one of the *Favorites* or *Frequently Visited* sites listed, or enter a website address in the Address Bar.

3. Click on this button next to the New Tab button to minimize all of the open tabs.

4. Move left and right to view all of the open tabs in thumbnail view. Click on one to view it at full size.

┌─ **A closer look** ────────────────────────────────

You can choose to show or hide your Favorites Bar by selecting View > Show Favorites Bar (or Hide Favorites Bar) from the Safari menu bar at the top of your window.

To manage the Favorites Bar, go to Safari > Preferences > General to find options for opening new pages with your Favorites list, and also specifying what is displayed within the Favorites.

└──

2 easy ways to protect your Mac from attack

Mac computers are certainly not immune from attacks from viruses and other forms of malicious software. So it's important to protect them with some form of third-party anti-virus software.

You can also turn on the macOS firewall from within System Preferences to provide protection from malicious software entering your Mac over the internet. To do this:

1. Access System Preferences > Security & Privacy.

2. Click on the *Firewall* tab.

3. Click on the padlock icon to make changes to your security settings.

4. Enter your Mac account login password to enable changes to be made. Click on the *Unlock* button.

5. Click on the *Turn On Firewall* button.

6. Click on the padlock icon to close it and apply the changes.

Staying secure

If your Mac is running slow, it's time to give it a little first aid. Click on the *Launchpad* icon on the Dock, and click on the *Utilities/Other* folder. Click on the *Disk Utility* app, and click on the *First Aid* button on the top toolbar to check for any errors on the hard drive. If any are found, the app will try and fix them.

You can also download third-party apps from the App Store to try and speed up a slow Mac and clear the cobwebs from the memory and file system. A few to check out are OS Cleaner, DaisyDisk, Disk Doctor, and System Cleaner.

Harness the power of your mighty tablet

Tablets — the perfect computer for folks over 50

Both tablets and laptops have become extremely popular in recent years, and it's easy to see why — they are mobile and powerful devices that can fulfill most computing needs.

But tablets are fast becoming the go-to device for many people, and they could be the perfect computer for the over 50 crowd. Here's why.

Mobility. While laptops are mobile, particularly around the home, tablets are the ultimate take-anywhere computing device. They're small enough to fit into a bag or large pocket. But they're also big enough to let you display your favorite websites, video chat with family and friends, or stay organized with your notes, address book, and calendar. Since tablets are lighter than laptops, they are much easier to carry around wherever you go.

Power. Tablets are powerful enough to perform all of your favorite computing tasks, and they are generally very efficient in terms of operation.

Ease of use. Once you get the hang of the interface on a tablet they are intuitive to use. There is no complicated file system, as with a laptop, and everything you do is self-contained within each app as it is accessed.

Expandable. iPads now have a range of accessories that can be used with them, such as external keyboards, and styluses for drawing on the screen. They are a definite option for all your productivity tasks.

When choosing a tablet, here are some of the areas you should consider.

- Screen size. Most tablets are approximately 10 inches (measured diagonally) in size, and this is a good compromise between mobility and screen viewing area.

- Battery life. Check how long the battery operates without being charged for different functions, such as surfing the web or making video calls using Wi-Fi.

- Wi-Fi/Cellular. All tablets can connect to the internet using Wi-Fi, and some can also connect to a cellular network in the same way as a smartphone. This requires a cellular service provider so it will be more expensive.

- Camera quality. Generally, the higher the pixel count for the camera (measured in megapixels), the better the quality.

Money-saver

When buying a tablet, look for one that is about a year old. Manufacturers release new models every year, so you can find bargains on the versions they are replacing. These will still be new and have good specifications, but they will be cheaper since they are not the very latest models.

---

iPad OS — the iPad's unique operating system

The iPad is essentially a large touch screen, which makes it ideal for using anywhere in the home, or for taking it with you if you are out and about.

The iPad has evolved considerably since the first model was released. You'll now find four different sizes of iPad and also a range of accessories, such as an external keyboard (Smart Keyboard) and a stylus (Apple Pencil).

You use these extra items to access the touch screen instead of using your finger. The Smart Keyboard and the Apple Pencil are sold separately from the iPad itself.

Here are the four main models of the iPad tablet.

iPad. This is the original version of the iPad and retains the standard iPad title. Its high-resolution Retina Display screen measures 10.2 inches (diagonally). The latest version is the 7th generation of the standard-size iPad and supports using the Smart Keyboard and the Apple Pencil.

iPad Air. Similar to the standard iPad, it has a 10.5-inch display. However, it is the thinnest of the iPad models and supports using the Smart Keyboard the Apple Pencil.

iPad mini. For those who like their tablets a bit smaller, the iPad mini has this area covered. Its 7.9-inch display is small enough to fit in a bag or large pocket, but large enough to provide the full iPad experience.

iPad Pro. This is the largest and most powerful iPad in the range. It comes in two sizes, 11-inch and 12.9-inch. The iPad Pro can also be used with the Smart Keyboard and the Apple Pencil.

In addition to having different models, the iPad is now powered by its own unique operating system, iPadOS. Previously, it used the same operating system as the iPhone, iOS.

While the two systems are similar, iPadOS has been specifically designed to take advantage of some of the new functions provided by the iPad's larger screen.

A closer look

To check the version of the operating system on an iPad, go to Settings > General > About. To see if there is an update available for iPad OS, have a look in Settings > General > Software Update.

Apple ID gets you up and running

When you first start using an iPad, you need to set the date and time, choose a language, and connect to your home Wi-Fi network so you can use the internet. If you're pressed for time, you can skip most of these items and set them up later in the Settings app.

Another option during the setup process is to create an Apple ID. This is an email address and a password registered with Apple that enables you to use a range of Apple services. These include:

- App Store for accessing and downloading more apps to the iPad.

- iCloud backup and sharing service. You can use it to make a copy of everything on your iPad, including the operating system. Have a look at the chapter *Save, protect, and share in the cloud* to find out more about using iCloud.

- Messages app for sending text messages.

- FaceTime app for video chatting with family and friends.

It is free to register for an Apple ID, which you can do during the setup process, or when you access functions that requires it. Or, you can register for an Apple ID on the Apple website at Apple ID *(appleid.apple.com)*. Here's how.

1. Tap on the *Create Your Apple ID* button at the top of the Apple ID web page.

2. Enter the details for the Create Your Apple ID step-by-step process to set up your Apple ID account.

Once you have created an Apple ID you will be able to use it on other Apple devices too, such as an iPhone or a Mac computer.

Navigate around the Home screen

The first screen you will see after you set up your iPad is the Home screen. This is also the screen that you will return to when you are not using any apps on the iPad. The Home screen has two main elements:

- The default apps for the iPad. These are the pre-installed apps that are included with the iPad. Tap on an app to open it.

- The Dock at the bottom of the screen. This serves as a short-cuts bar for accessing apps. It is split into two sections. The left-hand side contains your most frequently used apps. By default, these are Messages, Safari, Music, Mail, and Files, but these can be changed if required. The right-hand side displays the most recently used apps. The icons that are displayed here change as different apps are accessed on the iPad.

You can view the Home screen vertically, known as portrait mode, or horizontally, known as landscape mode.

┌─ A closer look ────────────────────────────────┐

Want to make your desktop a little more snazzy? iPadOS has
36 default wallpaper backgrounds you can use to liven up
your screen. Just look in Settings > Wallpaper. The options are
Dynamic, which means they appear to move independently
from the app icons when you tilt the iPad; and Stills, which
are static images. You can also use your own pictures from
the Photos app.

└──┘

Get to know the Home button

The Home button, located at the bottom-middle of the iPad, is an
important device for navigating around your iPad and accessing
certain functions.

- Click once on the Home button to return to the Home
  screen at any point.

- Double-click on the Home button to access the App Switcher
  window. This shows the most recently used and open apps.

- Press and hold on the Home button to access Siri, the digital
  voice assistant. This is an easy way to perform voice searches.
  Simply ask a question of Siri, for example, "Siri, what is
  today's weather forecast?"

5 gestures to cruise the iPad with ease

Since the iPad is a touch-screen device, much of the navigation is
done with gestures on the screen itself. Some of these include:

- Swiping between screens. Once you have added more apps to your iPad, they will fill up more screens. To move between these, swipe left or right with one or two fingers.

- Returning to the Home screen. Pinch together with thumb and four fingers to return to the Home screen from any open app. The Home screen can also be accessed by using a long swipe up from the bottom of any screen towards the top of the screen. (A short swipe brings up the Dock, and a slightly longer one brings up the App Switcher.)

- Swiping up and down. Swipe up and down with one finger to move up or down web pages, photos, maps, or documents. The content moves in the opposite direction of the swipe, that is, if you swipe up, the page will move down, and vice versa.

- Spreading. Spread outwards with thumb and forefinger to zoom in on a web page, photo, map or document. That will enlarge it and make it easier to see.

- Pinching. Pinch together with thumb and forefinger to zoom back out on a web page, photo, map, or document.

Lock and unlock — how to keep your tablet safe

As with all digital devices, it is important to keep the iPad locked when it's not in use. This means that it requires some form of authentication to unlock it so it can be used again. You can activate the Lock screen after a specified period of inactivity or by pressing the On/Off button once.

To unlock an iPad from the Lock screen, you first need to set up a passcode.

1. Settings > Touch ID & Passcode.

2. Tap on the *Turn Passcode On* button.

3. Enter a six-digit passcode. Confirm the passcode on the next screen.

4. The passcode is now required on the Lock screen whenever the iPad is locked.

An even more secure option for the Lock screen is to use the fingerprint identification option, known as Touch ID. Your Home button will then be used as a fingerprint sensor to unlock your iPad with the unique fingerprint you create. To use Touch ID:

1. Select Settings > Touch ID & Passcode.

2. Create a passcode as shown above in case the fingerprint with Touch ID does not work properly for any reason.

3. Tap on the *iPad Unlock* button to turn it On, and tap on the *Add a Fingerprint* option. This activates the Touch ID screen for adding your fingerprint.

4. Place your finger or thumb on the Home button several times to create the Touch ID fingerprint. The screen moves automatically after each part is captured, and the fingerprint icon starts to be filled in and turns red.

5. Once you create your Touch ID, you can unlock the iPad by pressing on the Home button with the finger you used to create the Touch ID in Step 4. It may take a little practice to create the correct pressure, but it's worth it as it is an effective system for securing your iPad.

Make the Dock your own

The Dock has been part of the iPad since it was introduced, and it can be customized to a certain extent.

By default there are five apps pinned to the Dock — Messages, Safari, Music, Mail, and Files. You can remove these default apps and add others whenever you want.

1. Press on an item on the Dock and drag it onto the main area of the Home screen.

2. Repeat the process for an app on the Home screen to drag it onto the Dock.

You can access the Dock from any app, not just from the Home screen. When you're in the app, simply do a short swipe up from the bottom of the screen.

App Switcher — the easy way to open and close apps

You have a feature in iPadOS called the App Switcher. It shows open apps and enables you to move between these and access them by tapping on the required item. It also enables you to close the apps.

You can access the App Switcher window from any screen on your iPad, as follows:

- double-click on the Home button, or

- swipe up from the bottom of any screen to the middle of the screen.

The iPad deals with open apps very efficiently, and they can be open in the background, in a state of semi-hibernation, until you need them. That means it is not essential to close apps when you move to something else. However, you may want to close them if you feel you have too many open, or if one stops working. To do this:

1. Access the App Switcher window. The currently open apps are displayed.

2. Press and hold on an app, and swipe it to the top of the screen to close it. This does not remove it from the iPad, and

it can be opened again in the usual way, by tapping on it on the Dock or the Home screen.

3. The app is removed from its position in the App Switcher window and the other apps move to fill the space.

A closer look

When you press and hold an app, all the apps on the screen start to wobble. You can then move them around the Home screen by pressing on them and dragging them into a new position.

If an app's icon has a small cross in the top left-hand corner, you can delete it by tapping on the cross. Apps that have been deleted can always be downloaded again, for free, from the App Store.

Control Center — your home base for accessing apps

The Control Center is a panel containing commonly used functions on the iPad. You can access a lot of them from the Settings app too, but the Control Center is quicker and easier. Access it with a swipe from any screen within iPadOS.

Just swipe down from the top right-hand corner of the Home screen to access the Control Center panel. The same action can be performed from any open app, or the Lock screen. This is what you'll see.

Control Center functions include:

- Music controls, which are accessed by pressing on the *Music* button. These include playing or pausing songs and changing the volume.

- Drag the buttons on the sun or loudspeaker icons to increase or decrease the screen brightness and the volume.

- Tap on individual buttons to turn items On or Off (they change color depending on their state).

The rest of the items in the Control Center are:

Airplane Mode. Tap on the airplane button to turn it On or Off. If it is Off the iPad cannot perform any form of network communication, such as connecting to the internet.

AirDrop. Tap on this button for sharing items with other AirDrop users, using Apple devices.

Wi-Fi. Tap on this button to turn the current Wi-Fi connection On or Off.

Bluetooth. Tap on this button to turn Bluetooth connections On or Off.

Screen rotation. Tap on the button with a padlock inside an arrow to lock or unlock the screen rotation. If it is locked, the screen will not change when you switch the orientation of your iPad.

Silent mode. Tap on the bell button to mute or unmute all sounds.

Do Not Disturb. Tap on the moon button to turn Do Not Disturb On or Off. If it is On, incoming calls and messages will be muted between certain hours.

Flashlight. Tap on the flashlight to turn it On or Off. This is operated using the iPad's back-facing camera — the one not on the screen of the iPad.

Camera. Press the camera button to access options for taking a selfie (self-portrait), recording a video, recording a slow-motion video, and taking a standard photo.

A closer look

You can customize the items in the Control Center by selecting Settings > Control Center > Customize Controls. If an item has a red icon next to it, tap on it to remove the item from the Control Center. If an item has a green icon next to it, tap on this to add the item to the Control Center.

Organize your iPad apps in a jiffy

Apps are the lifeblood of modern computing devices, and you'll find two types on the iPad.

- Pre-installed apps. They include the Safari web browser, Mail app, Camera app, Music app, Calendar app, Maps app, and the Notes app.

- App Store apps. These are apps you can download from the online App Store. There is a huge range of apps available, covering a variety of different categories. The apps in the App Store are updated and added to on a daily basis, so you'll always have new ones to explore.

The pre-installed apps on the iPad cover a wide range of functions, and you could happily use the device with just these apps.

However, there is no need to limit yourself to the pre-installed apps when the App Store is just a tap away. To use the App Store:

1. Tap on the *App Store* icon on the Home screen.

2. The App Store Home screen (Today) displays the latest recommended apps. Swipe up the page to see other recommendations.

3. Tap on the buttons on the bottom toolbar to view the apps according to the main categories of Today, Games, Apps, Arcade, and Search.

4. Once you have located an app you're interested in, tap on it to view its details. Swipe up the screen to view more information about the app, including user reviews and ratings.

When you identify an app you would like to use, you can download it to your iPad.

1. Tap on the button next to the app (this will say *Get* or display a price).

2. Tap on the *Install* button and enter your Apple ID account details to authorize the download.

3. Once the app has downloaded, it will appear on the next available space on one of the Home screens. Tap on the app to open and use it.

If you've downloaded so many apps that the Home screen looks cluttered, it's possible to organize them into folders. You do this by dragging one app over another to create the folder.

When you move the first app over the second one, the second one will expand to let the first one drop into the folder area. The folder is given a default name based on the category of apps, but you can change it by tapping on the text at the top of the folder and entering a new name.

You can add more items to the folder by dragging them over it. It's a great way to keep similar apps together, like your entertainment or travel apps. You can also add your folders to the Dock to keep it nice and tidy, too.

A closer look

The Contacts app acts as your address book on the iPad. Tap on this icon to open it.

Tap on the + button above the Contacts section to add a new contact and enter as much contact information as possible, such as email address and cell number.

Multitasking — how to work with 2 apps at the same time

The iPad has come a long way since the first model appeared. It still gives you a huge range of options, from accessing the internet to listening to music. But now it includes more productivity options so you can view more than one app at the same time. This is known as multitasking.

With iPadOS, this is done with the use of Split View. This function enables you to view and work with two apps within a single screen. Here's how to do it.

1. Open the first app that you want to use, such as Maps.

2. Perform a short swipe up from the bottom of the screen to access the Dock.

3. Press and hold an app on the Dock that you also want to use, and drag it to the right-hand, or left-hand, side of the screen. Release the app when a dark area appears below it.

4. Initially, the apps in Split View take up 50% of the screen and can be used independently of each other.

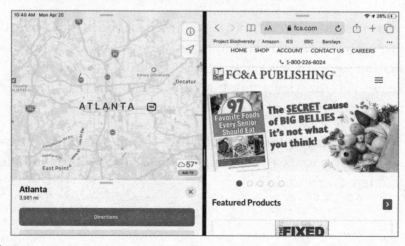

5. Drag on the middle bar to change the proportions of the two Split View panels.

6. Press and hold on the middle button and drag it away from the right-hand, or left-hand, edge of the screen to close one of the Split View apps.

Entertainment at your fingertips

You can enjoy entertainment on your iPad despite its smaller size. Check out these pre-installed apps that provide everything from music and movies to your favorite books.

iTunes Store. Tap on the *iTunes Store* app (sometimes located on the second Home screen) to access music, movies, and TV shows. Items you buy here will be available on any other Apple devices you have, such as a MacBook.

Music. Tap on the *Music* app to access your music library on the iPad. Tap on the *Library* button on the bottom tool-bar to see the items that are already in your library. Tap on the *Browse* button to find music to buy and have available on your iPad.

Tap on the *For You* button to access Apple Music, which is a sub-scription service. If you're interested, you can try it out with a three-month free trial. Radio stations are also available in the Music app via the *Radio* button on the bottom toolbar.

Movies and TV shows. Tap on the *Apple TV* app to access options for buying or renting movies and TV shows. There is also an option to subscribe to the Apple TV+ service, which offers a range of movies and TV shows, including original Apple content.

Books. Tap on the *Books* app to access the Book Store for downloading e-books, which are then stored in the Library section of the Books app, so you can then read them on your iPad.

Podcasts. Tap on the *Podcasts* app to access a huge range of podcasts (mostly audio broadcasts) that you can sub-scribe to, usually for free.

A closer look

If you have a subscription to a streaming service, such as Netflix or Amazon Prime Video, you can access these on your iPad, too. Go to the App Store and download the app for the relevant service. When you open the app you can sign in with your account details, and then start watching movies and TV shows right there on your iPad.

First step to using an Android tablet

Since Android is an operating system owned by Google, a Google Account is required when you first start using an Android device. This can be created in the following ways:

- during the initial setup of your Android tablet.

- when you first access one of the apps requiring a Google Account.

- from the Settings app, by accessing Settings > Users & accounts > Add account.

For each of the above, the process for creating the Google Account is the same.

1. If you already have an account, enter your sign-in details, or tap on the *Create account* option.

2. Enter the first and last name for the new account user, then tap on the *Next* button.

3. Enter a username (this will also become your Gmail email address), then tap on the *Next* button at the bottom of the screen.

4. Create a password for the account and then re-enter it for confirmation. Tap on the *Next* button at the bottom of the screen.

5. The account details are displayed. Tap on the *Next* button to sign in with your new account.

A closer look

Ever wondered why your Samsung tablet looks so different from your daughter's Sony tablet? It's because each manufacturer can customize Android tablets with their own design, known as a "skin."

So each company's Android device has a different visual appearance, even though they both use the same fundamental operating system. For a detailed look at the latest Android tablets, check out the website *android.com*.

Android Home screen — your home base for navigation

Once you have set up your Android tablet, the first screen you see will be the Home screen. This is also where you return each time you tap the Home button. The elements of the Home screen include the following:

- Notifications Bar and the Google Search box at the top of the screen. The Notifications Bar can be expanded by swiping down from the top of the screen.

- Home screen area. This is where the majority of your commonly used apps and widgets will be located.

- Favorites Tray at the bottom of the screen. This contains the most frequently used apps.

Take control of your tablet. You have three buttons at the bottom of the Home screen that you'll use to navigate around your tablet. On some Android tablets these are on the screen, and on others they are on the body of the tablet itself.

The Navigation buttons are, from left to right, as shown here.

- Back. Tap on the arrow to go back to the most recently visited page or screen.

- Home. Tap on the circle to go back to the Home screen at any point.

- Recents. Tap on the square to view the apps that you have used most recently. Tap on one of the apps to access it again. Swipe an app to the right or left of the screen to close it, or tap on the cross in the top right-hand corner of the app.

Navigating is a breeze. Getting around an Android tablet is generally similar to the iPad, although there are some differences.

- To move between Home screens on an Android tablet, swipe left or right on the touch screen.

- Tap on the *Home* button to return to the Home screen.

- Swipe up and down with one finger to move up or down web pages, photos, maps, or documents.

- Spread outwards with thumb and forefinger to zoom in on a web page, photo, map, or document. Pinch together with thumb and forefinger to zoom back out on the same items.

- To remove an app from the Home screen, press and hold on it, and drag it to the top of the screen. Drop it over the *Remove* button when it appears.

Learn to add and move your Android apps

The Home screen is where you manage your apps and view all of the available ones on your tablet. To do this:

1. Swipe upwards on the arrowhead on the Favorites Tray at the bottom of the screen.

2. All of the apps are displayed.

3. To add an app to the Home screen, press and hold it, then drag the app onto the Home screen you want it to appear on. Release the app at the required point.

4. The app is added to the Home screen.

5. Swipe left and right to move between the available Home screens.

With some versions of Android, the apps section is accessed by tapping on the *All Apps* button.

Once apps have been added to the Home screen they can be repositioned and moved to other Home screens. To do this:

1. Press and hold on an app to move it. Drag it into its new position. A light outline appears, indicating where the app will be positioned.

2. Release the app to drop it into its new position.

3. To move an app between Home screens, drag it to the edge of the Home screen. As the app reaches the edge of the Home screen it will automatically move to the next one. Add it to the new Home screen in the same way as in Step 2.

Explore your options in the Google Play Store

If you want more apps on your Android tablet, the Google Play Store is a great place to start. To access the Play Store and find more apps:

1. Tap on the *Play Store* app.

2. Tap on the *Apps* button on the bottom toolbar, and use the options at the top of the window to search for items using the Search box, or by tapping on one of the main headings.

3. Swipe up and down, or left and right, to see the full range of apps in the Play Store. Tap on an item to view further details about it, and tap on the *Install* button to download it to your Android tablet.

A closer look

Android widgets are similar to apps, except they generally display specific content or real-time information, like weather. You can add widgets from any Home screen. Press and hold on an empty area on the Home screen, and tap on the *Widgets* button from the options that appear. Press and hold on a widget and drop it onto a Home screen.

Put your favorites in a prime spot

The Favorites Tray at the bottom of the Home screen can be used to access the apps you use most frequently. This appears on all the Home screens. You can add or remove apps from the Favorites Tray whenever you want. To manage apps in the Favorites Tray:

1. Press and hold an app in the Favorites Tray, and drag it onto the Home screen to remove it from your Favorites.

2. If there is space on the Favorites Tray, repeat the process to select an app on the Home screen and drag it in. The Favorites Tray can only hold a certain number of apps, so if you try to add one too many, the app will spring back to its original location.

Quick settings get you going faster

While the full range of Android settings can be accessed from the Settings app, you also have a Quick Settings option that you access from the top of the screen. To use this:

1. Swipe down from any-
   where at the top of the
   screen to access the
   Quick Settings. They
   will look similar to this.

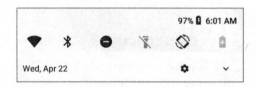

2. Tap on the downward arrow to view the full range of Quick Settings.

3. Tap on the pencil icon at the bottom of the expanded window to edit the items that appear in the Quick Settings.

4. Drag items from below the *Drag*
   to add tiles heading, to the section
   above, to include them in the
   Quick Settings. Reverse the
   process to remove an item from
   the Quick Settings.

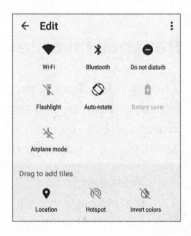

Android tablets offer a wealth of entertainment

You may see different entertainment apps on your tablet depending on which manufacturer made it. But you can use Google entertainment apps across all Android tablets, so you have plenty of options. The Google entertainment apps include:

- Music. Tap on the *Play Music* app to access the Google Play Music store for viewing music you already have, and for buying more.

- Movies and TV shows. Tap on the *Play Movies & TV* app to access the Google Play Movies & TV store for buying or renting movies and TV shows.

- Books. Tap on the *Play Books* app to access the Google Play Books store for buying e-books and audiobooks.

The Movies & TV and Books options can also be accessed from the Google Play Store by tapping on the *Movies & TV* and *Books* buttons on the bottom toolbar.

Tech talk — get smarter about your smartphone

Basic guide to your iPhone

Ever since cellphones had the word "smart" added to them they seem to be more complicated to use than some computers. This is partly because they essentially are computers, with the added function of making phone calls.

But help is at hand to unravel the mysteries of the smartphone, and this chapter will show how you can become the smart one when using an iPhone or Android cellphone.

Choose the latest models. The iPhone is a genuine phenomenon of the digital age and, since its introduction just over 10 years ago, it has transformed the perception of mobile devices in terms of communications, entertainment, and productivity.

The latest models of the iPhone run on the iOS 13 operating system and they are:

- iPhone 11, which has a 6.1-inch display (measured diagonally).

- iPhone 11 Pro, which has a 5.8-inch display.

- iPhone 11 Pro Max, which has a 6.5-inch display.

The main difference between the iPhone 11 and the iPhone 11 Pro and Pro Max is that the Pro models have a superior quality camera, with three lenses instead of two.

Options for setting it up. When you first turn on your iPhone there will be a series of setup screens. These include a range of options — creating an Apple ID account, setting up Face ID for unlocking an iPhone, and connecting to a Wi-Fi network for access to the internet. However, most of the options in the setup process can be applied, or modified, in the Settings app at a later time.

Around the Home screen. The iPhone Home screen is similar in appearance and operation to the iPad.

- Tap on an app on the Home screen to open it.

- Swipe left and right to move between available Home screens. As more apps are added to your iPhone, additional Home screens will be created.

- Press and hold on an app to move it around the Home screen. Drag an app to the edge of the screen to move it to the next Home screen.

- The Dock is located at the bottom of the Home screen. Press and hold an app on the Dock, and drag it onto the Home screen area to remove it from the Dock. Drag items onto the Dock if there is space.

- Press and hold an app on the Home screen until it starts to wobble. Tap on the cross in its top left-hand corner to remove it.

- Press and hold an app and drag it over another one to create a folder for both apps. Drag more items into the folder as required.

Money-saver

For a budget version of the iPhone, have a look at the iPhone SE. Although it still starts from $399 from the Apple website, it is considerably cheaper than the other flagship models.

iPhone 11 gestures you need to learn

The iPhone 11 models do not have a Home button. The functions you previously accessed by pressing the Home button are now performed by gestures on the screen and actions using the On/Off button. Gestures and actions for the iPhone include the following.

Turn on. Press and hold the On/Off button for a few seconds. Keep it pressed until the Apple icon appears.

Unlock the iPhone. This is done by using Face ID. Once you've set this up, raise the phone so the camera can view your face, and simultaneously swipe up from the bottom of the screen, to access the last viewed screen.

Return to the Home screen. Swipe up from the bar at the bottom of the screen. This can be done from any app.

Access the Notification Center. You can access the Notification Center by swiping down from the top left-hand corner, or the middle, of the screen.

Open the Control Center. The collection of icons for frequently used items is known as the Control Center, and you access this by swiping down from the top right-hand corner of the screen.

Call on Siri. Press and hold the On/Off button to access the iPhone's digital voice assistant, Siri.

Reachability. This is a function that makes it easier to reach the items on the iPhone's screen, particularly if you are using it one-handed. To use Reachability, which moves the items on the screen to the bottom half, swipe down from the bottom edge of the screen.

┌─ **A *closer* look** ─────────────────────────────

If you make a mistake while using your iPhone, such as deleting text in a note-taking app, shake the phone and tap on the
Undo button to revert back to the most recent version.

└──

Face ID: High-tech way to unlock your iPhone

With the removal of the Home button on the latest range of
iPhones, unlocking the phone is done through Face ID. To set
it up:

1. Access Settings > Face ID & Passcode.

2. Tap on the *Set Up Face ID* button.

3. Tap on the *Get started* button, and position your face in the
    center of the circle. Move your head slowly in a circle so the
    camera can record all elements of your face.

4. Tap on the *Continue* button after the first scan. A second scan
    will be done to complete the process.

5. Tap on the *Done* button to finish the Face ID setup process.

If you can't use Face ID to unlock your iPhone, you can use a
numerical passcode instead. This has to be set up at the same time
you create a Face ID. To do this:

1. Access Settings > Face ID & Passcode.

2. Tap on the *Turn Passcode On* button.

3. Enter a six-digit passcode. You'll use it to unlock your iPhone
    from the Lock screen.

To ensure that your iPhone cannot be accessed by anyone else, you can set the screen to auto-lock. This is the same as the Sleep option on a computer. To do this:

1. Access Settings > Display & Brightness.

2. Tap on the Auto-Lock option.

3. Tap on the time of inactivity after which you wish the screen to be locked, for example, 30 seconds or one minute.

Control center — the heart of your iPhone

Your phone's Control Center has a number of useful widgets that you can view instantly with a single gesture. Simply swipe down from the top right-hand corner of the screen.

On older iPhone models, you need to swipe up from the bottom of the screen, which now returns you to the Home screen. The options on the Control Center are the same as for the iPad, and the items there can also be customized in Settings > Control Center > Customize Controls.

Here's an example of a typical iPhone Control Center.

How to use app switcher on the iPhone

Remember the App Switcher from your iPad? It shows open apps and lets you move back and forth between them. It operates slightly differently on the iPhone.

1. Swipe up from the bottom of the screen to return to the iPhone Home screen. Swipe up from the bottom of the screen and pause in the middle of the screen to access the App Switcher.

2. From the App Switcher window, swipe left and right between open apps, and tap on one to make it the active app. Swipe an app to the top of the window in the App Switcher to close it.

Set up your Android smartphone for success

Unlike the iPhone, several manufacturers produce Android smart-phones, so you'll see a greater diversity in terms of appearance and pre-installed apps. For a detailed look at the latest Android smart-phones, check out the website *android.com*.

When you first turn on your Android smartphone (by pressing and holding the On/Off button) you will be taken through the setup process. This only has to be done once, and some of the steps can be completed or amended at a later time, usually within the Settings app.

Some of the elements that can be applied during the setup process include creating a Google Account, setting a security option for unlocking the smartphone, and linking to a Wi-Fi network for access to the internet.

Around the Home screen. Once you have set up your Android smartphone, the first screen you see will be the Home screen. This is also where you will return when you tap the Home button.

The elements of the Home screen include:

- Notifications Bar, at the top of the screen.

- Google Search box, in the middle of the screen.

- Home screen area, where the majority of your commonly used apps and widgets will be located.

- Favorites Tray, located at the bottom of the screen.

Easily manage your apps. The Home screen is where you can add and manage your apps.

1. Swipe up from the bottom of the screen, or tap on the *Apps* button, depending on the type of Android smartphone.

2. All of the built-in apps are displayed. Tap on an app to open it.

3. To add an app to the Home screen, press and hold on it.

4. Drag the app onto the Home screen on which you want it to appear and release it. The app is added to the Home screen.

5. Swipe left and right to move between the available Home screens.

6. Press and hold an app in the Favorites Tray, at the bottom of the Home screen, and drag it onto the Home screen to remove it from the Favorites Tray.

7. Press and hold an app on the Home screen, and drag it onto a space in the Favorites Tray to add it there.

A *closer* look

Tap on the Google Play Store app to access a huge range of apps that can be downloaded to your Android smartphone.

Protect your Android phone with a digital lock

You can place a digital lock on your smartphone screen to prevent unauthorized access to your device. To do this:

1. Tap on the *Settings* app.

2. Tap on the *Security & location* button.

3. Tap on the *Screen lock* button to set a method for unlocking the screen.

4. The methods for unlocking the screen are Swipe, Pattern, PIN, Password, None, and Fingerprint (if applicable). Tap on the required method to select it and set its attributes.

Just beware — if you select the Swipe or None options for unlocking an Android smartphone, anyone can gain access to it.

Add a SIM card for full network access

A SIM card is a small card that contains a chip. You need one in your phone so you can access the local mobile network to place or receive calls or send texts. You can remove it and transfer it to other phones if necessary.

117

Adding a SIM card to an iPhone. The SIM card for the iPhone will be provided by your mobile carrier — the company that provides your cellular phone and data services. Without it, you could still communicate with your iPhone, but only via Wi-Fi.

Some iPhones come with the SIM pre-installed, but you can also insert one yourself. Here's how.

1. The SIM tool is provided in the iPhone box. It looks like this.

2. Insert the SIM tool into the small hole on the SIM slot, on the side of the iPhone.

3. Press the tool firmly into the hole, so that the SIM tray pops out and starts to appear. Pull the SIM tray fully out.

4. Place the SIM card into the SIM tray. It should fit flush, resting on a narrow ridge underneath it, with the diagonal cut on the card matching the cut in the tray.

5. Place your thumb over the bottom of the SIM tray, covering the SIM card, and place the tray into the SIM slot, with the metal contacts facing the back of the phone. Push the tray firmly into the slot until it clicks into place.

Adding a SIM card to an Android smartphone. This is similar to the process described for adding a SIM to an iPhone.

1. The SIM tray is located on the side of the phone, with a small hole at the end of it.

2. Use the SIM tool that should be provided with the phone to open the SIM tray, by pressing firmly into the hole in Step 1.

3. Pull out the SIM tray and remove it fully from the phone.

4. Insert the SIM card into the SIM tray and return it into the slot on the phone.

4 top cellphone service providers

Now that you have your smartphone, there's one more critical thing you need — a cellular network to use it on. Mobile networks use 4G or 5G technology. The G stands for Generation and the higher the number the faster the network operates.

You gain access to a mobile network through a telecom company. The top cellphone providers include AT&T, Sprint, T-Mobile, and Verizon. Their range of cellphone plans can be found at their respective websites — *att.com, sprint.com, t-mobile.com*, and *verizonwireless.com*.

You can also choose from dozens of smaller cellphone service providers, many of which use the networks of the larger companies.

Secrets to cutting your cellphone bill in half

Let's face it, cellphone bills can be expensive. That's why it pays to look around and compare services. Here are some things to consider when looking for a service provider for your smartphone.

Buy your smartphone separately. Generally, it is cheaper to buy your own smartphone and then find a plan that covers access to a mobile network. This will require a larger initial outlay but should be cheaper over the duration of the plan.

Get rid of a long contract. If you have a contract for a year, or even two years, you could be locked into paying more than you need to for an extended period. Instead, look for a month-to-month plan.

Look for a deal that waives activation fees. You usually have to pay a fee to get your contract up and running. Most companies will be so keen to get you signed up that they should agree to waive it if you ask.

Find the right plan. Work out what you want to use your phone for (in terms of calls, texts and data), and find the appropriate plan. Don't pay for services you won't use. Go to *whistleout.com* to compare cellphone plans.

Watch your data usage. Most plans give you a certain amount of data each month for accessing the web and online services. If you go over the plan data limit you will be charged. Try to limit your data usage to just texts, emails, and browsing the web. If you want to do more data intensive tasks, such as downloading music or streaming movies, wait until you are connected to Wi-Fi. Better still, try and find a plan that has unlimited data usage.

Switch to another carrier. A competitor may be so eager to get new business that they will pay any early termination fee, in effect buying out your contract. The larger companies should offer this if you ask them. A smaller company that does this is Boost Mobile. Check them out at *boostmobile.com* to see what they offer.

How to handle calls from an unknown number

Unwanted calls can be the scourge of the smartphone, so what do you do if you get a call and don't recognize the caller ID? The single smartest thing is just not to answer it and let it go to voicemail. If it is important, the caller will leave a message. If not, you've saved yourself a lot of grief.

Many unwanted calls are known as robocalls. These automated calls are scams offering fake prizes or false warnings about bank accounts or tax returns. If you receive these types of calls, ignore them but take note of the number.

Here's an easy way to try and find out who's been calling. Use Google to see if there is any information online about the number, as most scam calls will have generated some comments online.

An even better option is to block the annoying robocalls altogether. This can be done with a robocall prevention app. Most phone service providers use their own apps for this purpose, so get in touch with your wireless provider, then download the app to your smartphone.

Contacts app: Your virtual address book

You can make calls and send messages with your smartphone by entering your friend's or family's details directly into the phone or messaging app. But who wants to do that over and over again?

A quicker option is to add a person's details as a contact in your smartphone's address book app, so it will be recognized whenever you want to call or message the person.

Adding contacts on an iPhone. To add a contact on an iPhone so you can access it from the Phone or Messages apps:

1. Tap on the *Contacts* app. Any contacts that you already have are displayed.

2. Tap on the plus sign button to add a new contact.

3. Enter the name for the contact at the top of the window in the First name and Last name fields.

4. Tap in one of the Phone fields, or tap once on the *add phone* button, to add a new phone field.

5. Enter the phone number with the number pad that is activated when you tap in a Phone field. Enter any other useful details, such as an email address.

6. Tap on the *Done* button to add the new contact.

7. Tap on a contact to view their full details. You can use the buttons at the top of the window to send them a text, make a voice call, make a video call, and send them an email (if their email address is included).

| message | call | video | mail |

Adding contacts on an Android smartphone. To add a contact on an Android smartphone so you can access it from the Phone or Messages apps:

1. Tap on the *Contacts* app.

2. Tap on the plus sign button to add a new contact to your Contacts list.

3. Select where you want to store the contact. This can be your Google Account, which means that the contact details will be stored in the Google cloud so you can access them wherever you are, and on different devices. You can also store a number on the phone or SIM card. If it is stored on the SIM, you can take it with you if you change phones.

4. Enter the details for the new contact and tap on the *Save* button.

5. The new contact is added to the Contacts app (which is also accessed from the Contacts tab in the Phone app).

6. Tap on a contact to see their details.

Simple steps to make and receive calls on your iPhone

Despite all the amazing things smartphones can do, they still manage to successfully fulfill their basic function of making and receiving calls. Once you have a service provider and a SIM card on your phone, you can talk to friends and family with the touch of a button.

To make a call by dialing a specific number:

1. First tap on the *Phone* app on the Dock.

2. Tap on the *Keypad* button at the bottom of the window.

3. Tap on the numbers on the keypad to enter the number, which appears at the top of the window. If you make a mistake, tap on the X button to delete the number.

4. Tap on the phone in the green circle to make the call.

To call someone you've added to your Contacts app:

1. Open the *Phone* app, and tap on the Contacts button at the bottom of the window. The *Contacts* app opens, with the Phone toolbar still visible at the bottom of the window.

2. Tap on a contact. The full details for the contact are displayed.

3. Tap on the phone button at the top of the window to call the number of the contact.

To receive a call with an iPhone:

1. When your phone rings, the person's name, photo (if you've added it to your Contacts app), and number appears on the screen. You'll have the choice to accept, decline, set a reminder, or send a message.

2. Tap on the *Accept* button (or if the phone is locked, drag the *slide to answer* button to the right) to take the call.

3. Tap on the *Decline* button to refuse the call. If the phone is locked when a call comes in, press the phone's On/Off button to decline the call. This message is then displayed at the top of the window.

4. Tap on the *Remind Me* button to decline the call but set a reminder for yourself that the person has called.

5. Tap on the *Message* button to decline the call but send the person a text message instead. Tap on the text message you want to send, as shown, or tap on the *Custom* button to create your own message.

Phone calls are a snap on your Android

On an Android smartphone, you can make a call by accessing the phone dialer and typing a contact's number on the keypad. To do this:

1. Tap on the *Phone* app on the Favorites Tray.

2. Tap on the *Keypad* button. Type the person's number on the keypad. As you enter the number, you'll see corresponding names from your Contacts list.

3. Tap on the contact's name to display their full number.

4. Tap on the phone icon to call the number.

Once you have added someone to your Contacts list, you can easily access them and then call them. To do this:

1. Tap on the *Phone* app.

2. Tap on the *Contacts* tab. At the top of the Contacts list is a Search box.

3. Tap in the Search box and type a name you want to find.

4. All matching results are shown. The more characters of a name that you type, the more the search results will be narrowed down. Tap on the contact you want to call.

To receive a call on an Android smartphone:

1. When a call is received, the caller's name is displayed (if they have been added as a contact) along with their phone number. Swipe the left-hand phone button to the right to accept a call, or swipe the right-hand button to the left to reject it.

2. Once you accept a call, you'll see these buttons at the bottom of the window. They'll give you options to use during your call.

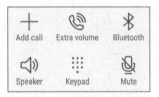

3. For example, tap on the *Keypad* button to access a keypad you can use to select options during an automated customer service call. Tap on the *Speaker* button to activate the speaker so you can hear the call without holding the phone to your ear.

Text messages — quick and easy way to communicate

Text messaging is one function that really increased the popularity of smartphones. It is a quick way to keep in touch with family and friends, and you can add fun attachments like pictures, videos, and emojis to your text. Both the iPhone and Android smartphones are highly effective when it comes to text messaging.

Messaging with an iPhone. Text messages sent with the iPhone's Messages app can either be iMessages or SMS (Short Message Service) text messages, depending on how they are sent.

iMessages are sent via Wi-Fi to other users with an Apple ID, using an iPhone, iPad, or Mac computer. SMS text messages are sent via your cellular (mobile) carrier. When you send an iMessage it appears in a blue bubble in the Messages app. SMS text messages appear in a green bubble. To send a text message:

1. Tap on the *Messages* app on the Dock.

2. Tap on this button to create a new message, and start a new conversation.

3. Tap on this button to select someone from your contacts.

4. Tap on a contact to select them as the recipient of the new message.

5. Tap in the text box above the keyboard and type the message.

6. Tap on this button to send the message.

7. As the conversation progresses, each message is displayed in the main window.

Messaging with an Android smartphone. To text a contact directly from the Messages app:

1. Tap on the *Messages* app.

2. Tap on this button to start a new message.

3. In the Contacts section, select a recipient, or search for one in the Search box.

4. Enter the text for the message and tap on the *Send* button.

A closer look

Have a long message to type? Make it easy on yourself and speak it instead. When typing a message on an iPhone or Android smartphone, simply tap on the microphone icon next to the text box to record a message by voice rather than text.

Smartphones use virtual keyboards, which appear whenever text needs to be entered. You can set your keyboard to do handy tasks like automatically capitalize words at the beginning of sentences, check spelling, and enable predictive text so the keyboard guesses at words as you type them.

To look at the keyboard settings on an iPhone, go to Settings > General > Keyboard. For an Android smartphone, go to Settings > System > Language & input, and tap on one of the keyboard options, depending on the type of Android device.

Where things get really smart — getting online

What initially transformed the humble cellphone into a smartphone was being able to access the internet. This was a game-changer and the final piece in the jigsaw that has made smartphones indispensable for so many people.

For both iPhones and Android smartphones, the process for connecting to the internet is the same.

- Use a Wi-Fi network, either at home or a Wi-Fi hotspot when you are away from home. Wi-Fi can be set up in Settings > Wi-Fi for both iPhone and Android.

- Access a cellular network through your smartphone service provider.

Once you make a connection, you can access the web with a pre-installed browser. Safari is the default browser for iPhone, and Chrome is the default for an Android smartphone.

6 activities to enjoy on your smartphone

Smartphones really are very clever and at times there seems no limit to their talents. Here are some of the things you can do, usually without having to download any additional apps.

Play music. On the iPhone, use the Music app; on an Android smartphone, use the Google Play Music app.

Watch movies and TV shows. On the iPhone, use the Apple TV app or the iTunes Store app; on an Android smartphone, use the Google Play Movies & TV app.

Read books. On the iPhone, use the Books app; on an Android smartphone, use the Google Play Books app.

View and edit photos and videos. On the iPhone, use the Photos app; on an Android smartphone, use the Google Photos app.

Get around with maps. On the iPhone, use the Maps app; on an Android smartphone, use the Google Maps app.

Monitor your health and fitness. On the iPhone, use the Health app; on an Android smartphone, use the Google Fit app.

Money-saver

Smartphones are valuable devices, so why risk breaking the phone or its screen? For a few dollars you can protect both, saving you money in the long run.

- A phone cover can protect the back and sides of the phone. Some, with a fold-over cover, also shield the front of the phone. A cover not only cushions the phone if it is dropped on the ground, it also makes it easier to hold.

- A screen protector is a piece of clear, hardened plastic that attaches to the screen of the phone. If you drop the phone, the screen protector may crack, but the screen itself should survive the fall.

Protect your cellphone from being hacked

Since smartphones are essentially small computers, they can be hacked just like any other computing device, in some cases even more easily. Here are some signs to watch out for:

- strange apps appearing on the Home screen.

- the phone shuts itself down randomly.

- the battery drains unusually quickly.

- pop-up messages appear on the Home screen and in the smartphone's web browser.

- apps refuse to open, or close unexpectedly.

If any of these things happen, or you see other unexplained behavior, immediately download an anti-malware app. That's the best way to protect your privacy, your security, and your bank account from malicious phone pirates.

Go to the App Store or the Google Play Store, enter "anti-malware" or "anti-virus" into the search box, and select one of the options. Or select several apps and test them on your smartphone to see which one you like best. For the best protection, do this when you first start using your smartphone.

Never fear — here's how to locate a lost smartphone

Your smartphone may be one of the most valuable objects you own. You'd hate to see it get lost or, worse, stolen. But don't worry — if the unthinkable happens, help is at hand.

Both iPhones and Android smartphones have a Find Phone function that will locate your missing phone. You have to set it up first, but after that you can use it to locate a lost smartphone through a web browser.

Locating a lost iPhone. To set up the Find Phone function on an iPhone:

1. Access Settings > Apple ID > iCloud.

2. Tap on the *Find My* button.

3. Tap on the *Find My iPhone* button.

4. Drag the *Find My iPhone* button to On.

5. Drag the *Send Last Location* button to On. If the iPhone is turned off, or the battery dies, it will send its last known location.

If your iPhone goes missing you can try and locate it as follows:

1. On a web browser, log in to the iCloud website at *icloud.com* with your Apple ID.

2. Click on the *Find iPhone* button. If the iPhone can be located, it will be shown on the map.

3. Click on the iPhone name to access options to send a sound to the iPhone, lock it with a password so no one can gain unauthorized access, or erase its contents if you are concerned they could be compromised.

Locating a lost Android smartphone. To set up the Find Phone function on an Android smartphone:

1. Access Settings > Security & location.

2. Tap on the *Find My Device* button. Drag the button to On.

3. Make sure that *Location* is On also, at Settings > Security & location > Location.

If your Android smartphone goes missing, you can try and locate it as follows:

1. On a web browser, go to *android.com/find* and log in with your Google Account details. If the Android smartphone can be located, it will be shown on the map.

2. Select options to send a sound to the Android smartphone, lock it with a password so no one can gain unauthorized access, or erase its contents if you're concerned they could be compromised.

┌─ **Staying secure** ─────────────────────────

When you're setting up the Find feature on your phone, don't forget about your tablet. The Find My iPhone function works in the same way for an iPad as an iPhone. And the Find My Device function will protect your Android tablet just as well as your Android phone.

7 tricks for making your cellphone battery last longer

One of the main complaints about smartphones is that the batteries run down too quickly. But help is at hand, with a few handy hints for preserving battery power. Most of these options can be accessed from the device's settings.

- Put the battery into Low Power Mode.

- Turn your smartphone off at night.

- Turn down the screen brightness.

- Activate the Lock screen sooner.

- Turn off Wi-Fi and Bluetooth.

- Turn off Location Services.

- Turn off background app refresh.

┌─ **Money-saver** ─────────────────────────

You may not want to spend extra money on accessories for your phone, but a few items will help you get even more out of your investment. Look for a mobile battery pack for backup battery power, a spare charger, a dock for charging your smartphone, and a stand to support it, such as when you're having a video chat.

15 most useful — and free — cellphone apps for seniors

The hands-down best thing about apps is how much easier they make your life. Here are 15 helpful apps you'll want to download now.

AccuWeather. For top-quality weather forecasts.

Evernote. A powerful note-taking app.

Facebook. Get the most popular social media app on your smartphone.

Flightradar24. Track flights around the world.

GasBuddy. Get the best gas prices from around the country.

Magnifying Glass with Light. Use your smartphone's screen as a magnifying glass, complete with flashlight.

MapMyWalk. Track the exact distance whenever you go for a walk.

Medisafe. Get updates and reminders for taking medication.

Pocket. Save web pages so you can read them offline, when you are not connected to the internet.

Relaxing Sounds. Soothing sounds to help you relax and fall asleep.

Snapseed. An easy-to-use and powerful photo editor.

Tip Calculator Free. Never worry about how much to tip again.

Waze. Get directions to wherever you are going, and avoid frustrating traffic jams.

Wi-Fi Finder. Free Internet. Find free Wi-Fi access when you are out and about.

Words with Friends. Challenge your friends in this fun game of word play.

What not to do with your smartphone

Smartphones are undoubtedly wonderful things, and they can improve your life in numerous ways. But they can definitely be misused, too. Avoid letting your smartphone cause you, or people around you, any unnecessary annoyance or injury. Here are some of the major faux-pas to look out for.

- Using your phone while driving. It's dangerous to you and other road users and illegal in most states.

- Texting while walking. If you must text when you are out somewhere, find a spot where you're not in the way of anyone else, stop walking, and then compose your message.

- Using your phone while crossing the road.

- Conversing in the cinema or theater, or during a meal in a restaurant.

- Keeping your phone on at night. If you turn your phone off, chances are you will get a better night's sleep.

- Discussing important details on your phone in public, such as online banking details or debit or credit card numbers.

- Loud keyboard sounds. Don't have the keyboard sounds activated if you are texting around other people. The "clicks" can be extremely annoying, so turn them off in your phone's Sounds settings.

Slick tricks to simplify your device

Nifty features that make your device easier to use

Everyone should be able to use computing devices to their full potential, regardless of issues with sight, hearing, or motor skills. Fortunately, desktop computers, laptops, tablets, and smartphones all have a range of accessibility options that address these issues. Here's what to look for on your device.

Zooming. Poor eyesight is generally a result of the aging process. Therefore, it's helpful to increase the size of whatever is on your screen. This can either be for a specific item, particularly text, or for everything on the screen.

Narration. For anyone with vision problems, having a computing device speak what is on the screen is a valuable feature. This is available through the narrator option. It usually covers the text that is on the screen, and also the controls, such as buttons and check boxes.

Dictation. If you have issues with your hands, it may be painful to type for prolonged periods of time, either on a virtual keyboard or a physical one. To overcome this, you can speak your words through dictation rather than write them.

Closed captions. When watching movies, TV shows, or videos (such as those on YouTube), closed captions (subtitles) can be a useful feature for people with hearing issues. Closed captions will only work on some apps though. If an app supports closed captions, there will be an option to turn it on within the app.

Inverting screen color. Traditionally, computer screens display text as black on a white background. However, this does not suit everyone, and some people find it easier to read text on different colored backgrounds. To help with this, you can invert the screen colors on a computing device. On some platforms, it is also possible to change the overall color scheme to make elements easier to see.

Flash alerts. If you're hard of hearing, sound alerts and notifications on your device won't do you much good. To overcome this, look for an option to display screen flashes to indicate a new alert or notification.

Hearing. For hearing aid users, the iPad and iPhone have some options that can help improve sound quality. Check with the manufacturer of the hearing aid to see if they have any specific recommendations.

Keyboard and mouse. On desktop computers and laptops, you'll find accessibility options to customize the keyboard and mouse to make them easier and more comfortable to handle.

Read on to find out how you can use these features on all your devices.

A closer look

You're excited to learn your device has special features to make it easier to use. So where do you go to find all these great options?

- On an iPad or iPhone, look in Settings > Accessibility.

- On an Android tablet or smartphone, look in Settings > Accessibility.

- On a Windows 10 desktop computer or laptop, look in Settings > Ease of Access.

- On a macOS iMac or MacBook, look in System Preferences > Accessibility.

Put your squinting days behind you

Having trouble seeing those tiny words on your iPhone or iPad? Or maybe it's hard to see the letters on that bright white screen. Try these options to make your screen easier to view.

Zoom in to enlarge your text. On an iPad or iPhone, the function for zooming in is a good way to magnify certain areas of your screen.

1. In the Accessibility settings, tap on the *Zoom* button in the Vision section.

2. Drag the *Zoom* button to On.

3. The Zoom function activates a window that can be dragged around the screen, and it magnifies everything underneath it.

4. Double-tap with three fingers to zoom in and out. Drag the zoom panel with three fingers to move it around the screen.

5. Tap on the *Zoom Region* option.

6. Select whether to zoom using a specific area of the screen (pinned), the whole screen, or the area passed over by the zoom window.

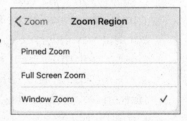

7. Drag the *Maximum Zoom Level* slider to specify the amount of zoom used.

Magnify everything on your screen. Not only can the iPad and iPhone increase the size of elements on the screen, they can also be used as a magnifying glass, so you can zoom in on items such as books or articles that you are reading. To do this:

1. In the Accessibility settings, tap on the *Magnifier* button in the Vision section.

2. Drag the *Magnifier* button to On.

3. Once the magnifier has been turned On, it can be activated at any time by triple-clicking the Home button (iPad) or triple-clicking the On/Off button (iPhone). This opens the camera and enables you to zoom in on whatever the camera is pointed at. Drag the slider at the side of the camera up and down to change the level of magnification.

Change the size and style of text. The Display & Text Size accessibility options for the iPad and iPhone are an excellent way to get the text on the screen looking exactly how you want it.

1. In the Accessibility settings, tap on the *Display & Text* button in the Vision section.

2. Drag the options *On* or *Off* for the different options, as required.

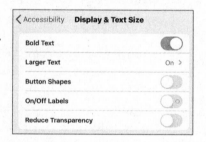

3. The Display & Text Size options can be used to select bold text for the whole screen, increase the size of the text for the whole screen (tap on the *Larger Text* button and select the required text size), reduce the transparency between certain items so they appear clearer, and increase the contrast between the foregrounds and backgrounds of apps so items appear clearer.

Invert colors for more comfortable viewing. The on-screen colors can have a significant effect on anyone with color blindness or who has difficulty reading text on certain colored backgrounds. The accessibility options for the iPad and iPhone offer a number of options for customizing this.

1. In the Accessibility settings, tap on the *Display & Text* button in the Vision section.

2. Drag the *Classic Invert* button to On to reverse the colors of the display.

3. Drag the *Smart Invert* button to On to reverse the colors of the background and the text on the screen, but keep other elements the same, such as images and app icons.

4. Tap on the *Color Filters* option.

5. Drag the *Color Filters* button to On, and select a color to apply this as the screen color filter.

6. Drag the slider at the bottom of the window to determine the intensity of the filter.

A closer look

If you'll be doing a lot of dictation, it would be worth looking at a dedicated dictation app. For Apple and Android devices, try Dragon Anywhere. For Windows 10, one option is the Dictation App that is available in the Microsoft Store.

Let your phone talk to you

If you can't make out what's on your screen, just let your phone or tablet tell you. To enable an iPad or iPhone to speak what is on the screen:

1. In the Accessibility settings, tap on the *VoiceOver* button in the Vision section.

2. Drag the *VoiceOver* button to On to enable the narrator.

3. Drag the *Speaking Rate* slider to specify the speed of the narrator.

4. Tap on the *Speech* and *Verbosity* options to specify these settings for the narrator.

5. To turn off *VoiceOver*, tap once on the *VoiceOver* button to select it, and double-tap to turn it Off.

You can also let your phone speak for you. Tell your iPad or iPhone what you want to say by using the Dictation feature.

Instead of entering text via the virtual keyboard, you can activate Dictation directly from the keyboard of a compatible app by tapping on the microphone icon.

Fingers a little achy? You'll love the touch options

The AssistiveTouch function for the iPad and iPhone is an excellent option if you don't want to use all the physical gestures for getting around the device, such as pressing the Home button. To use this:

1. In the Accessibility settings, tap on the *Touch* button in the Physical and Motor section.

2. Tap on the *AssistiveTouch* option, and drag the *AssistiveTouch* button to On.

3. The *AssistiveTouch* icon appears on the screen. Press and hold on the icon and drag it to a different location on the screen, as required.

4. Tap on the *AssistiveTouch* icon to view its options.

5. Tap on the items to access them. For example, open the Control Center rather than having to swipe on the screen.

6. Tap on the *Device* option to access more functions to use via AssistiveTouch, rather than using gestures on the screen or the body of the device, such as the volume buttons.

The Home button on an iPad can be customized in terms of how it reacts when it is double-clicked or triple-clicked for certain actions. To do this:

1. In the Accessibility settings, tap on the *Home Button* option in the Physical and Motor section.

2. In the *Click Speed* section, select a speed for clicking the Home button, either Default, Slow, or Slowest.

On an iPhone without a Home button, the same function is accessed from Settings > Accessibility > Side Button.

A closer look

One of the useful functions of AssistiveTouch is to take a screenshot on an iPad or iPhone, without having to worry about pressing a combination of buttons on the body of your device. A screenshot captures an image of what is exactly on the screen.

To do this with AssistiveTouch, navigate to the screen you want to capture. Tap on the AssistiveTouch icon, and select Device > More. Tap on the *Screenshot* button to capture what is on the screen. (The AssistiveTouch items will not appear in the screenshot.)

Fabulous features for the hearing impaired

Just because you're a little hard of hearing doesn't mean you shouldn't enjoy all the features your iPhone or iPad has to offer. Here are some options you need to try.

Flash alerts. You like to get notifications when you receive calls or messages, but sometimes you don't hear the alerts. Good news — Apple devices have an option to flash the screen instead.

1. In the Accessibility settings, tap on the *Audio & Visual* button in the Hearing section.

2. Drag the *LED Flash for Alerts* button to On to activate a flash on the screen when a notification is received.

Hearing aids. If you use hearing aids, you have an option to link certain devices to an iPad or iPhone. To do this:

1. In the Accessibility settings, tap on the *Hearing Devices* button in the Hearing section.

2. Under the *MFI Hearing Aids* option, tap on a compatible bluetooth hearing aid to link to your iPad or iPhone.

3. Drag the *Hearing Aid Compatibility* button to On to improve sound quality with compatible hearing aids. Check with the manufacturer of the hearing aid to see which devices support this.

Closed captions. You're a big fan of the show *Outlander*, but it sure is hard to understand those Scottish accents. How would you like to see exactly what they're saying? Just use the closed captions and subtitles feature.

1. In the Accessibility settings, tap on the *Subtitles & Captioning* button in the Hearing section.

2. Drag the *Closed Captions + SDH* button to On to activate this, when using a compatible app that supports closed captioning.

6 ways Android makes your device easier to use

As the owner of an Android tablet or phone, you have just as many accessibility options as an Apple aficionado. Look for these features to make your experience more enjoyable.

Magnification. To enlarge what is on the screen for an Android device:

1. In the Accessibility settings, tap on the *Magnification* button.

2. Tap on one of the Magnification options, and tap on its button to turn it On.

3. If *Magnify with triple-tap* is turned On, the screen items can be magnified by tapping three times quickly on the screen. Tap three times again to go back to the original magnification level.

4. If *Magnify with button* is turned On, tap on this accessibility icon next to the Android control buttons at the bottom of the screen.

5. Tap anywhere on the screen to magnify it. Drag with two fingers to move around the magnified screen. Tap on the accessibility icon again to return to normal magnification.

Narration. To get an Android device to read what is on the screen, or what you've selected:

1. In the Accessibility settings, tap on the *Text-to-speech* output button.

2. Apply the required settings for the narrator (engine) to use for converting text to speech, the language to use, the speech rate, and the pitch. Tap on the *Play* button to hear a sample.

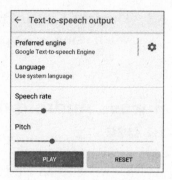

Dictation. Dictation can be activated directly from the keyboard of a compatible app by tapping on the microphone icon.

Inverting colors. To change the color appearance of an Android device, go to the Accessibility settings, and tap the *High contrast text* or *Color inversion* buttons to On to apply these features.

Flash alerts. For Android devices, the best option for flash alerts is to download an appropriate app from the Google Play Store. Search for "flash alerts" in the Play Store. These apps operate by using the device's camera to produce a flash alert when a sound notification is received.

Closed captions. To use closed captions and subtitles:

1. In the Accessibility settings, tap on the *Captions* button.

2. Drag the *Captions* button to On to activate it when using a compatible app that supports closed captioning. Make appropriate selections for how the *Language, Text size, and Caption style* options operate by tapping on each item.

Size up to see everything better

Your computer may be much larger than a tablet or cellphone, but it still can be difficult to read the small print. Here's how to make text larger on the screen of a Windows desktop computer or laptop.

1. In the Ease of Access settings, click on the *Display* button in the left-hand panel.

2. Under the *Make text bigger* heading, drag the slider to change the size of the on-screen text. Click on the *Apply* button to make the change.

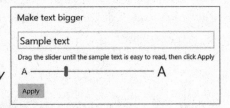

3. Under the *Make everything bigger* heading, click in the box and select a size for everything on the screen, not just the text.

Like the smaller devices, Windows desktops and laptops have an option for zooming in on areas of the screen. You can also change the magnification level of the zoom function.

1. In the Ease of Access settings, click on the *Magnifier* button in the left-hand panel.

2. Drag the *Turn on Magnifier* button to On.

3. This activates a window (lens) that magnifies everything it passes over. The window can be dragged around the screen to magnify items as required.

4. Use the *Magnification* panel to decrease, or increase, the amount of magnification used in the magnification window.

5. Set the required options for the Magnifier.

6. Click in the *Change Magnifier* view box to select the type of magnification that is used. The options are for *Lens*, which is the default option of the on-screen window; *Docked*, which inserts a bar across the top of the screen — everything the cursor passes over is magnified in this bar; and *Full screen*, which magnifies the whole screen.

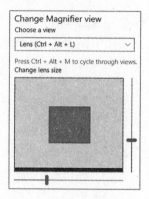

Change Magnifier view

Choose a view

Lens (Ctrl + Alt + L)

Press Ctrl + Alt + M to cycle through views.
Change lens size

How to narrate and dictate in Windows

Let Windows read what's on your screen so you don't have to squint to see it. To enable Windows to do this:

1. In the Ease of Access settings, click on the *Narrator* button in the left-hand panel.

2. Drag the *Turn on narrator* button to On.

3. The item that is being read is highlighted with a blue box, and the narrator gives a description of what it is, for example, "On, Narrator, toggle switch."

4. Use the *Personalize Narrator's voice* settings to specify a voice for the narrator, the speed of speech, the pitch, and whether there are pauses in the intonation.

Windows also has a keyboard shortcut that can activate the dictation function.

1. In an appropriate app, such as a word processing or notes app, press the Win key+H.

2. The dictation bar is activated.

3. Speak what you want to appear on the screen. You can add punctuation by saying "period" or "comma," and give general commands such as "Select All." Say "Stop dictating" when you are finished.

2 Windows settings you need to adjust

The keyboard and mouse are the two devices you use most when working with a desktop computer. You might as well be comfortable when handling them.

To specify the operation of the keyboard in Windows:

1. In the Ease of Access settings, click on the *Keyboard* option in the left-hand panel.

2. Make selections for the keyboard as required. These include *Use the On-Screen Keyboard*, which is a virtual keyboard that appears on the screen once it has been activated.

To specify the operation of the mouse in Windows:

1. In the Ease of Access settings, click on the *Mouse* option in the left-hand panel.

2. Make selections for the mouse as required. These include enabling the numbers pad to be used to move the mouse pointer (cursor) around the screen.

Hearing or vision problems? Make the screen your friend

Your computer screen can be your best friend if you have problems with vision or hearing. Just make a few simple adjustments. Here are some of the things it can do.

Alert you with flashes. To enable the Windows screen to flash when you receive an audio alert for something:

1. In the Ease of Access settings, click on the *Audio* button in the left-hand panel.

2. Click in the *Show audio alerts visually* box.

3. Select an option for how the visual notification works.

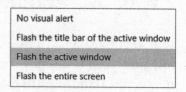

Supply captions to make speech clearer. To show closed captions and subtitles in Windows:

1. In the Ease of Access settings, click on the *Closed captions* option in the left-hand panel.

2. Select the required closed captions settings. These will be displayed in apps that support closed captions.

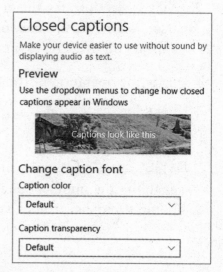

Invert screen colors for easier viewing. You have a number of options for changing the screen color in Windows.

1. In the Ease of Access settings, click on the *High contrast* button in the left-hand panel.

2. Drag the *Turn on high contrast* button to On.

3. Click in the *Choose a theme* box.

4. Select a color theme. This will be applied to elements such as scroll bars, icons, desktop, and menu bars.

5. Click on the *Apply* button to see the new color theme.

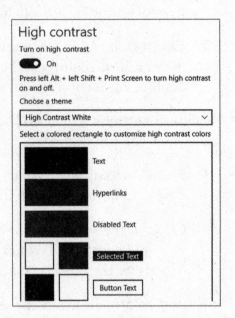

8 super Mac settings that simplify your life

If you have a Mac computer, you probably loved how easy it was to use right out of the box. Here are eight settings that will make things even better for your aging eyes and hands.

Zooming. To zoom in on areas of the screen on a Mac using macOS:

1. In the Accessibility System Preferences, click on the *Zoom* button in the left-hand panel.

2. Check the box *Use keyboard shortcuts to zoom* to activate the zoom function from these keys.

Mouse settings. To specify the operation of the mouse in macOS:

1. In the Accessibility System Preferences, click on the *Pointer Control* button in the left-hand panel.

2. Click on the *Mouse & Trackpad* tab, and make selections for the mouse as required. These include the speed at which a double-click action is activated.

Keyboard settings. A virtual keyboard can be used with macOS, rather than the physical one.

1. In the Accessibility System Preferences, click on the *Keyboard* button in the left-hand panel.

2. Click on the *Accessibility Keyboard* tab at the top of the window, and check the box next to *Enable Accessibility Keyboard* to activate the on-screen keyboard.

Inverting colors. To invert the screen colors with macOS to make items easier to read:

1. In the Accessibility System Preferences, click on the *Display* button in the left-hand panel.

2. Click on the *Display* tab, and check the *Invert colors* checkbox to On. Make any other selections, as required, such as for *Increase contrast*. Drag the *Display contrast* slider to determine the amount of contrast for the screen elements.

Using the macOS narrator. To enable macOS to read what is on the screen:

1. In the Accessibility System Preferences, click on the *VoiceOver* button.

2. Check the *Enable VoiceOver* checkbox On to enable the narrator.

Voice commands. To use your voice to specify certain actions with macOS:

1. In the Accessibility System Preferences, click on the *Voice Control* button.

2. Check the *Enable Voice Control* button to On to activate voice control. Once this has been done, you can perform a range of actions with your voice, such as closing a window by saying, "Close window." Click on the *Commands* button to see the full range of voice control commands, and also create your own.

Flash alerts. To enable the macOS screen to flash when you receive an audio alert:

1. In the Accessibility System Preferences, click on the *Audio* button in the left-hand panel.

2. Check the *Flash the screen when an alert sound occurs* checkbox to On. Click on the *Test Screen Flash* button to preview the effect.

Closed captions. To use closed captions and subtitles:

1. In the Accessibility System Preferences, click on the *Captions* button in the left-hand panel.

2. Check the *Prefer closed captions and SDH* checkbox to On to use closed captions rather than standard subtitles.

A closer look

Dictation can also be used with macOS devices to enter text by speaking, rather than having to type it. To do this, go to System Preferences > Keyboard, and click on the *Dictation* tab. Next to the *Dictation* option, click in the *On* box. Once dictation has been turned on, it can be activated in a compatible app by selecting File > Start Dictation from the Menu bar.

Save, protect, and share with the cloud

How to crash-proof your computer files

The best way to give yourself the confidence to explore new computing features is to make sure everything is safe and secure, by backing up all of your valuable documents, such as photos and family records.

One option is to store copies of your important documents with an online cloud service. This involves copying the files from the computer in your home onto the storage computers (known as servers) used by the company providing the cloud service.

Some cloud services are proprietary ones. That means they are linked to specific operating systems, such as the OneDrive cloud service for Windows computers; iCloud for Mac computers, iPads, and iPhones; and Google Drive for Android devices.

There are also third-party cloud services, such as Dropbox, which can be used from a computer using any operating system. Most cloud services offer a free amount of storage, but you can buy more if you need it.

Once you know your files are stored in the cloud, you can be confident in whatever you do, safe in the knowledge that you'll never, ever lose a precious photo or document — even from theft, fire, or flood.

OneDrive: Windows service in the cloud

Windows 10 cloud service is known as OneDrive. Items can be saved here from your Windows 10 desktop computer or laptop and then opened on another Windows 10 device, or accessed online at *onedrive.live.com*. By default, you get 5GB of free storage in OneDrive. This can be upgraded to 100GB for $1.99 a month.

You need a Microsoft Account before you can set up OneDrive. You then have the option to access OneDrive through the app or through File Explorer. Both display the same content.

To access the OneDrive app:

1. Click on the *Start* button, and click on the *OneDrive* icon on the Start menu. (This icon is colored blue on the Start menu).

2. In the *Setup OneDrive* window enter your Microsoft Account email address, and click on the *Sign in* button.

3. Enter your Microsoft Account password, and click on the *Sign in* button.

4. Click on the *Next* button.

5. Select the folders that you want to use with OneDrive by checking the On boxes next to them. Click on the *Next* button.

6. The OneDrive app displays the folders and files within it.

To access OneDrive through File Explorer:

1. Click on the *Start* button, and click on the File Explorer OneDrive icon (the one with a folder behind it).

2. The OneDrive folder opens in File Explorer. This contains the same content as the OneDrive app. If content is added to either version it will be available in the other one, too.

OneDrive has its own range of settings, which can be accessed from the Notification area of the Taskbar (at the right-hand side).

1. Right-click on the OneDrive icon in the Notification area on the Taskbar, and click on the *Settings* option.

2. Click on the *Settings* tab for General settings and Notifications settings.

3. Click on the *Account* tab.

4. Click on the *Choose folders* button to specify which folders are used with OneDrive (the same way you set it up in the first instance).

5. Check the files On or Off, as required, and click on the *OK* button.

Remembering to back up all your important files on a regular basis can be a bit tedious. OneDrive is aware of this and offers some help with an *Auto Save* function, which can be used to automatically save some types of content to OneDrive. To use this:

1. Right-click on the OneDrive icon in the Notification area on the Taskbar, and click on the Settings option.

2. Click on the Backup tab at the top of the window.

3. Click on the Manage backup button.

4. Click on the required folders to select them. Once you do this, the content in these folders will automatically be copied to OneDrive whenever it is changed, providing there is enough storage space. Click on the Start backup button.

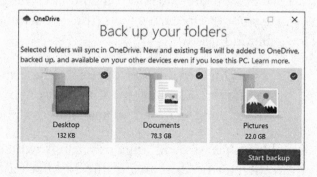

A *closer* look

If the OneDrive icon is not on the Taskbar, open Settings > Personalization > Taskbar and, under the *Notification area* heading, click on the *Select which icons appear on the taskbar* option. Drag the *Microsoft OneDrive* button to On.

2 easy ways to add files to OneDrive

Once you set up OneDrive, you can add files to it by saving, or copying, them into the OneDrive folder in File Explorer on your Windows 10 desktop computer or laptop. You can also do it directly through the OneDrive app.

To add files to the OneDrive folder in File Explorer.

1. Create a document and save it. Then select File > Save As from the Menu bar.

2. Click on the OneDrive icon at the top of the Navigation pane in File Explorer.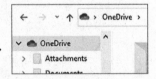

3. The OneDrive folders are displayed in the main window. Double-click on the folder where you want to save the file.

4. Click on the *Save* button.

5. To copy an item into the OneDrive folder, right-click on it in File Explorer, and select the *Copy* option.

6. Navigate to the required location in the OneDrive folder, right-click on an empty space, and select the *Paste* option.

To add files directly to the OneDrive app:

1. Open the OneDrive app from the Start menu, and click on the arrow button to upload files or a folder into OneDrive.

2. Select whether to upload *Files* or a *Folder*.

3. Navigate to the required item in File Explorer, click on it to select it, and click on the *Select Folder* (or *Open* for a file) button.

How to access OneDrive online

It's easy to work with OneDrive online. To view files and add new ones in the online version:

1. Access OneDrive at *onedrive.live.com*, and log in with your Microsoft Account details.

2. Click on the *Sign in* button.

3. The files and folder structure should be the same as for OneDrive on your Windows desktop computer or laptop.

4. Click on a folder to open it, or click on a file to view it.

5. Click on the *Upload* button on the top toolbar to upload files from the device you are using.

6. Click on the *New* button to create a new item in OneDrive. This will be available in the OneDrive folder and app on your Windows desktop computer or laptop.

To check your storage in OneDrive:

1. Right-click on the OneDrive icon in the Notification area on the Taskbar, and click on the *Settings* option.

2. Click on the *Account* tab. The amount of used storage is shown at the top of the window.

Let iCloud give you peace of mind

For Mac, iPadOS, and iOS users, iCloud is the invisible, but powerful, force that helps you back up and share the content on your Apple devices. After you set it up, you can:

- back up all of the content on your device.

- back up content from specific apps.

- access content that has been created on one device, and edit it on another.

- share items with family members.

- share photos directly from the Photos app.

Once you have an Apple ID, an iCloud account is automatically created, too. This is linked to your Apple ID. You can then specify how you would like iCloud to operate.

1. Open the *Settings* app on an iPad or iPhone, or *System Preferences* on a Mac.

2. Select the *Apple ID* button.

3. Tap on the *iCloud* button.

4. Drag the buttons to On or Off for the items whose content you want to store in iCloud. They will then be available on other compatible Apple devices. For instance, it you specify you want Notes to use iCloud, you can create a Note on your iPhone, and then pick it up and continue with it on your iPad.

Once you set up iCloud, you can leave it alone without worrying about it, giving you the peace of mind to get on with other things.

157

┌─ A *closer look* ──────────────────────────

One of the best things about iCloud is that you can share content with your family by setting up *Family Sharing*. You can use it to invite up to five family members to share your favorite apps, music, books, and more.

Want to show them those great vacation photos you took? For iPadOS/iOS, select *Photos* in the Settings, and drag the *iCloud Photos* button to On. For macOS, open the Photos app, select Photos > Preferences from the menu bar, click on the *iCloud* tab, and check the *iCloud Photos* checkbox.

└──────────────────────────────────

Safeguard your docs in the cloud

In addition to storing items such as notes, calendars, addresses, and Safari browser settings, iCloud can also be used to store documents. Documents are stored in the Files app, which is part of iCloud Drive. You'll set this up in the iCloud section of Settings.

1. Access Settings > Apple ID > iCloud and drag the *iCloud Drive* button to On.

2. Once iCloud Drive has been activated, the apps that can use it are displayed below the iCloud Drive button. Drag the buttons to On for the items you want to use. These will be the apps whose content is stored in iCloud Drive.

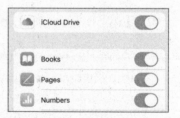

Simple steps to access iCloud online

Once you set up iCloud and specify the types of content you would like saved there, you can access these items online wherever you are.

1. Go to the iCloud website at *icloud.com*, and log in with your Apple ID details. All of the iCloud items are displayed.

2. Click on an item to view the content within it. For instance, if you have created notes on an iPad, these will be available from the Notes icon on the iCloud website.

3. You can also create new content in the online version of iCloud. Write a new note there, and it will show up on all of your iCloud-enabled devices.

To check your storage in iCloud:

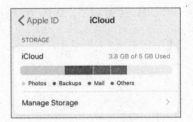

1. Access Settings > Apple ID > iCloud. The amount of used and free storage space is displayed at the top of the window.

2. Tap on the *Manage Storage* button to view how much storage specific apps are using. Click on the *Change Storage Plan* button to upgrade your iCloud storage.

By default, you get 5GB of free iCloud storage. This can be upgraded to 50GB for $0.99 a month, 200GB for $2.99 a month, and 2TB for $9.99 a month.

Google Drive — Android's solution to your cloud needs

Android devices have their own cloud service for backing up and sharing files. The Google Drive app gives you 15GB of free storage for your documents, photos, and other files.

As with other cloud services, content within Google Drive can be accessed from any online computer, tablet, or smartphone, providing you have online access. To use Google Drive:

1. Access the All Apps section on your Android device, and tap on the *Drive* app.

2. Sign in to Google Drive with your Google Account login and password.

3. The Drive app opens at the *My Drive* home page, which displays the content that has been added.

4. Tap on the *Home* button on the bottom toolbar to view the latest items that have been added.

5. Tap on the *Files* button on the bottom toolbar to view all the files and folders in Google Drive.

Here's how to add files to Google Drive.

1. Tap on the plus sign button in the Drive app to add items to Google Drive.

2. Select an option for the new items. You can upload an existing file by tapping on the *Upload* button, create a new scanned file with the *Scan* button, or create new files with the Google Docs, Google Sheets, or Google Slides apps.

Secrets to using Google Drive online

You've added files to Google Drive on your Android device. Now how do you access them online? And how can you tell how much storage you've used? Just take these easy steps.

1. Go to the website at *google.com/drive*, and click on the *Go to Drive* button.

2. Log in with your Google Account details.

3. Click on the *My Drive* button to view the contents of your Google Drive. These should mirror the contents of the Drive app on your Android device.

4. Click on the *New* button to upload items to Google Drive from the device you are using, or create new content in the same way as using the Google Drive app.

To check your storage in Google Drive:

1. Open the Drive app on your Android device, and tap on the menu button (three horizontal lines) to the left of the *Search in Drive* box.

2. The amount of used storage is shown under the *Upgrade storage* heading. Tap on this button to view details about the amount of storage used.

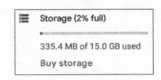

You can upgrade the 15GB of free storage for your Google Drive to 100GB for $1.99 a month, or 2TB for $9.99 a month.

Backup is a snap with a Google account

You can set many of your apps to automatically back up to Google Drive on your Android device. You must be signed in to your Google Account to use this, but once you set it up, content on your Android tablet will synchronize with Google Drive on a regular basis (at least daily).

To specify which items you would like backed up on your Android device:

1. Access Settings > Google > Backup.

2. Drag the *Backup to Google Drive* button to On.

3. Tap on the *Backup now* button.

Dropbox — a cloud service for everyone

In addition to the cloud services linked to specific operating systems, you can use an independent cloud service on your device. The most widely used is Dropbox. It can be accessed on any platform or device, and it is an excellent option for backing up and sharing your files. To use Dropbox:

1. Download the *Dropbox* app from the Apple App Store, the Microsoft Store, or the Google Play Store.

2. Create a user account with an email username and a password.

3. Click on the *Home* button on the bottom toolbar to view the most recent activity in your account.

4. Click on the *Files* button on the bottom toolbar to view the file structure in your Dropbox account, and access items.

5. Tap on the *Create* button on the bottom toolbar, and select one of the options for uploading content, or creating new folders, within Dropbox.

The standard, free, Dropbox account provides 2GB of storage space. You get an extra 500MB for anyone you refer to Dropbox, once they create an account. You can also upgrade to Dropbox Plus, which offers 2TB of storage for $9.99 a month for existing users, or $11.99 a month for new users.

To use the online version of Dropbox:

1. Go to the Dropbox website at *dropbox.com*, and sign in with your Dropbox account details.

2. Click on the *Files* button in the left-hand panel to view your Dropbox folders and files.

3. Any changes you make to the online version of Dropbox will show up in any other versions, such as the Dropbox app.

Hitch a ride on iDrive and pCloud

Dropbox isn't the only third-party cloud service in town. Here are two more to try.

iDrive. This service offers a range of possibilities for backing up content from desktop computers, laptops, tablets, and smartphones. Check out some of its great features.

- It's multi-platform, which means it can be used with Windows, macOS, iPadOS, iOS, and Android.

- Information is synchronized across all devices linked to the account.

- It has a high level of encryption for added peace of mind.

- It performs incremental backups to save time. Each time content is backed up, iDrive only downloads new, or changed, items rather than also copying items that are already there.

iDrive offers a free basic account with storage up to 5GB. The iDrive app can be downloaded from the Apple App Store, the Google Play Store, and the Microsoft Store. Look for this icon.

pCloud. This service offers a similar range of options to iDrive. Here are some of its features.

- It's multi-platform. pCloud can be used with Windows, macOS, iPadOS, iOS, and Android.

- It has a function for sharing files and also working on the same document with someone else.

- It has high levels of encryption.

pCloud offers a free account with storage up to 10GB. You can download the pCloud app from the Apple App Store or the Google Play Store. Download a Windows version at the pCloud website at *pcloud.com*. Look for this icon.

Staying secure

Even if you're happy with your system's cloud service, there's no reason you can't use another as well. It's just an added layer of protection. You can save your important documents and photos into both for extra security and peace of mind.

Cloud sharing — the icing on the cake

You love the idea of backing up your valuable files, documents, and photos and accessing them from all your devices. But the best thing about cloud services may be the ability to share those files with your family and friends. You do it from the online versions of the various services.

OneDrive. To share content from the online version of OneDrive:

1. Go to the OneDrive website at *onedrive.live.com*, and sign in with your Microsoft Account details.

2. Open a folder, and click on the items you want to share. (Click in the circle in the top right-hand corner to select items.)

3. Click on the *Share* button on the top toolbar.

4. Enter an email address for the recipient of the shared item, and click on the *Send* button.

5. The recipient will receive a message saying you have shared an item in OneDrive with them, together with a link to view it online and edit it, if you have given this permission.

iCloud. To share content from the online version of iCloud:

1. Go to the iCloud website at *icloud.com*, and sign in with your Apple ID details.

2. Select the required item to share, such as a photo or word document, and click on the *Share* button.

3. Select the method for sharing the selected item, such as by email or copying the link.

4. Enter the details of the person with whom you would like to share the item, and send the invitation. If you copy a link to them, they can view the item within your iCloud structure.

Google Drive. To share content from the online version of Google Drive:

1. Go to the Google Drive website at *google.com/drive*, and sign in with your Google Account login details.

2. In the My Drive section, right-click on an item, and click on the *Share* button.

3. Enter an email address for the recipient, and click on the *Done* button.

4. Click on the *Send an invitation* button to email the recipient, and invite them to view the shared item.

Dropbox. To share content from the online version of Dropbox:

1. Go to the Dropbox website at *dropbox.com*, and sign in with your account details.

2. To share an item, click on the menu button next to it, and click on the *Share* button.

3. Enter the email address for the recipient of the shared file, and specify their permissions. For example, they can view only via a link, or view and edit.

4. Click on the *Share* button. The recipient will receive an invitation to view the shared item.

┌─ **A closer look** ─────────────────────

How would you like to share your iCloud photo albums with family and friends? Easy peasy. Simply open the Photos app and tap on the *Albums* button. Tap on the plus sign button at the top of the window, and tap on the *New Shared Album* button.

Enter a name for the shared album, and tap on the *Next* button. Enter the recipient's details, such as their email address, and tap on the *Create* button.

The recipient will then receive an invitation to view the shared album. Whenever you add new photos to the album, everyone who has access to it will be notified.

Video chats — face-to-face calling keeps you close

Video calls — a lifeline in good times and bad

If there is one positive to come out of the terrible events of the COVID-19 pandemic that started in 2020, it is the realization that technology has an increasingly important role to play in society, particularly when people are confined to their homes for a prolonged period of time.

One element of technology that has thrived as a result is video chatting, where you use your device to see and hear someone rather than just talk to them on a phone. During the pandemic, it became one of the main ways for families and friends to keep in touch — and get to see each other.

Video chatting is now firmly embedded as one of our most important means of communication, as it provides a vital link with the outside world during good times and bad. The good news is you probably already have everything you need to dive straight into this exciting world. Here's your checklist.

- Desktop computer, laptop, tablet, or smartphone. A tablet is probably the best option for video chatting because it isn't too large and is easy to carry around.

- Camera or webcam. A lot of computing devices now have these built in, particularly tablets and smartphones. If not, a webcam can be connected to a desktop computer or a laptop using a USB cable.

- Microphone. These are built in to most computing devices, but if you want to upgrade the microphone, an external one can be attached via a USB cable.

- Video chatting app. Many computers already have these pre-installed. If not, you can download them from your device's app store. Apple uses its own FaceTime app for video chatting, but you have other options too, such as Skype, Zoom, and Facebook Messenger. When making a video call, the person at the other end needs to use the same app as you.

- Internet connection using Wi-Fi. One of the great things about video chatting is that it is free if you use a connection over Wi-Fi.

Caution

Out and about? You can make a video call on your smartphone using your cellular network connection. But watch out. If you don't have a mobile plan with unlimited data, you may be charged for data usage. And that long video chat with your grandson could end up costing you a pretty penny.

What's all the hype about Skype?

Skype is one of the premier services for free video and voice calls (to other Skype users, using Wi-Fi) and instant messaging for text messages. It is owned by Microsoft, so it is the default video chatting app on Windows 10 desktop computers and laptops.

However, one of the advantages of Skype is that it is multi-platform, which means it can also be used on Mac computers using macOS, iPads using iPadOS, iPhones using iOS, and Android tablets and smartphones.

Before you can start video chatting with Skype you have to obtain the app and create an account.

1. Download the Skype app from the app store linked to your device — Microsoft Store for Windows 10 devices if not already installed, App Store for Apple devices, and Google Play Store for Android devices. Tap (or click) on the *Skype* app to open it.

2. Tap on the *Sign in or create* button to create a new account.

3. If you already have a Skype account you can sign in with these details or with your Microsoft Account details.

Manage your Skype profile. After you have logged in to your new Skype account the first thing to do is to create your profile. This will help your family and friends find you if they are looking for you on Skype. It will also let other people know a bit about yourself. To do this:

1. Tap on your own profile icon on the Skype home page in the top left-hand corner.

2. Tap on the *Settings* button to access the range of settings that can be applied for your Skype account.

3. Tap on the *Account & Profile* button in the left-hand panel.

4. Tap on the *Profile picture* button to add a picture for your Skype profile.

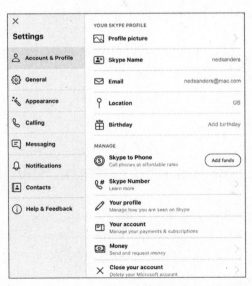

5. Tap on the *Your profile* button to add a description about yourself, which will be seen by other Skype users.

Find contacts. The first step to making a video call is finding someone to call. To do this:

1. In the main Skype window, tap on the *People, groups & messages* search box.

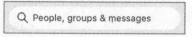

2. Enter the name of the person you want to contact.

3. Tap on one of the results.

4. Tap on the *Say hi* button to invite the person to add you as a contact. Once they have accepted your invitation you will be able to contact them for video, audio, and text chats.

Indicate your availability. It is possible to show people whether you are available for a Skype call, or not. To do this:

1. Tap on your profile picture on the *Chats* page.

2. Tap on this button below your account details.

3. Select one of the options for indicating your availability.

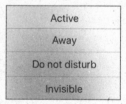

The ins and outs of Skype calls

You've got Skype all set up. Now you're anxious to start chatting with your grandchildren across the country. Here's what you need to know about making and receiving calls.

Starting a Skype call. Get your tablet and follow these instructions.

1. Tap on the *Chats* button on the bottom toolbar.

2. Recent conversations are listed in the left-hand panel. Tap on a recent conversation to contact that person again.

3. Otherwise, tap on the *Contacts* button to view your Skype contacts. Tap on one to start a video or voice chat, or send them a text message.

4. Tap on the video icon to start a video chat, or the phone icon to start a voice call.

5. Once a video chat has been connected, your contact's video feed will appear in the main window, and your own one will appear in a thumbnail window.

6. During a video call, use these buttons on the screen to, from left to right: mute or unmute your microphone; show or hide your video feed; and end a video chat.

7. Tap on the menu button in the bottom right-hand corner to access options for allowing incoming video, displaying subtitles, adding more people to the call, recording the current video chat, sending a heart graphic, and sharing your screen.

8. During a call, tap on these buttons in the bottom left-hand corner to send a text message to the other person or take a photo of the other person's video feed.

9. Tap on your own video feed to switch the camera between the front-facing and back-facing cameras.

Receiving a Skype call. If someone calls you via Skype, it is straightforward to start chatting with them. Just tap on the *Accept* button and you will be connected. It's as easy as that. If you do not want to take the call, tap on the *Decline* button.

Staying secure

It is best not to use the *Away* option for indicating your Skype availability. Someone may take it to mean your home is empty. A better option is to use *Do not disturb* if you want to indicate that you are not available for a call.

Another way to stay safe is to refuse Skype requests from people you don't know. If you receive one of these, tap on the *Decline* button when someone sends you a request.

Mac users: Take advantage of FaceTime

You can use the FaceTime app for video chats with other Apple users on a Mac device with macOS, and also an iPad and an iPhone. To start using FaceTime for video chatting, you need to turn it On for the device you are using.

For macOS devices, you do this in the FaceTime app, from FaceTime > Preferences on the top menu bar. For your iPad and iPhone, you'll do it in Settings > FaceTime. This is so FaceTime knows the Apple ID account that is using the app. If you do not have an Apple ID at this point, you will be prompted to create one.

To start making video calls with FaceTime:

1. Tap on the *FaceTime* app.

2. Recent video chats are shown in the left-hand panel. Tap on one to start another chat with that person.

3. Tap on the + button to look for new contacts.

4. Enter the name of a contact, or tap on the + button to look for contacts in the Contacts app.

5. Once a contact has been selected, tap on the *Video* button to make a FaceTime call. The recipient must have FaceTime on their Apple device.

6. When you have connected, your contact's video feed appears in the main window, and yours appears in a picture-in-picture thumbnail in the corner.

7. Use these buttons during a call to, from left to right: turn the video feed on or off for the call (audio will still be available); mute or unmute the microphone; switch the camera view between the front-facing and back-facing cameras; and end the call. Swipe down on the top of the panel to hide these buttons.

A closer look

Don't want to be disturbed? You can silence incoming FaceTime calls and other alerts whenever you want peace and quiet. You do this within the Do Not Disturb section in the Settings app (System Preferences > Notification with macOS).

Drag the *Scheduled* button to On to specify times during which you do not want to receive notifications for calls or messages. If required, calls from selected people can still be enabled via the *Allow Calls From* option, under the *Phone* heading.

'Zoom' in to video chatting with this popular app

Although Zoom is a relative newcomer to the world of video chatting, it has quickly risen to become one of the biggest players in the market. It is aimed primarily at video conferencing for businesses, but it is also an excellent option for video chats with family and friends.

You can use Zoom on a Windows desktop computer or laptop, a Mac computer or laptop, a tablet, and a smartphone. The Windows and macOS versions can be downloaded from the Zoom website at *zoom.us*. The Zoom app can be downloaded from the App Store for iPads and iPhones, or the Google Play Store for Android tablets and smartphones.

Once you have downloaded Zoom, you can sign up with account details for a Google Account or a Facebook account. Alternatively, you can create a free Zoom account, which gives you a greater range of options with the service. Once you have entered your sign-in details you will be sent an activation email. Tap on the *Activate Account* button to get started with Zoom.

After signing in, the first screen you will see is the Home screen. This is where you will start and manage meetings (video chats) with other people. But the first thing to do is to have a look in the Zoom settings.

1. Tap on the *Settings* button in the bottom left-hand corner of the Home screen.

    Settings

2. Tap on the *Meetings* button.

3. Apply the audio and video settings as required, such as for turning the video feed on or off.

Caution

The free Zoom plan gives you unlimited video calls for 40 minutes for up to 100 participants. That's great if you have a big family — but not if they're big talkers. If you want to have video calls longer than 40 minutes, you need to get a paid plan.

Handy tips make you a Zoom pro in no time

Zoom can be a fun way to keep in touch with family and friends. With the gallery view, everyone's pictures show up on the screen just like the Brady Bunch or Hollywood Squares. Here's how to start or schedule one yourself.

Start a Zoom chat. To create a video chat using Zoom:

1. On the Home screen, tap on the *New Meeting* button.

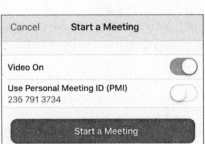

2. Make sure the *Video On* button is turned On.

3. Tap on the *Start a Meeting* button.

4. Tap on the *Call using Internet Audio* button.

5. At this point you will be the only person in the meeting, and you will see your video feed on the screen.

Cancel	Start a Meeting	
Video On		⬤
Use Personal Meeting ID (PMI) 235 791 3734		○
	Start a Meeting	

6. Tap on your video feed, and tap on the *Participants* button on the top toolbar.

175

7. Tap on the *Invite* button.

8. Select one of the options for inviting someone to the Zoom video call, such as by email or text message.

9. Enter the details for the person you want to invite, and send the email or text message.

10. When the recipient gets the message, they can join the meeting by tapping on the *Join Zoom Meeting* link.

Schedule a Zoom video chat. Another option for setting up a Zoom video chat is to schedule it for a specific time. This can be useful if you have a regular chat with a family member, or if you want to get several people together. Creating a scheduled meeting lets everyone know what time it is going to take place. To schedule a meeting for a specific time:

1. On the Zoom Home screen, tap on the *Schedule* button.

2. Make selections for the elements of the scheduled video chat, including *Start, Duration, Repeat* and *Required Meeting Password*. The Repeat option is a good one to use if you plan to have a regular video chat with someone at the same time every week.

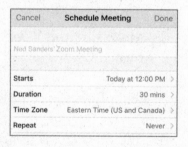

3. Once you've entered the details for the scheduled chat, tap on the *Done* button.

4. An email is created with the details for the meeting. Enter the email address for all the people you want to include in the video chat, and tap on this button to send the email invitation.

5. To start a scheduled meeting, tap on the *Meetings* button in the left-hand panel on the Zoom Home screen.

6. Tap on the Start button next to the meeting you want to begin. (You can start a meeting before the scheduled time.) The recipient joins the meeting by clicking on the link in the email they received.

Staying secure

If you've been invited to a Zoom meeting, look for a Meeting ID on your invitation. It is generated when a new meeting is scheduled and has to be entered before you can join in. Use the *Join* button on the Zoom home page to enter the meeting. A password may also be included for extra security.

Surprise: Facebook Messenger is not just for texting

You may not have known you could use Facebook for video chatting, but its Messenger app is ideal for making video calls. You can download and use it separately from Facebook, although you still sign in to the Messenger app with your Facebook account details.

You can make video calls from your tablet and smartphone in addition to your desktop computer or laptop. Here's how to do it with your tablet or phone.

1. Tap on the *Messenger* app to open it.

2. From the *Chats* menu, tap on the pencil icon.

3. Enter the name of a Facebook contact.

4. Tap on the video icon to start a video chat with the elected contact.

Facebook also has something called the Facebook Portal that can be used for video chatting. However, this is a more expensive option as the Portal device, which looks similar to a tablet, has to be bought separately.

Staying secure

Hackers have been known to sneak into private video chats. Don't let it happen to you. Here are three things you can do to make sure your conversations remain private.

- Use passwords if available. Zoom has a function where you can include a password when you first create a video chat meeting. You send the password to the recipient, and they enter it to join the chat.

- Turn off Location Services for the video app. Look in the app's settings, or the main settings for the device being used, and turn the Location Services option Off, so that your location cannot be identified via the video app.

- Don't discuss any sensitive information, such as financial or login details for online accounts, while you're chatting, even with family and friends.

How to have a video chat party

One of the more recent developments with video chatting is that it can now be done with multiple people, not just one-to-one. To do this on different platforms:

- On Skype, start a video call with one person, and tap on the menu button in the bottom right-hand corner. Tap on the *Add people* button to invite more people, up to 50.

- On FaceTime, start a video call with one person, swipe up on the panel of controls, and tap on the *Add Person* button, up to 32.

- On Zoom, start a video call with one person, tap on the *Participants* button on the top toolbar, select one of your Zoom contacts, and tap on the *Invite* button. Also, when a new meeting is scheduled, you can add multiple recipients in the scheduling email. The free version of Zoom allows for up to 100 people on a call, should your ever need that many.

- On Facebook Messenger, start a video call with one person, and tap on the + icon to invite more people, up to 50, although only six will be shown at a time.

Caution

Be prepared for some distractions, and maybe a bit of frustration, while participating in a video chat. For example, if you FaceTime with multiple people, all the video windows move around the screen, which may get annoying after a while. If something bothers you, remember you can sign off at any time.

Photo fundamentals — take and edit perfect pictures

Get the best shot every time

Smartphones and tablets can both be used to capture, view, manage, and edit photos. However, they both specialize in different areas of digital photography.

Smartphones are a better option for taking photos, as the cameras are generally of higher quality and are more portable. But tablets, due to their larger screens, are a better option for viewing photos, and for editing them so you can create the perfect image.

Here's what you need to think about to get that perfect picture on your smartphone or tablet.

Proper focus. Good focusing is one of the essential elements of any photo. If a scene is not properly in focus then the resulting photo will be ruined regardless of how perfect the lighting is, or how well the shot is composed. Therefore it is important to be confident when focusing shots on a smartphone camera. This can be done by choosing where you want the focus area in a photo. To do this:

1. Open the camera app and compose a scene.

2. Press and hold on the screen on the area that you want to be the main focal area.

3. A colored square appears over the focal area. This can be used to lock the focus, and the exposure, of the photo at this

point. The camera will measure the amount of light within the square and use this to create the best lighting conditions for the whole photo.

4. Keep holding on the screen until the *AE/AF Lock* button appears at the top of the screen. (AE is for the exposure of the photo, AF is for the Auto-Focus.) This indicates the focal point has been set and will remain there once you remove your finger from the screen and move the camera.

Zooming. Being able to zoom in and out on a scene is an element of photography that can make significant differences to the composition of a photo, by making subjects appear larger on the camera's screen. This can generally be done in two ways.

- Zoom by spreading. You can zoom in and out on scenes by spreading and pinching on the screen. Spread outwards with thumb and forefinger to zoom in on a scene with the camera app; pinch inwards with thumb and forefinger to zoom out on a scene.

- Zoom options. Some smartphone cameras also have buttons that can change the amount of zoom by specific factors, such as x2 enlargement. If this option is available, tap on the zoom button in the camera app.

Light. Using light effectively is another important element in producing eye-catching photos. Here are some specific techniques you can use.

- Wait for the best light. Patience is a significant asset when trying to capture great photos, and this is definitely the case when looking to use the best light. A few minutes, or even seconds, can mean the difference between a dull photo, and one that is perfectly lit, due to the sun moving its position or emerging from behind a cloud.

- Avoid glare. If you are taking photos on a sunny day, glare from the sun can be a problem. To overcome this, use your hand over the top of the smartphone to shade the camera and remove the glare. Just be careful that your hand doesn't put a shadow over the camera on the screen.

Portrait or landscape. One of the most effective techniques in terms of composing photos with a smartphone camera is also one of the most simple. Just rotating the smartphone 90 degrees can result in two dramatically different photos. This is known as taking photos in either landscape or portrait mode.

- Landscape mode is ideal for taking photos of its namesake, and also photos of cityscapes.

- Portrait mode can be used for effective portraits of people and statues, and also items such as buildings and towers.

Caution

Digital photos are made up of small colored dots called pixels. If you zoom in on a scene with your smartphone camera — known as digital zoom — it increases the size of the pixels in the photo. If you zoom in too much, the individual pixels will become visible, making the photo look blurry. This is known as pixelization.

To avoid this, try taking the picture as it appears, then enlarging and cropping it in edit mode to get a close-up view.

---

2 special techniques to enhance your photos

Photography is not always an exact science. Some of the best photos can be taken on the spur of the moment or because someone has a good eye for a scene. However, you can also use more formal techniques to ensure you can confidently approach any photo opportunity.

Use a grid for composing. One of these techniques is known as the Rule of Thirds. This consists of looking at a scene as if it has been overlaid with a grid consisting of three lines horizontally and three lines vertically. This creates a grid with nine separate segments.

The advantage of the Rule of Thirds is that the grid can be used to position subjects within a composition to give it a more balanced effect. Subjects can be positioned at different points where the grid lines intersect.

Some camera apps can have a Rule of Thirds grid superimposed on the screen. Look in the camera's settings to see if this is available.

Create your own frames. Photos or pictures always look better in an appropriate and attractive frame, and the same is true for photos when they are taken. If you frame the main subject in an interesting or artistic way, it can add considerable impact to the final photo. Framing options exist with natural or man-made elements.

- Use branches of trees to frame a landmark or a landscape scene.

- Use architectural elements, such as towers or spires, to frame specific items.

- Use an existing man-made frame, or doorway, to create a ready-made frame for a photo.

A closer look

One of the most common lighting techniques involves taking photos as the sun rises or sets. This is known as the Golden Hour, and occurs approximately one hour after the sun rises, and one hour before it sets. At these times of day, the light has a much richer texture to it rather than the harsh sunlight effects from strong, overhead sunlight. As the name suggests, it can produce a rich, golden color that can result in outstanding photos.

Embrace the selfie stick for better self-portraits

Selfies are very much a phenomenon of the smartphone camera age. These are self portraits you take using the front-facing camera on a smartphone. That's the one you see when you look at the screen of the smartphone.

To expand the area in a selfie, you can use a selfie stick. You attach your smartphone to this telescopic device and then extend it so it can take the picture from a greater distance. Selfie sticks can be operated via a cable which attaches to the smartphone, or via a wireless bluetooth connection.

To use a cable selfie stick:

1. Insert the smartphone into the top clamp, and connect the cable to the smartphone's microphone jack.

2. Open the smartphone's camera app, and press the shutter button on the handle of the selfie stick to take the photo.

Bluetooth selfie sticks are slightly more sophisticated than their cable counterparts, but they perform the same task. However, the connection between the smartphone and the selfie stick is a wireless bluetooth one, rather than a physical one with a cable.

To use a bluetooth selfie stick, attach the smartphone to the selfie stick, and turn on *Bluetooth* in the smartphone's settings. Select the selfie stick in the bluetooth settings to connect it (pair) with the smartphone. You can then take your photo with the shutter button on the selfie stick.

A closer look

Do you have problems trying to take a selfie with one hand? It's easier than you think. Just use the volume button to snap the picture. Open the camera app, and press either of the volume buttons on the side of the smartphone to take a photo.

The art of picking your subjects

Outings with friends, family celebrations, and fabulous vacations all provide an endless supply of photo opportunities. Trying to decide just what pictures to take can be tough. Here are three areas to focus on.

Group shots. Organizing a group of people for a photo can sometimes be a stressful task. Use these tips to get the best pictures.

1. Try and avoid a shot with everyone standing with their arms at their sides looking directly at the camera.

2. Ask people to stand side-on, or at an angle, in a more relaxed fashion.

3. Ask the group to perform a prearranged action, such as on the count of three everyone throws their arms up in the air, at which point you take the photo.

4. Include yourself in the shot using the camera app's self-timer. Set it for the maximum amount of time, so you can easily get into the shot.

Panoramas. When faced with an impressive landscape or cityscape, one good photographic option is to take a panorama. This is a photo where two or more photos are combined to provide a wider final photo that is captured in a single shot. Some smartphone cameras have a function to create panoramas automatically using the camera app. To do this:

1. Open the Camera app, and tap on the *Pano* option.

2. Tap on the Shutter button.

3. Move the smartphone camera slowly along the whole panoramic subject.

4. Tap on the Shutter button again to complete the panorama.

Buildings. When taking photos of buildings, a straight-on shot does not always do them justice. Here are a few easy techniques you can use to transform your plain-jane building into a work of art.

• Emphasize the immense size of a building by capturing a photo from directly below it.

- Look for details. Photos of smaller elements of a building can help to show its character.

- The foreground can be an important factor in photos and should be treated as a composition feature in its own right. Foreground objects can include natural elements such as trees or flowers, or man-made items like a stone wall or wrought-iron gate.

Caution

As much as you'd like that super scenic shot, it's not worth getting hurt over. There have been instances around the world where people have come to harm by taking selfies in dangerous locations, such as near the edge of cliffs. Never put yourself, or others, in danger when trying to take a selfie. If you are near a drop of any kind, always make sure you know where your feet are in relation to the edge.

Guide to managing your smartphone photos

The Photos app on the iPhone can be used to store, edit, and share photos. This is regardless of whether it is linked to iCloud or not. If it is linked to iCloud, photos will be backed up and stored there. To use the Photos app:

1. Tap on the *Photos* app.

2. Tap on the *Photos* button on the bottom toolbar to view all of the photos on your iPhone.

3. Tap on these buttons to view photos according to Years, Months, Days, or All Photos.

4. Tap on the *Albums* button on the bottom toolbar to view albums that have been created to store similar photos. Tap on the + button to create a new album.

5. Tap on the *For You* button on the bottom toolbar to view collections of photos that have been collated automatically by the Photos app, such as featured photos and Memories.

6. Tap on one of the *Memories* to view it, and display it as a slideshow with transitions and music.

On an Android smartphone, you'll use the Google Photos app to work with photos.

1. Tap on the *Photos* app to open it.

2. Tap on the *Photos* button on the bottom toolbar to view photos that have been taken, according to the dates on which they were captured. Tap on a photo to view it at full size.

3. Tap on the *Albums* button on the bottom toolbar to view and create albums for storing photos of similar type. Tap on the *New album* button to create a new album.

4. Tap on the *For you* button on the bottom toolbar to access options for using your photos creatively, such as in photo books and collages.

Make your photo perfect with an editing app

Want to make your photo look extra special? Let an editing app work its magic. Tablets are your best option for editing photos because of the larger screen, but you can also do it on your smartphone. Editing tasks you can perform include:

• enhancing the overall color of a photo, in one tap.

- enabling sophisticated tools to manually improve all aspects of the color in a photo.

- adding filters to transform a photo.

- cropping a photo so the main subject stands out.

- fixing red-eye, when someone's eyes appear red as a result of the flash reflecting in them.

- adding text to photos. This can be customized in a variety of ways in terms of font and style.

- applying artistic special effects, such as converting a photo into a watercolor painting.

- applying fun special effects, such as transforming someone's face into a cartoon character.

Tips to make iPhone editing a snap

The iPad and iPhone use the built-in Photos app for managing photos that have been captured with the device's camera, or obtained through other methods, such as downloading from an email. In addition to managing and displaying photos, the Photos app can also be used to edit them.

1. Tap on the *Photos* app to access your photos.

2. Tap on the *Photos* button on the bottom toolbar to view all of the photos, and tap on one to open it at full size.

3. Tap on the *Edit* button in the top right-hand corner.

4. The main editing categories are accessed from these buttons on the bottom toolbar.

5. Tap on this button on the bottom toolbar to access the color editing options.

6. Tap on one of the color editing options. For each option, drag on the slider to apply the required amount of the selected effect.

7. Tap on this button on the bottom toolbar to access the filter effects options.

8. Swipe along the panel of thumbnails to view the filter effects, and tap on one to apply it to the current photo.

9. Tap on this button on the bottom toolbar to access the straighten and rotation options, including cropping the image, by dragging on the resizing handles in each corner.

Simple steps to edit your Android photos

Android tablets and smartphones can use the Google Photos app for managing and editing photos on the device. To do this:

1. Tap on the *Photos* app to access your photos.

2. Tap on the *Photos* button on the bottom toolbar to view all of the photos, and tap on one to open it at full size.

3. Tap on this button to edit the photo.

4. The main editing categories are accessed from these buttons on the bottom toolbar.

5. Tap on this button on the bottom toolbar to access the filter options.

6. Swipe on the filter's thumbnails to view the options.

7. Select a filter as required, and tap on the *Save* button to save the photo with the current filter applied.

8. Tap on this button on the bottom toolbar to access the color editing options.

9. Tap on each item to access additional options. Drag the slider to apply the effect for each item.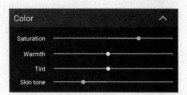

10. Tap on this button on the bottom toolbar to access options for rotating the photo.

11. Tap on this button to rotate the photo in 90-degree increments.

12. Tap on this button on the bottom toolbar to access options for adding drawings and text to a photo. Select the drawing tools to create a freehand drawing on the photo.

13. Tap on this button to add text to a photo.

Free photo app you don't want to miss

Snapseed is a comprehensive photo editing app that has an array of tools for enhancing photos on your tablet or smartphone. It can be downloaded for free from the Apple App Store or the Google Play Store. To use Snapseed:

1. Tap on the *Snapseed* app to open it.

2. Tap on the *Open* button to access photos.

3. Select where you want to access photos from. Tap on the *Open from Device* button to access the photos already on your tablet or smartphone. Tap on a photo to view it at full size.

4. Tap on the *Looks* button on the bottom toolbar to access filters.

5. Swipe on the filters bar to view the range of available filters.

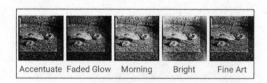

6. Tap on one of the filters to select it. Tap on the check mark to apply it to the photo, or the cross to reject it.

7. Tap on the *Tools* button on the bottom toolbar to access the editing tools.

8. Tap on one of the available tools to use it on the currently open photo.

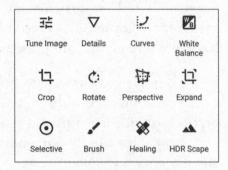

9. Tap on the *Export* button on the bottom toolbar to access options for sharing, saving, and exporting the current photo.

A closer look

Feel like having a little fun? Photo editing doesn't have to be limited to fine tuning the elements that are already in a photo. It is perfectly possible, and at times preferable, to add special effects that will give you a whole new image. Some of the creative effects you can add are:

- themes.

- filters.

- lighting effects.

- frames and borders.

- stickers and graphics.

- fun effects.

To find apps for creative effects, look in the App Store or the Google Play Store, and enter "fun photo effects" or "creative photo effects" into the search box.

No. 1 most important thing to do for your photos

Photos of family and friends are priceless and irreplaceable. It therefore makes sense to keep them as safe as possible, so you never have to worry about losing them.

In the digital age, it is easy to forget about photos when they are stored on computers, tablets, and smartphones. Backing up your precious photos is essential if you want to make sure you never lose them. This can be done both manually and to an online cloud service.

- To back up photos manually, save them from your computer to an external device such as a USB flash drive or an external hard drive.

- For Apple devices, use iCloud to back up your photos. To do this, go to Settings > Apple ID > iCloud > Photos, and drag the *iCloud Photos* button to On.

- For Android devices, access Settings > Google > Backup > Google Photos > Back up & sync, and drag the *Back up & sync* button to On.

Share your fun with friends and family

It certainly is fun to share your photos. And you can do it as soon as you've snapped one, so your family and friends can see it almost immediately.

Sharing from an iPad or iPhone. The process for sharing photos from an iPad or an iPhone is the same:

1. Open the *Photos* app, and tap on the *Photos* button on the bottom toolbar.

2. Tap on the *Select* button on the top toolbar.

3. Tap on the photos you want to share. You can pick one or more.

4. Tap on this button in the bottom left-hand corner to share the photo.

5. Select one of the options for sharing the selected photo.

6. Complete the selected option to share the photo, such as completing an email, and send it to someone with the photo attached.

Sharing from an Android device. To share photos from an Android tablet or smartphone:

1. Open the Google *Photos* app, and tap on the *Photos* button on the bottom toolbar.

2. Press and hold on a photo to select it. Tap on other photos to select them along with the initial selection.

3. Tap on this button on the top toolbar.

4. Select the method for sharing the photo, or tap on one of your contacts to share it directly with them.

5. Complete the selected method to share the photo.

Bring your photos into the 21st century

If you have boxes of old photos, it's not too late to turn them into a beautiful album — complete with labels showing who or what you're looking at. Don't bother with an old-fashioned book — do it the high-tech way and scan them into a digital photo album.

You can use a regular scanner to convert old photos into digital ones, or you can download an app and scan photos directly onto your tablet or smartphone. You'll preserve them for years and can make prints whenever you want, without a negative.

If you really want a hardcover book, you can upload your photos to an online printing service or a photo printing app, which will turn them into an album, complete with text descriptions for your photos. Popsa and FreePrints Photobooks are two apps to check out.

Some apps can also convert old photos back to their former glory. Three to have a look at are Photo Scanner, Photo Scan, and Colorize.

Money-saver

You love having all those pictures on your phone that you can enjoy any time you want. But now you'd like to frame a few prints for your living room. No problem.

You'll find dozens of printing services online, and they're cheaper than printing your own photos on a color printer with photo-quality paper. You can register on a site for free, then simply upload your photos and select how you would like them to be printed. Choose from prints, albums, calendars, cards, canvas — even cushions and mugs.

Online printing services offer good value for your money, and they frequently offer specials. Some sites to look at are Snapfish at *snapfish.com*, Shutterfly at *shutterfly.com*, and Walmart Photo at *photos3.walmart.com*.

Get connected — internet secrets you need to know

Connect online and have the world at your fingertips

The days of having to spend hours getting connected to the internet are, thankfully, long gone. Most modern computing devices are designed to be internet-ready, and once they are turned on, you need just a few steps to get online.

1. Find an Internet Service Provider (ISP) who will provide the connection to the internet. This could include cable companies.

2. The ISP should provide you with a Wi-Fi router, which is the device through which you will connect to the internet. Plug this in according to its instructions. The router should have a password on it, which you'll use to connect via your desktop computer, laptop, tablet, or smartphone.

3. Open the *Settings* app on your device.

4. Access the *Wi-Fi* section.

5. Select the appropriate network. This will usually be a variation of the name of your ISP.

6. Enter the password for the Wi-Fi router.

7. That should be it. Open a web page in a browser to check that the connection has been made.

┌─ A *closer* look ─────────────────────────────────

The terms "internet" and "web" can sometimes be confused.
The internet is the global collection of computing devices that
are interconnected and used for tasks such as sending emails
and viewing web pages. The web refers to the World Wide
Web (WWW), which is the collection of pages that are
viewed through a browser such as Microsoft Edge, Safari,
or Google Chrome.

└──

Find the browser that fits your needs

All computing devices have their own default browsers for viewing
web content — Microsoft Edge for Windows; Safari for macOS,
iPadOS, and iOS; and Google Chrome for Android devices.

But you don't have to stick with the default browser. You can
download several browsers and see which one you like best. Here
are some browsers to look at.

Chrome. Although this is the default browser on a lot of Android
devices, there are also versions for Windows, macOS, iPadOS, and
iOS devices. Try it by downloading the appropriate version at
google.com/chrome, or download the app from your app store.

Firefox. This is one of the most widely used browsers on the web,
and comes in desktop and mobile versions. It has a range of security
features and prides itself in protecting online rights. Try it by downloading the appropriate version at *mozilla.org*, or as an app version.

Opera. With versions for all platforms, this is a slick, well-designed
browser that comes with a built-in ad-blocking feature. Try it by
downloading the appropriate version at *opera.com*, or from your
app store.

Money-saver

Wouldn't it be great if you had a list of all the places you could find free Wi-Fi when you are away from home? Thankfully, the hard work for this has already been done, and there are several apps that display this exact information.

Type "wifi finder" into the Search box of whichever app store you use for your device, and pick one from the results. Four to check out are WiFi Finder in USA, WiFi Finder — Connect Internet, WiFi Finder + Map, and Boingo Wi-Finder.

Home sweet home: Choose the page to open first

When you first open a web browser on your device, it will bring you to the browser's default home page. This will inevitably be something the browser's developer wants you to see, but you don't have to keep it. You can choose whichever web page you want and set this as your home page.

Windows 10. To set a home page with Microsoft Edge:

1. Open the Microsoft Edge browser, and click on the menu button (three horizontal dots) in the top right-hand corner of the browser window.

2. Click on the *Settings* option at the bottom of the menu.

3. Click in the *Open Microsoft Edge with* box, and click on the *A specific page or pages* option.

4. Enter the website address you want to use as your home page in the *Enter a URL* box. This does not need to be the full address. For example, you can enter just *fca.com*.

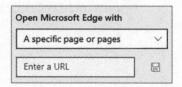

macOS. To set a home page with Safari in macOS:

1. Open Safari, and navigate to the web page you want to use as your home page.

2. Select Safari > Preferences from the top menu bar.

3. Click on the *General* tab.

4. In the *Homepage* field, enter the website address to use or click on the *Set to Current Page* button, which is the currently active one in the browser.

iPadOS/iOS. You don't have an option to set a specific home page with an iPad or iPhone. However, you can add an icon to the Home screen that will open at your favorite web page. To do this:

1. On an iPad or iPhone, open Safari and navigate to the page you want to use as a home page.

2. Tap on this button (on the top toolbar on an iPad, and on the bottom toolbar on an iPhone).

3. Swipe up the window, and tap on the *Add to Home Screen* button.

5. An icon is added to your Home screen. Tap on it to open your favorite web page in Safari.

Google Chrome. Android devices also have an option for adding an icon to the Home screen.

1. Open Chrome, navigate to the page to use, and tap on the menu button (three vertical dots) in the top right-hand corner of the screen.

2. Tap on the *Add to Home screen* option.

> Add to Home screen
>
> **a** Amazon
>
> Cancel   Add

3. Enter a name for the page, and tap on the *Add* button.

4. An icon is added to your Home screen. Tap on it to open your favorite web page in Chrome.

Staying secure

When you are away from home and can't access your home Wi-Fi network to connect to the web, help is at hand in the form of Wi-Fi hotspots. These are Wi-Fi connections provided by a wide range of public establishments, from restaurants to airports.

But beware. Public Wi-Fi hotspots are not as secure as using your home network. They are more susceptible to hackers, particularly if they're not protected by a password.

Things you definitely shouldn't do on public Wi-Fi include making online purchases with credit or debit cards; entering personal details into an online form, such as for online banking; or entering general personal login details into a website, such as for logging into your email account.

Always have your favorite websites a click away

Everyone has the same web pages they visit again and again. These can be for news, sports, lifestyle, finance, and hundreds of other topics, depending on your hobbies and interests.

Rather than having to navigate to them by typing in a web address each time, it's much easier to set them as a favorite — or bookmark — so you can access them in a couple of clicks.

Check out the chapters *Windows — an old favorite with new features* and *Amazing tips to master your Mac* for instructions on adding favorites in Windows 10 and MacOs. Here's how to do it on your tablet or smartphone.

iPadOS/iOS favorites. To add favorites (bookmarks) in Safari on an iPad or iPhone:

1. Navigate to the required page, and tap on this button (on the top toolbar on an iPad, and on the bottom toolbar on an iPhone).

2. Tap on the *Add Bookmark* button.

3. Enter a name for the bookmarked page, and tap on the *Save* button.

4. To view bookmarked web pages, tap on this button (on the top toolbar on an iPad, and on the bottom toolbar on an iPhone).

5. Tap on this button to view all of the book-marked web pages.

Google Chrome favorites. To set favorites (bookmarks) with Google Chrome on an Android device:

1. Navigate to the required page, and tap on the menu button (three vertical dots).

2. Tap on the star icon so that it appears solid.

3. Tap on the *Bookmarks* button on the main menu, accessed in Step 1, to view all of the bookmarks that have been added. If they are added to the *Mobile bookmarks* folder, you will be able to access them on other devices with your Google Account.

Keep tabs on all your web pages

As you surf the web, you can't help but open multiple web pages. But if you open a separate browser window for each new site, you're working harder than you need to. There is a much neater solution — tabs. Using tabs allows you to open multiple websites within a single browser window.

Windows 10 tabs. To use tabs in the Microsoft Edge browser:

1. Open the Edge browser. It will open at its Start page, or a Home page if this has been specified.

2. Click on the + button to open a new tab, or press Ctrl+T on the keyboard. To specify what happens when a new tab is opened, go to Menu > Settings and under the *Open new tabs with* heading, select what you want to appear when a new tab is created. The options are for *Top sites* and *A blank page*.

3. Tap on one of the thumbnail suggestions on the new tab page, or enter a website address in the search box.

macOS tabs. In the chapter *Amazing tips to master your Mac* you learned how to open new tabs in Safari using macOS. You can also determine how the tabs operate with settings in Safari.

1. Open Safari, and click on Safari > Preferences from the top menu bar.

2. Click on the *Tabs* tab, and make the required selections for how tabs operate, such as for opening tabs and switching between them.

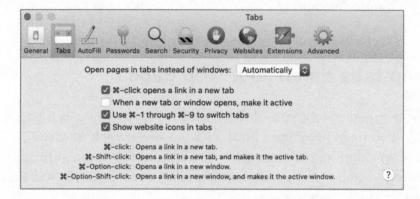

iPadOS/iOS tabs. To use tabs in Safari on an iPad or iPhone:

1. On an iPad, tap on the + button on the top toolbar. On an iPhone, tap on this button on the bottom toolbar, and then tap on the + button.

2. Select a page to open, or enter a website address into the address bar.

3. Tap on this button to view thumbnails of all of the currently active tabs.

Google Chrome tabs. To use tabs with Google Chrome on an Android device:

1. Click on this button to add a new tab.

2. The start page displays the Google Search box and recommended sites. Tap on one to make it the active page.

3. To view tabs that have been recently closed, tap on the menu
   button, and tap on the *Recent tabs* option.

A closer look

To determine what appears when a new tab is first opened
on your iPad or iPhone, go to Settings > Safari, and tap on
the *Favorites* option. This contains the folders that have been
created for your favorite bookmarks. The default is *Favorites*,
but click on another if you want this to appear as the option
when you open a new tab.

Easiest way to get rid of annoying pop-up ads — and it's free

You may be tired of seeing ads pop up every time you go to a new
web page. Let's face it, they're pretty annoying. But there is an easy
solution — ad blockers. In fact, most modern browsers have these
pre-installed.

- For Microsoft Edge, click on the
  menu button at the right-hand side
  of the top toolbar, and click on the
  AdBlock button to view its settings
  and details of ads it has blocked.

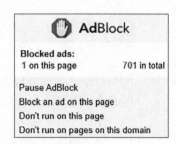

- For Safari on macOS, open Safari, and select Safari >
  Preferences from the top menu bar. Click on the *Security* tab,
  and check the *Block pop-up windows* checkbox.

- For Safari using iPadOS/iOS, go to Settings > Safari, and drag the *Block Pop-ups* button to On.

- For Chrome on an Android device, open Chrome and tap on the menu button. Select Settings > Site settings > Pop-ups and redirects, and drag the *Pop-ups and redirects* button to Off.

8 best websites for seniors

Once you connect to the web, there are literally hundreds of thousands, if not more, great websites to look at, covering every subject imaginable. It's worth surfing around just to see what you come across, but here are eight of the best sites to get you started.

- BenefitsCheckUp, by the National Council on Aging, at *benefitscheckup.org*. There are approximately 50 to 70 government programs in your state alone — all designed to benefit older adults. Simple ways to sort through them all, and get what you deserve, are revealed on this excellent and comprehensive website.

- Administration for Community Living (ACL), at *acl.gov*. Information and advice for communal living, for seniors and people with disabilities.

- Grandfolk, at *grandfolk.com*. Commonsense advice about buying a variety of items, from cars to insurance.

- Money, at *money.com*. Keep your personal finances in robust health with this comprehensive finance site.

- Retire Wow, at *retirewow.com*. A site covering a wide range of retirement issues, including activities, finance, and health.

- Seniorly, at *seniorly.com*. Aimed at helping seniors find the best assisted living in the community.

- Senior List, at *theseniorlist.com*. A range of advice for people continuing to live in their own homes, from medical alert systems to care alternatives.

- SavvySenior, at *savvysenior.org*. Syndicated media information covering all of the topics important to seniors.

Research on the web — discover your family history

Genealogy (researching family history) is an ideal hobby for exploring on the web, and learning about your ancestors has never been so simple — especially now that other folks have done so much of the legwork.

You'll be amazed at how many online genealogy sites are available to look up your family history, find genealogy research help, and see some of the connections that have already been made by other people.

You can trace your family's roots through government records and ship's logs dating back to the 1800s. Most genealogy websites have companion apps that can perform similar tasks. Here are some to check out.

- Ancestry, at *ancestry.com*. This is the world's largest genealogy site, with over 10 billion historical records covering births, deaths, marriages, census records, military records, and much more.

- MyHeritage, at *myheritage.com*. This can be used to create your family tree, and you also have an option for taking a DNA test to help trace your heritage. Basic searches can be undertaken for free, and a reasonable amount of research can be done in this way.

- FamilySearch, at *familysearch.org*. Another popular site that allows you to search records and family trees, and also has access to the FamilySearch Wiki, where people can add their own family tree information with a view to creating a global family tree.

- Genealogy and Family History, at *usa.gov*. This is an official United States government website that provides official records relating to ancestors and descendants and also U.S. Census Data and Statistics.

- National Archives, at *archives.gov*. Another government site that can be a useful resource for genealogy research, including tips on how to conduct this type of work, and also links to other useful websites.

A closer look

Another great way to find old friends and long-lost relatives can be a few clicks away, simply by searching with Google. Just type someone's name into the Google Search box, and include the name in quotes so the exact name is searched for.

To add more information, click on the *Settings* button on the Google home page, and click on the *Advanced search* button. Enter any additional information you know about the person, such as where they live or their approximate age.

The search results will cover a range of sites, from social media to genealogy, so it may take a bit of time to sort through them. However, this is an excellent starting point if you are trying to reconnect with long-lost family and friends.

Behold 8 more super sites for seniors

There's no need to climb every mountain in search of fabulous websites. Visit these instead. Here are more outstanding websites for seniors, covering areas including travel, gardening, consumer goods, and investing.

- American Discount Cruises & Travel, at *americandiscount cruises.com*. A good starting point if you are looking at getting the best travel deals, particularly on cruises.

- Consumer Reports, at *consumerreports.org*. Get the lowdown on a huge number of different types of consumer goods.

- Evergreen, at *evergreenclub.com*. Excellent value accommodation if you are traveling in the U.S. and Canada.

- Investopedia, at *investopedia.com*. Make your finances go further with this comprehensive investment site.

- GardenWeb, at *gardenweb.com*. Learn how to grow anything, inside or out, with the help of this great gardening site.

- Garden Guides, at *gardenguides.com*. Another great gardening option.

- Road Scholar, at *roadscholar.com*. A not-for-profit website, aimed at inspiring adults to travel to exciting destinations around the world.

- SmarterTravel at *smartertravel.com*. A travel site with expert tips, news, and deals, including a section for seniors.

Search smarter, better, and faster with Google

It's like having a library right in your home

Google has become synonymous with searching the web, and you've undoubtedly used it at one point or another just like millions of others.

But Google is so much more than a search engine. It contains such a wide range of content and information that it removes the need for most other reference material. Dictionaries, encyclopedias, maps, news, almanacs, phone books, recipes, statistics, even translators are all free on the web. And you can find them all through Google.

Dictionary. You need never be stuck for knowing the meaning of a word again. Type the word followed by "definition" to see a Google dictionary definition.

Encyclopedias and almanacs. Enter a search word for the subject you want to research, and sit back and view the results. Add the word "encyclopedia" or "almanac" as part of the search to view the results from these reference sources. For instance, enter "george washington almanac" to find a treasure trove of information about America's first president.

News. With Google, you don't even have to enter any search details to get the latest news. A separate category exists right on the Google home page that will get you up to speed with the latest events at home and around the world. On the News page, enter specific topics you want to read about.

Phone books. No need to have a bulky phone book in your home. Enter a phone number, or a person's name with the words "phone number," to see the results. In a lot of cases, Google will point you towards online phone directories to find the exact details (some of which you need to pay for). Google is particularly useful for identifying scam numbers and robocalls, and also locating area codes.

Recipes. One of Google's many talents is of a culinary nature. Enter a type of food followed by "recipe" to see the suggestions. Alternatively, enter the name of a specific dish to view the recipes for it.

Translators. Google is truly multilingual and can effortlessly translate languages from around the world into English, and vice versa. (Google will even inform you that vice versa is Italian for "the other way around.")

When a word or phrase is entered for translation, the result will include a speaker icon, so you can hear the pronunciation of the word or phrase.

Finding your way around. Google Maps is an excellent option for finding locations and directions whether it's at home or further afield. Simply type a location into the Google Search box, or a particular site such as a tourist attraction, and a map should be displayed in the search results.

Statistics and math. No need to be a math genius if you have Google at hand. In fact, you'll quickly look like a genius yourself.

Type a sum into the search box, for example, "square root of 256," and the answer will be displayed complete with a calculator for any calculations you want to do manually. Google can also handle much more complicated calculations and statistical analysis.

Conversions. Google is highly adept at converting a whole range of items, from money to temperatures. Just type in a command such as "convert 20 ounces to grams."

Weather. Google is an expert meteorologist and can give weather forecasts for locations around the world, and also local forecasts for the current day and the week ahead.

Tipping. Working out the correct tip can be an awkward task, particularly if several people are splitting the bill. Google takes all the hassle out of it. Simply type in an amount with the $ symbol followed by "tip" to see the result.

Having a Doodle. Google is known for its sense of humor, and the Google Doodles that appear at the top of the home page to commemorate holidays and special events are known for their quirky and entertaining designs. Keep an eye out for these as they appear on a regular basis.

A closer look

Never wonder about the lyrics of your favorite songs again. Type "lyrics of" and the name of a song into the Google Search box, and the lyrics will be listed.

Another good option for Google is tracking packages and flights. If you have a package being delivered, and it has a tracking number, you can follow its progress simply by entering the tracking number into the Search box, as long as the delivery or courier company supports this service.

For flights, enter the flight number, such as "American AA 345 to Atlanta." The results will show the scheduled arrival time, any delays, the terminal, and gate number.

9 tips to find exactly what you're looking for on the web

Google does such a good job searching for items that it's easy to get a bit lazy when defining searches. If what you're looking for does not immediately show up on the first page of search results, here are a few options you can try to help you google more effectively.

Search using the Google categories. Google has expanded so much over the years that it now offers numerous categories to search, rather than looking at the whole web. The different categories are displayed at the top of the results page and include All, Maps, News, Images, Videos, Shopping, Books, Flights, and Finance.

Click or tap on one of the categories to conduct a search or see the results for the current search in relation to the selected category. For instance, if you select the Flights category, you can look for, and book, flights to specific destinations.

Look for an exact phrase. In a normal search, Google will look for all the words in a search query. To search for an exact phrase as it appears in its actual location, use quotation marks around the search words, "outdoor furniture" for example. This instructs Google to look for the exact phrase, rather than just any occurrences of the words.

Exclude items. Sometimes a search query will result in delivering some of the items you are looking for, but also include something that you don't want. To solve this, you can exclude certain words by putting a hyphen in front of them. So if you do not want search results containing "fruit" to be included, enter "-fruit" at the end of the search query, as in "Apple -fruit."

Search specific sites. To narrow down the number of sites searched by Google, use a colon and the name of a specific site, such as "computer books:fca.com." This will only show search results from the selected site.

Use the wild card. The wild card in Google is denoted by the asterisk symbol *. This instructs Google to fill this space with what it thinks is the most appropriate word. It is frequently used for items such as song titles or poems if you can't remember the whole thing. For instance, for the search request "the owl and the *" Google will correctly predict that the missing word is "pussycat" and return that result.

Look for similar sites. Most people get into regular habits in terms of the websites they visit. However, to expand your horizons, you can look for sites that are similar to your favorites and so find a wider range of information than you may otherwise have seen.

To perform this type of search, use the word "related" followed by a colon, and the name of the website, such as "related:nationalgeo-graphic.com" with no spaces. The actual website address should be used, not just the name of the website.

Find it locally, wherever you are. Use the word "nearby" in a search to enable Google to give you results that are near to you. For instance, enter "coffee places nearby" and Google will give you a list of, and directions to, the nearest coffee houses. This works best on a smartphone when you are away from home. Location Services needs to be turned On in order for this to work.

Cut out redundant words. Google generally ignores words such as "a," "and," "the," and "it." Therefore you can cut them out of search queries and save time. Instead of typing, "Where are the best places to see the sunrise and sunset," try "best sunrise sunset" instead.

See if you feel lucky. The Google home page sports an I'm Feeling Lucky button. This is not some sort of lucky dip option, where you are offered random results for your search query. Rather, it opens the top search result from the query.

The idea is that you feel certain you will find what you are looking for on the first try, instead of having to look through a lot of search results. It's worth trying, if only to see what is offered, but in reality it is usually more productive to view a range of search results.

Images — a unique way to explore

Google not only finds results using a text search, it can also search using images. For instance, if you see a photo on the web that looks familiar, but you can't quite place where it is, you can ask Google to search over the image.

You can also use your own images for the *Search by image* function. This can be done using Google on a desktop computer, a laptop, or a tablet, but not on a smartphone. Here's how.

1. Access the Google home page, and click on the *Images* button on the top toolbar.

2. The Google Search box is converted into the *Google images* Search box. Click on the camera icon.

3. Click on the *Upload an image* tab.

4. Click on the *Choose File* button.

5. Select whether to take a new photo or video or use one from the photo library on your device.

6. Navigate to an image, and click on the *Open* button to upload it.

7. A description, or best guess, of the image will be displayed, as well as links to other images based on the description provided by Google images.

┌─ A closer look ─────────────────────────────────┐

If you want to use Google on your smartphone or tablet, the experience is similar to using it on a desktop computer or laptop.

1. Access the Google website at *google.com* to view the standard Google Search box.

2. Begin typing a word or phrase. As you type, corresponding suggestions will appear.

3. As you continue to type, the suggestions will become more defined.

4. Tap on a result to view details about it.

└──┘

Instantly unleash the power of Google

With your tablet or smartphone, you don't even need a web browser to have Google just a tap, or a voice command, away. You can use an app to unleash the power of Google.

Download the Google app from either the Apple App Store or the Google Play Store. You can then use it in the same way as the website version in terms of performing searches.

In addition, it can be set up for voice searches (except on an iPhone). To do this:

1. Tap on the *Google* app to open it.

2. The regular Google Search box is displayed. This includes a microphone icon. Tap on the microphone to make a voice

search, although you can change
it so there is no need to even tap
the icon.

3. Tap on the *More* button in the bottom right-hand corner.

4. Tap on the *Settings* button.

5. Tap on the *Voice* button.

6. Drag the *"OK Google" hotword* button to On. This will
    enable the use of voice searching without the need to tap the
    microphone icon. The phrase "Hey Google" can also be used
    to activate voice searches.

Voice query — the simplest way to search

After the Google app has been set up for voice commands, it can
be used without the need to access the keyboard at all.

1. Open the *Google* app, and start by saying "OK Google" or
    "Hey Google."

2. If OK Google is available, the *Speak now* screen will appear.
    If you do not say anything immediately, the screen will dis-
    play *Listening*.

3. Speak your query.

4. OK Google is designed to be conversational so that you can
    ask several related questions one after another, just as you
    would when talking to a person. However, you have to start
    each question with "OK Google."

5. Your device will read out the result of your OK Google voice query.

A closer look

The Google Assistant app is another option for using text and voice searches with Google. It operates in a similar way to the Google app, except that it aims to give a tailored approach so you can use it for all your daily activities. Voice commands are activated with "OK Google" or "Hey Google," and the results are spoken by the Assistant.

---

7 ways voice search can make your life easier

With OK Google up and running, you can use it for a number of handy tasks. Just pick your favorite helper — the Google app or the Google Assistant app.

Open apps. Simply say to Google "OK Google, open Calendar" or "OK Google, open Calendar app," and it should do the work for you.

Set reminders and appointments. OK Google is an excellent option for setting regular reminders. For instance, say "OK Google, set a reminder to take vitamins every day at 11 a.m."

Get the daily news. OK Google is a great way to start your day with a news update, simply by saying "OK Google, latest news."

Check out the weather. Just ask Google what the weather is like for your location to see the forecast. Refine the results by asking for a specific time or date.

Play music. Take the effort out of playing music on your device. Ask Google to play a particular track or album, and it will become your personal music presenter.

Send text messages. For digital devices, OK Google can be particularly useful for certain tasks when you cannot access the keyboard. One of these is sending text messages with your voice rather than typing it.

Ask OK Google to send a text message to a specific person. If they are in your address book they will be displayed. If they have more than one number associated with them you will be asked which one to use.

After you have spoken the message it will appear at the top of the screen with a prompt to send it. Just say "Send" and that's it, job done.

Get directions. If you are out and about, getting directions to places is a few words away with OK Google. Ask for directions to a certain location, and a map will be displayed with a route to follow.

Tap on the *Go* button to start following the route, which changes as you progress along it, until you get to your destination.

Beyond Google — more exciting search options

Google is definitely not the only option when it comes to looking for content on the web. Some other services to look at include:

- Bing. This is Microsoft's own search engine, and it is the default one used on Windows devices. It is one of the most-used search engines globally, although still far behind Google.

- Yahoo! In the 1990s Yahoo! was one of the top search engines. Although it has now fallen well behind Google, it is still a good option in the world of web searching.

- DuckDuckGo. This search engine differentiates itself from its competitors by emphasizing privacy and security for its users. It also aims to avoid presenting personalized results based on a user's search and web history. The DuckDuckGo search results for each query are the same for all users.

A closer look

Most web browsers have an option for specifying a default search engine to use. You'll find this in the browser's Settings.

- For a Windows 10 device, open the Microsoft Edge browser, and select Menu > Settings > Default browser > Change my default.

- For a macOS device, open the Safari browser, and select Safari > Preferences > Search from the top menu bar, and click in the *Search engine* box to select one of the options.

- For options on an iPad or iPhone, look in Settings > Safari > Search Engine.

- For an Android laptop or smartphone using the Chrome browser, look in Menu > Settings > Search engine.

Email — an easy way to stay in touch

Choose the best email service for you

Despite the proliferation of text messaging apps and social media sites, email remains a popular, fast, and reliable means of digital communication. There are two main ways of using email.

Proprietary apps. These apps are linked to the device you are using, and the email is connected to the account that is being used with the device. For instance, Windows with a Microsoft Account has its own Mail app, and so do Apple devices.

Once you set up your account, the email account will automatically be created. Proprietary apps on Windows and Apple devices can also be used to link to a range of web-based email services.

Web-based email services. These are email services that can be used on any device and operating system. They are cloud-based services, meaning they operate in an online environment and are not physically located on a specific device. The most widely used web-based email is Gmail.

Manage your email on Windows 10

Windows 10 comes with the Mail app, which can be used to manage all of your email needs. To use the Mail app:

1. Ensure that a Microsoft Account has been created.

2. Click on the *Start* button, and select the *Mail* app (or click on it on the Taskbar).

3. The left-hand panel of the Mail app contains links to email accounts and folders. Click on an account name, then the *Inbox* button.

4. Messages are displayed in the middle panel. Click on a message to view its contents in the right-hand panel.

5. Use the buttons above a message to *Reply* to the sender; *Reply all*, to reply to everyone who was included in the original email; *Forward* the message to someone else; *Archive* it; or *Delete* it.

To create a new email:

1. In the left-hand panel, click on the *New mail* button to start a new email.

2. Enter a recipient in the *To* box. If the recipient and their email address are already in your Windows 10 address book, the People app, they will appear as an option as you begin to type their name. Click on their name to add them in the *To* box.

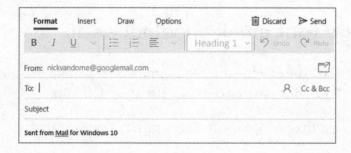

3. Enter a title for the email in the *Subject* box.

4. Enter the body text for the email below the *Subject* box.

5. Click on the *Format* tab at the top of the Mail window to select options for font size and color, alignment, and pre-formatted styles for the text of the email. Before formatting text, drag over it with the cursor to select it.

6. Click on the *Insert* tab to add any attachments, such as photos.

7. Click on the *Send* button.

Simple steps to send messages on your Mac

Mac computers using macOS come with their own email app, called Mail. This covers all of the email functionality that most people could need. To start using Mail:

1. Ensure that an Apple ID has been created, and click on the *Mail* app on the Dock.

2. The left-hand panel contains links to the Inbox and various folders within the app.

3. Click on an email in the middle panel to view its details in the right-hand panel.

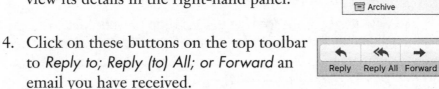

4. Click on these buttons on the top toolbar to *Reply to; Reply (to) All;* or *Forward* an email you have received.

5. Click on the trash can button to move the email to the *Trash.*

To create a new email:

1. Click on the *New Message* button to create a new email.

2. Enter a recipient in the To field. If they are already in your address book (the Contacts app) their email address will be inserted as you type their name (as long as the email address has been added in their contact information).

3. Enter a title for the email in the *Subject* field, and enter the text in the main Mail window.

4. Select text as required by clicking and dragging over it with the cursor.

5. Click on this button to show the text formatting options.

6. Use these buttons to select font and font size, font color, bold, italic, underlining, strikethrough, and alignment options.

7. Click on the paperclip button to browse your folders to attach photos or documents to your email.

A closer look

To view text with the icons in the Mail app on your Mac, Ctrl+click on the icon, and select the *Icon and Text* option.

Send emails from anywhere with your iPhone

You can send an email no matter where you are, as long as you have your tablet or phone with you. Here's how to do it on an iPad using iPadOS, or an iPhone using iOS.

1. Ensure an Apple ID has been created, and tap on the *Mail* app on the Dock. (If there is a red icon in the corner, this displays the number of unread emails in your Inbox.)

2. Tap on a message to display it.

3. Use these buttons to, from left to right, delete the current message or move it to another folder. For an iPad these are located on the top toolbar, and for an iPhone they are located on the bottom toolbar.

4. Tap on this button on the bottom toolbar for both iPad and iPhone.

5. Select the options to reply to a message, reply to all recipients in a message, forward it to a new recipient, delete it, flag it for additional actions, mark it as read or unread, or move it to another folder.

To create and send an email:

1. Tap on this button to create a new message, for both iPad and iPhone.

2. In the *To* box, enter the recipient's email address, or type the recipient's name (if they are in your Contacts app), and tap on one of the suggestions to select it.

3. Enter a title in the *Subject* box.

4. Enter the body text in the area below the Subject box.

5. For both iPad and iPhone, tap on this button to send the email to the recipient.

┌─ **A closer look** ────────────────────────────────┐

If you use the Mail app on a Mac computer and an iPad or iPhone, you'll be able to access your emails on all of these devices, providing you use the same Apple ID on all of them.

└───┘

Gmail — the best option for Android fans

Your best choice for emailing on an Android tablet or smartphone is the popular Gmail. This can be used with your Google Account that you set up when you first started using the Android device. You can access Gmail using either the Gmail app or the online version at *gmail.com*.

To use the Gmail app:

1. Download the *Gmail* app from the Apple App Store or the Google Play Store.

2. Tap on the Gmail app, and sign in with your Google Account details.

3. Click on this button to view the Gmail menu.

4. The Gmail menu contains links to the Inbox and other Gmail folders. Tap on the *Inbox* button.

5. Tap on an email to view its details in the main window.

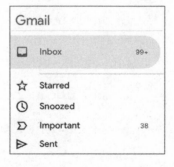

6. Tap on this button to reply to an email.

To create a new email in the Gmail app:

1. Tap on this button at the bottom of the Inbox.

2. In the *To* box, enter the recipient's email address, or type the recipient's name (if they are in your Contacts app), and tap on one of the suggestions to select it.

3. Enter a title in the *Subject* box.

4. Enter the body text in the area below the Subject box.

5. Tap on this button to add attachments to the email.

6. Tap on this button to send the email to the selected recipient.

To create a new email with the online version of Gmail, using any web browser:

1. Access the Gmail website at *gmail.com*, and sign in with your Google Account details.

2. Click or tap on the *Inbox* option to view your emails, which are displayed in the main panel.

3. Click or tap on an email heading in the Inbox to view its details.

4. Click or tap on the *Compose* button to create a new email.

5. Enter a recipient's email address in the *To* box, add a subject, then write the body text of the email.

6. Click or tap on the *A* button on the bottom toolbar to access text formatting options.

7. Click or tap on this button on the bottom toolbar to attach an item to the email from your device, such as a photo or a file.

8. Click or tap on this button on the bottom toolbar to attach a photo from your Google Account photos.

9. Click or tap on the *Send* button to send the email.

A closer look

You don't have to use an Android device to take advantage of Gmail. It's available for Windows desktop computers or laptops, and for Apple devices using macOS, iPadOS, or iOS. You can access it by going to the Gmail website at *gmail.com*, or by downloading the Gmail app.

Email accounts — the more the merrier

If you use one email service, it doesn't mean you can't add another one and access the content from the email app you're already using.

This can be useful if you want to have a second email account to use when registering for online shopping websites and other services. That will keep you from receiving a lot of unwanted emails on your personal account. Here's how to add email accounts for different operating systems.

- For Microsoft, open the Mail app, and click on the *Add Account* button.

- For macOS, open the Mail app, and select Mail > Add Account from the top menu bar.

- For iPadOS/iOS, access Settings > Passwords & Accounts, and tap on the *Add Account* button.

- For Android devices, access Settings > Users & accounts, and tap on the *Add account* button.

For each of these options you will be able to link to an existing account that you have. For instance, if you use the iCloud account on an iPad or iPhone, you can add a Gmail account, and all your emails will be available within the Mail app, under their own account headings in the Inbox.

3 easy ways to streamline your Inbox

In some ways, email is like the ultimate storage cupboard — it gets filled up easily, things get left there, and then you just forget about them. This can result in your Inbox storing hundreds of emails.

Over time it can take up a certain amount of storage on your device, particularly if you have a lot of emails with attachments. To avoid being overwhelmed by your Inbox, use some of these options to get it organized.

Mailboxes. Create mailboxes for similar types of content, such as Finances and Family. Once you receive an email on one of these subjects and you have read it, move it into the relevant mailbox.

Most email apps have a button like this for moving messages into a mailbox. Open the email, and click or tap on the *Move to Mailbox* button, and select the mailbox into which you want to move the email.

Flags. You can attach flags to emails so you can quickly identify important messages. Some email apps use flags of different colors, so you can apply the same color for emails covering a similar topic.

229

Delete. As with many cleaning tasks, sometimes it's a good thing to just throw things away. Try going through your Inbox and deleting any emails you no longer need. If you think you want to keep one, move it into a mailbox so it no longer takes up space in your Inbox.

Staying secure

Junk email, or spam, is one of the great frustrations of modern computing. It usually comes in two forms:

- unsolicited junk mail from spammers trying to sell you something, or worse, trying to trick you out of your personal financial details.

- marketing junk mail from companies or websites with which you have registered to buy items online.

All email apps have an option for marking emails as junk and moving them to the Junk mailbox with an icon such as this.

It is worth doing this as it trains the app to recognize junk emails. Over time, it will move them directly into the Junk folder without them showing up in your Inbox first.

---

10 terrific tips to get rid of annoying junk mail

People are saying "bye" to junk emails — for good. Take these steps to "de-spam" your Inbox, and you can join them. It's easier than you think.

Never reply to junk email from spammers. Even to try and unsubscribe. All that does is confirm to them that it is an active email address and encourages them to send more spam.

Unsubscribe from marketing emails. You can unsubscribe from companies you have done business with online. The Unsubscribe option is usually at the bottom of the marketing email.

Ignore any offers in junk email. This is particularly true of financial emails. For instance, an email may say, "Your account with XXX has been locked. Please click here to enter your details and unlock your account." Never, ever click on these types of links.

Use a "junk" email address for online transactions. This is an active email address (best created with a web-mail service such as Gmail) that you can use when registering with online retail sites. This way, you can still have access to details about your purchases, but any marketing emails will be sent to this account and not your personal one used for communicating with family and friends.

Set up an email filter. Is your email account suffering from junk mail overload? Using a filter will help de-spam your Inbox. You can create one from within your email app. Check in the Settings section of your email account for specific security settings relating to spam, and make sure your privacy settings are as robust as possible.

Make your email address harder to guess. Some spammers operate by trying to guess email addresses, such as john_smith@ gmail.com. To try and avoid this, insert numbers and symbols into your email address, like john!_smith8458$@gmail.com.

Even though this may look complicated, once family and friends have it in their address books they will not have to remember it.

Use spam-blocking software. There is a range of spam-blocking software on the market. Search using "spam blocking" on the web, and research the options carefully before you settle on one product. Try looking at MailWasher at *mailwasher.net*, SPAMfighter at *spamfighter.com*, and SpamHero at *spamhero.com*.

Check out the latest spam information on the FTC website.
The Federal Trade Commission (FTC) no longer has an email
address where you can send examples of spam, but they do collect
spam from the internet and take actions against it. Check them out
at *consumer.ftc.gov/articles/0038-spam*.

Be cautious of strange emails from your friends. If you get a
random email from one of your contacts this could mean their
computer has a virus and is sending out spam. Delete the email,
and contact the person to let them know what has happened.

Change your ISP. If problems with spam persist, consider changing
your Internet Service Provider (ISP), as it may not have sufficient
defenses in place.

Be considerate — follow good email etiquette

Email does not involve some of the pitfalls that come with instant
messaging and communicating via social media. However, you
should still be polite and courteous in your email communications.
Follow these tips to ensure you have the best email etiquette.

Be careful with Reply All. If you receive an email with multiple
recipients, such as a family group letter or club invitation, take care
how you send a reply. Do you need to reply to one person or all of
the recipients? If it is the former, use the Reply option so the other
recipients are not overwhelmed with replies.

Use an appropriate greeting. Since email is more formal than a
text message, but generally less formal than a written letter, the
method of greeting can be tricky. Generally, the safest way to intro-
duce an email is just to use the person's first name, either on its
own or preceded by "Hello" or "Hi." If it is a more formal corre-
spondence, use the method of greeting for a written letter.

Watch the length of your emails. Just because email technology allows you to write emails as long as you like doesn't mean you should. Say what you need to say as concisely as possible. If you need to have a longer discussion, contact the person in another way, such as by phone or video chat.

Don't go overboard with formatting. Most email apps have options for formatting text in terms of font type, size, and color; bold; underlining; and lists. A certain amount of formatting can make elements of an email stand out, but don't overdo it, or it may look too confusing.

Create an interesting signature. You can have text added automatically at the end of all your emails. It does not have to be your name. You can add an extra flourish by including your favorite quote or scripture, or even a cute picture.

For Windows Mail, add a signature from Settings > Signature. For macOS Mail, select Mail > Preferences > Signatures from the top menu bar, and click on the + button. For iPadOS/iOS Mail, add a signature from Settings > Mail > Signature.

For the online version of Gmail, add a signature from Settings > Signature > Create new. For the Gmail app, add a signature from Menu > Settings > Account name > Signature settings, and turn Mobile Signature to On.

Top tips to navigate social media

Learn the lingo to be one of the group

For something that has been around less than two decades (Facebook was founded in 2004), social media has taken a remarkable hold around the world. In fact, it's become an accepted part of daily life for millions of people.

Given the nature of social media sites, it's not surprising they have created a whole new language of their own. If you want to participate, it helps to be familiar with it. Here are some of the terms to know.

Friend request. The process of linking to another person on Facebook. A friend request is sent by one person, and once it has been accepted, both people can see what the other is saying on their page.

Posts. Refers to anything you put on your social media page. Originally, it was generally just a text comment, but now posts include photos, humorous images (known as memes), and videos.

Hashtags. The symbol (#) that is added to posts on social media sites, usually Facebook and Twitter, to identify specific topics. The intention is to create enough other posts with the same hashtag that the topic starts to "trend."

Trending. When a topic has such a large number of hashtags that it becomes one of the most popular items on the site. Social media sites usually list the top trending topics, and these change on a regular basis.

Following. On Twitter, you can see other people's comments on your own page by following them. You can look at what other people are saying without following them, by looking at their pages, but they will only appear on your page if you decide to actively follow them.

Tweet. A post you put on your own Twitter page. Twitter is designed to be a concise means of communication, and tweets are limited to 280 characters.

Trolling. When people are attacked on social media with abusive or derogatory comments. It can be a major problem and is something that deters some people from engaging with social media sites.

Flaming. An argument on a social media site. It can start with an inoffensive comment, but quickly escalate if someone takes a comment the wrong way. A drawn-out argument between two people on a social media site is known as a flame war.

Follow the golden rule when you're online

One of the big problems with social media sites is people posting rude, abusive, and insensitive comments. Many feel emboldened to do so because they can hide behind a computer screen.

A general rule when using social media is to not post anything to someone, or about someone, that you would not say to them in person. Keep these points in mind.

- Be respectful of other people's views and opinions. You may not always agree with someone, but being negative or rude is never a good approach. Always think about what you post, and the effect it could have on other people.

- Be careful with humor. Something that you may think is hilarious may be offensive to someone else. If in doubt, don't post it.

- Be responsive to questions. If someone asks a specific question, such as "What time shall we meet tomorrow?" it is polite to send some form of reply.

Caution

False and fake news has become a major issue in digital communications. False news on social media sites comes in two main forms — individuals posting false information about something, and organizations promoting false news for their own purposes.

Because social media is so unreliable, you should never rely solely on these sites for your news. This is especially true with major security alerts or natural disasters, since a lot of false details are spread on social media. If you want information during a major incident, check the local or national TV news channels, rather than just relying on social media.

Another option for checking news items that you see on social media sites, or other media outlets, is a fact-checking website. Two to look at are FactCheck at *factcheck.org*, and Politifact at *politifact.com*.

The ins and outs of Facebook

Facebook has become the dominant force in the world of social media, and for millions of users, it is a valuable option for keeping in touch with family and friends.

Along with posting comments, Facebook is also excellent for publishing photos and videos. It is definitely a social media site that covers all the bases.

Get up and running. When you first start using Facebook, it pays to become familiar with the site, so you can be confident about using it. It is also important to be aware of the security features, so you can protect your privacy online as much as possible.

A Facebook account can be created for free with a username and password. Once you do this, you can get started with the exciting world of social media.

1. Visit the Facebook website at *facebook.com*, or download the Facebook app, and log in with your account details.

2. Click on this button on the top toolbar.

3. Click on your own account icon in the left-hand panel. Your timeline home page is displayed.

4. Click on the *Profile picture* box to add, or update, your profile photo.

5. Click on the *Add Cover Photo* button to add a main photo for your timeline.

6. Click on the *About* button on the top toolbar to update your profile information.

Add your friends. Facebook is nothing without family and friends. To connect, you need to send someone a friend request, or reply to one that you have been sent. To do this:

1. Click on this icon on the top toolbar.

2. Enter a name into the *Search Facebook* box.

3. Once you have located a friend, click on the *Add Friend* button.

4. The *Friend Request Sent* button is displayed. Once the person accepts your request, you have your first Facebook friend.

5. Once you have added your first friend, you will start to get suggestions for more friends to add, based on the ones you already have.

Create a post. It's time to tell everyone what you've been up to. To add a post to your timeline:

1. Click on the + button on the top toolbar.

2. Click on the *Post* button.

3. Type in the *Create Post* text box. Use the buttons below the text to add videos, add photos, and tag friends, so the post is displayed on their timeline. Then add your location.

4. Click on the *Post* button to add it to your timeline.

Caution

As a general rule, don't accept a friend request from someone you don't know and who isn't already a friend of one of your existing Facebook friends. Fraudsters and scammers operate within the social media world in the same way as in other online environments. They're out to con people out of their money or steal their identity.

Special way to send messages

In addition to your timeline, Facebook also has its own built-in messaging app, Messenger. This can be used to send messages to individuals, or groups, either through Facebook, or by using the Messenger app on an iPadOS/iOS or Android device. To use Messenger within Facebook:

1. Click on this button on the top toolbar.

2. Select one of your friends to send a message to.

3. Type the message in the text box, and click on this button to send the message.

4. Click on this button in the bottom right-hand corner to use the live chat panel to chat to someone in real-time.

No. 1 priority when setting up Facebook

Although it is tempting to dive straight into some of the exciting options that Facebook has to offer, the first stopping-off point should be the Privacy settings, which can be used to determine who gets to see your information on Facebook and how people can interact with you. To do this:

1. Click on this button on the top toolbar.

2. Click on the *Settings & Privacy* option.

3. Click on the *Settings* button.

4. Click on the *Privacy* button in the left-hand panel.

5. The Privacy section contains a range of options for how people interact with you, as shown below.

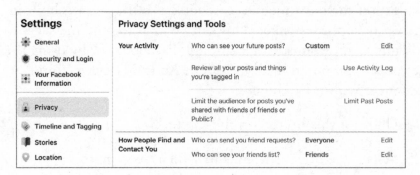

6. For each item, click on the *Edit* button.

7. Click in this box for the selected item, and choose the required option. In general, selecting *Public* is not a good idea as it makes an item available to anyone, whether they have a Facebook account or not. If an item is public, it can show up in a web search and be accessible from the search results.

8. Go through all of the Privacy items and make selections accordingly. These can always be changed at a later date. If possible, limit access for most items to family and/or friends.

The more time you spend initially in the Privacy settings, the more time you may save yourself during your Facebook interactions, and the safer you'll be.

What you should never post on social media

Criminals monitor social media sites looking for anything that can provide information for a variety of criminal activities, from fraud to identify theft. Therefore it is important to avoid certain types of information on your social media sites.

One popular feature on Facebook is the announcement of your birthday to all your friends, so they can send you virtual birthday wishes. As much as you might enjoy all the attention, it's the one place you should never announce your birthday.

Birth dates are one of the prime items identity theft criminals try and obtain. If the wrong people see it, they could steal your identity.

Since you have to enter your date of birth when you first register for Facebook, how do you avoid it being displayed to everyone? The answer lies in the Privacy section, where you can hide your birthday details. To do this using the Facebook website at *facebook.com*:

1. On your timeline, click on the *About* button on the top toolbar.

2. Click on the *Contact and Basic Info* option in the About panel.

3. In the Basic Info section, click on this button next to your date of birth.

4. Select an option for who can see your birthday. The most secure is *Only me*.

5. Repeat the process for the *Birth Year* option, and click on the *Save* button at the bottom of the page.

Other things you should never share or post on Facebook:

*   Vacation details, or photos while on vacation. Criminals look at social media sites, just waiting for someone to tell them there is going to be an empty home.

241

- Personal details about family and friends. Just as you shouldn't give away any sensitive details about yourself, the same is true for family and friends.

- Financial details. Don't post anything in relation to your financial situation, and never reveal any bank account details or login information for online accounts of any kind. Also, be careful not to leave anything like bank or credit cards in the background of photos.

Popular app lets you share your life through photos

A number of photo-sharing social media sites have emerged over the years, but the dominant one is Instagram, known colloquially as Insta. Founded in 2010 and now owned by Facebook, it was initially launched as an app to be used on iPhones.

It has since expanded and is now widely available on all platforms with app and website options. Because it's designed for users to upload photos instantly from wherever they are, the app version on a tablet or smartphone is probably your best option.

You can download the Instagram app from the Apple App Store for iPads and iPhones, and the Google Play Store for Android tablets and smartphones. Create a free account using an email address and a password. Then you're ready to start sharing and viewing photos and videos.

1. Tap on the *Instagram* app, and log in with your account details to get started. You can also log in with your Facebook account details.

2. To view someone's photos you have to follow them. The home page displays suggested people to follow, and you can also find your own family and friends by tapping on the *Find People to Follow* button.

3. You can also search for people and photos. To do this, tap on this button on the bottom toolbar. Enter someone's name in the Search box at the top of the window, and tap on one of the results to view that person's photos and details.

4. Tap on the *Follow* button for the person you want to follow. This means you will be able to see their existing photos and videos and also new ones that they post.

5. Tap on this button on the bottom toolbar to view the latest items that have been posted by people you are following.

Snap and share photos on Instagram

Since the main function of Instagram is to share photos and videos, this is probably one of the first things you will want to do. To get started:

1. Open the Instagram app, and tap on this button on the bottom toolbar to access existing photos from the photo library on your tablet or smartphone.

2. Tap on the *Next* button in the top right-hand corner of the screen.

3. Select any editing options for the photo as required, and tap on the *Next* button.

4. Write a caption for the photo, and tap on the *Tag People* or *Add Location* options. If you tag any of your contacts, the photo will show up on their Instagram page.

5. Tap on the *Share* button to add the photo to your home page, from where other people will be able to view it.

To take a photo with your device's camera, and share it to Instagram:

1. Open the Instagram app, and tap on this button in the top left-hand corner.

2. Tap on the *Enable Camera Access* and *Enable Microphone Access* buttons, for taking photos and videos.

3. Swipe along the icons at the bottom of the screen to add a filter for the photo. The active filter operates as the shutter button for taking the photo.

4. Take the photo or video.

5. Tap on the *Send To* button, in the bottom right-hand corner.

6. Select how you want to share the photo or video, from *Your Story*, or *Close Friends Only*.

7. Tap on the *Share* button.

Fantastic filters make your Instagram pictures shine

One of the most popular features on Instagram is the ability to add filters to photos. This can produce dramatic and artistic effects. It has also created the phrase "no filter applied," which people use to indicate that they have not edited a photo. In addition to filters, there are also some other editing options for photos on Instagram.

1. Share a photo from your photo library. In the Edit section, tap on the *Filter* button on the bottom toolbar.

2. Swipe along the filter options, and tap on one to apply it to the photo.

3. Tap on the *Edit* button on the bottom toolbar.

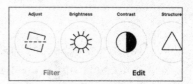

4. Tap on one of the editing options.

5. Drag the slider to apply the editing effect. Tap on the *Done* button.

6. Tap on the *Next* button to continue sharing the edited photo.

A closer look

When you take a photo with your device's camera to share on Instagram, tap on this bar at the top of the photo window to access editing options including creative filters, stickers, freehand drawings, and text.

Keep your Instagram photos private

To set security and privacy settings in Instagram, such as determining who can follow you or view your photos:

1. Tap on this button on the bottom toolbar.

2. Tap on the menu button in the top right-hand corner.

3. Tap on the *Settings* button.

4. Tap on the *Privacy* button, and make the required selections for how people can interact with your Instagram account.

5. Tap on the *Security* button on the main Settings page to select options for logging in and managing how your data is used.

A closer look

Hashtags (#) can be added to words within a tweet on Twitter to identify them as a popular subject. The most popular hashtags become a trending topic on Twitter.

Hashtags can be created by combining several words, such as #myfirsttweet, but they have to be continuous, with no spaces. To create a hashtag when you are writing a tweet, add the hashtag symbol before the word to be used.

Twitter — it's not just for the birds

Launched in 2006, Twitter is a site that is designed to enable you to display and share short messages, up to 280 characters. This is also known as micro-blogging.

Messages on Twitter are known as tweets. You have to register on Twitter to post tweets, but you can read them without registering. Photos and videos can also be shared on Twitter.

Get up and running. Twitter can be accessed from its app in the Apple App Store or the Google Play Store, or online at *twitter.com*. You can create a user account for free, using an email address and a password.

Once this has been done you can start tweeting your thoughts and seeing what other people are saying. Twitter opens up at your home page, also known as your Twitter feed.

How to follow people. Before you start tweeting it is best to follow people on Twitter. You can do this with family and friends, and also celebrities if you want to see what they are saying. To start following people:

1. Tap on this button on the bottom toolbar.

2. Enter the name of the person you want to follow.

3. Navigate to the required person, and tap on the *Follow* button.

4. The number of people who you are following, and vice versa, is displayed at the top of your Twitter feed.

Post a tweet. When you want to say something on Twitter it will be seen by your followers. (When someone you are following tweets something, it will appear on your Twitter feed.) To send a tweet:

1. Tap on this button.

2. Write the tweet, and tap on these buttons to add a photo or a video, add an animated GIF image, create a Twitter poll, or add your location.

3. Tap on the *Tweet* button to publish the tweet.

Reply to tweets. If a tweet appears on your Twitter feed you can do the following:

1. Tap on this button to reply to a tweet.

2. Tap on this button to retweet it, either on its own or with an additional comment. This is like publishing it on your own Twitter feed, in which case all your followers will see it.

3. Tap on this button to mark it as a favorite, which can be used by the person who published it to see how popular the tweet is.

How to keep things private. To select security and privacy options on Twitter:

1. Tap on your own profile button.

2. Tap on the *Settings and privacy* button.

3. Tap on the *Privacy and safety* button, and make selections as required.

4 more fun social media sites to try

Even though you may not use a lot of the social media options that are out there, it is good to be aware of them, if only to keep up with what your grandchildren are talking about. Here are some favorites.

Snapchat. A messaging service that allows users to send text, photos, and videos to their Snapchat friends, or groups of people. Once these are accessed, they generally remain visible for a short period of time, and then they are deleted. Users can also create stories of chronological content.

TikTok. A video-sharing social media site that has gained great popularity through the fun and quirky videos that are posted there.

Pinterest. A virtual pinboard where users can upload and "pin" items of interest, such as text posts and images. It is designed to enable users to find a range of interests and ideas.

Reddit. A social media news aggregation site. Users can post links, text posts, and images, and the site's users vote on them in terms of popularity. They are then ranked on the site accordingly.

10 tips for staying safe on social media

Hanging out on social media can be a lot of fun and a great way to keep up with friends and family. Here are some reminders on how to stay safe and secure so you can enjoy it for many years to come.

- Don't become friends with people you don't know.

- Never give out sensitive information such as bank details or online login information.

- Never reply to unknown requests of any kind.

- Use different passwords for separate social media sites.

- Always think twice before posting something.

- Never give an indication that you are going to be away from home.

- Never post anything that could be offensive, or even illegal.

- Check any photos you post to make sure they don't contain any sensitive information.

- Check any news stories on a social media site with at least one other independent source.

- Always log out at the end of a session in case someone tries to add content to your social media site, pretending to be you.

Digital security — how to protect yourself online

7 warning signs that you're under attack

Being secure in any aspect of your life helps you to be more confident, and the same is true in the world of technology. The more you're aware of what could go wrong, the more prepared you can be to prevent it.

This is particularly true in the world of online digital security, where malware (malicious software) poses a considerable threat to computer users. Not sure you'll know if you're under attack? Here are some danger signs to watch out for.

- The operating system fails to start. This is a serious problem since, obviously, you will not be able to gain access to your device. In cases such as this, look for a software security expert in your area.

- Slow performance in terms of opening apps and accessing items.

- Error messages keep appearing for no apparent reason.

- Files and folders disappear without explanation.

- Random emails are generated and sent to all of the contacts in your address book.

- Your device crashes or freezes with monotonous regularity.

- Apps launch themselves with no input from you.

The dangers of the digital and online world can appear frightening and daunting at times. However, understanding these dangers and taking steps to protect yourself is the best way to gain the confidence to carry on safely with the rest of your computing activities.

A closer look

Computer viruses have been around for almost as long as computers themselves. They operate by infecting computing devices and performing various malicious acts.

Viruses install themselves on the victim's computer without their knowledge. When they are opened, either automatically by the virus itself, or by an act such as clicking on an affected attachment in an email, the virus then conducts its malicious mission.

Any erratic or unexplained behavior that suddenly starts happening regularly could mean your device has a virus. If this happens you should investigate immediately.

Vaccinate your computer against damaging viruses

As with many threats in the real or online world, being aware of the problem is the first step to preventing it. The good news is that there are companies dedicated to providing excellent anti-virus protection.

Unfortunately, the hackers and fraudsters are very determined and increasingly sophisticated, and you can never be 100% secure all of the time. But if you remain constantly vigilant, you will give yourself the best chance of a safe and secure computing environment. Here are some steps to take to protect your information and your investment.

Use anti-virus software to identify any malicious attacks. This is your first and most important step. There are both free and paid versions available, and you should always use one on your device if you plan to connect to the internet.

Never open an attachment if you receive an email from some-one you don't know. This includes clicking or tapping on any links in the email. It's one of the most common ways that hackers deploy viruses. If you get an email like this, do not access anything in it, and instead delete it immediately.

Look for a Wi-Fi router with a built-in firewall. The aim is to use the router to stop viruses before they get the chance to access your computing devices. Check the specifications of the router before you buy it to see if it has a built-in firewall.

Use a software firewall on your computer for detecting malicious items trying to access your device via the internet. For Windows and macOS devices, these can be deployed in the Settings section, and separate firewalls can also be used with anti-virus apps.

Keep on top of information about new viruses. Anti-virus soft-ware sites, such as McAfee at *mcafee.com* and Norton at *norton.com*, usually have news about the latest viruses as well as products to protect against them. Details about particularly widespread viruses also sometimes appear in the national news.

How to get anti-virus software for your computer that really works — for free

All of the major anti-virus companies have free options of their products, although these do not have as extensive a range of fea-tures as the paid-for versions. Check out these free anti-virus options that offer good protection against viruses and malware.

- Avast at *avast.com*

- Panda at *pandasecurity.com*

- Spybot Search & Destroy at *safer-networking.org/products/spybot-free-edition*

- SpywareBlaster at *brightfort.com/spywareblaster*

- SUPERAntiSpyware at *superantispyware.com/free-edition.html*

Free versions of anti-virus software can usually be upgraded to more powerful, paid-for, versions.

Windows users have a built-in anti-virus option that can scan for viruses, and it also provides a free firewall that protects against malicious software accessing your desktop computer or laptop. You'll find it within the Windows Security section of the Settings app. To use it:

1. Access Settings > Update & Security.

2. Click on the *Windows Security* option in the left-hand panel.

3. Click on the *Open Windows Security* button.

4. Click on the *Virus & threat protection* option to view general details of the most recent scan.

5. Click on the *Scan options* button to view greater details about the most recent scan, including any current threats. Select options for how you want scans to be performed, from *Quick scan, Full scan*, or *Custom scan*.

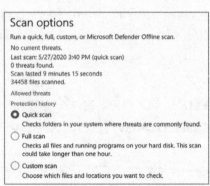

6. Click on the back arrow button to go back to the main *Windows Security* page.

7. Click on the *Manage settings* option under the *Virus & threat protection settings* heading to determine how the virus

checker works. Drag the *Real-time protection* button to On to ensure that Windows Security checks regularly for viruses and malicious software.

8. Click on the *Check for updates* button under the *Virus & threat protection updates* heading on the main Windows Security page to see the last time that anti-virus definition files were updated. This is an important check because these are the files that look for the latest viruses. If the anti-virus definitions are not up to date, then you may miss recent viruses even if you scan your computer and it appears to be free of malicious software. Click on the *Check for updates* button to perform a manual check for new definitions.

> ↻ Virus & threat protection updates
> Security intelligence is up to date.
> Last update: 6/5/2020 10:39 AM
> Check for updates

9. On the main Windows Security page, click on the *Firewall & network protection* option.

10. The firewall options can be used to activate individual firewalls, which help protect your computer when connected to a network, such as via your home Wi-Fi router. By default, the firewalls should be turned On for all of the available networks. If a firewall has been turned Off, click on the *Restore settings* button to turn it back On.

> ((ᵖ)) Firewall & network protection
> Who and what can access your networks.
> ⊗ Microsoft Defender Firewall is using settings that may make your device unsafe.
> Restoring default settings will remove all Windows Defender Firewall settings that you have configured for all network locations. This might cause some apps to stop working.
> Restore settings
> ⧉ Domain network
> Firewall is on.

5 common security mistakes: Are you making 1 of them?

The digital world is full of potential dangers. But if you're aware of some of the common mistakes that can lead to compromised security, you can take steps to avoid them and improve your defenses against unwanted attacks.

Creating short passwords. The shorter the length of a password, the easier it is for hackers to break it. Try and create passwords that are a minimum of eight characters in length, and use a combination of letters, numbers, and symbols. Have a look at the chapter *Simple steps to fight fraud, scams, and ID theft* for more information about creating passwords, including using a password manager.

Using the same password for all your devices and online accounts. It is tempting to use the same password for everything, and it seems logical as you have less chance of forgetting it. But it's highly risky because if someone gets hold of your password they can then access all your devices and online accounts. A much more secure option is to create different passwords for different devices and accounts and store them securely, ideally in a home safe.

Not using two-factor authentication for sensitive websites. This security method sends you a code, usually to your smartphone, after you have signed in to a website and entered your password. This code is then used as the second part of authentication for gaining access to the website. Two-factor authentication is used on websites where there is sensitive financial information. If a website offers this, you should use it.

Accessing public Wi-Fi for financial transactions. If you are away from home you can connect to the web using public Wi-Fi networks, known as hotspots. However, you should not use these to access any websites where you have to enter sensitive information or financial details. These hotspots can be compromised by nearby hackers, who can then access any details that you enter while linked to the hotspot.

Not updating operating systems. If you do not have the latest version of your device's operating system, you will also not have the latest updates that offer protection against viruses and online threats. Therefore it is important to keep your operating systems as up to date as possible.

For Windows, look for the latest updates in Settings > Update & Security > Windows Update. For macOS, look for updates in System Preferences > Software Update. For iPadOS and iOS, look for updates in Settings > General > Software Update. For Android devices, look for updates in Settings > Security & location > Security update.

A closer look

Can't access your favorite website no matter how many times you try? The site could be experiencing a Denial of Service (DoS) attack. This is an industrial form of computer hacking, where websites are inundated by so many requests for pages that they crash.

DoS attacks are usually automated operations performed by large numbers of computers. It is not something that should affect your own computing devices, but it may impact some of the sites you look at on the web.

Smart defense against malicious malware

Malware is just what it sounds like — malicious software. Its purpose is to damage or exploit a computer, server, or network or to steal your identity or other valuable information. These are the most common infectious programs you need to watch out for.

Worms wriggle their way in. Unlike the squirmy creatures you may find in the backyard, the digital versions are much more malicious. They're a form of virus that actively works to spread itself, rather than waiting to be activated through a particular action or on a specific date.

257

Worms spread themselves automatically from computer to computer over the internet. Like viruses, they perform similar destructive and irritating tasks. One of their specialties is to replicate themselves via email by accessing your computer's address book to send itself to all of your contacts.

Trojans are on the march. Trojans are another form of virus, and they get their name from the wooden horse of Troy, where a malicious force (the Trojans) was hidden inside an innocent looking gift (the wooden horse). In computing terms, the Trojans are still the malicious force, frequently hidden in apparently friendly items, such as games apps.

Trojans generally have a different purpose from viruses, which try to destroy elements of your digital world. Instead, they are more intent on gathering information from the infected device. This could be bank or credit card details, which they obtain by creating a fake advertisement on your computer offering something that requires you to enter your bank account details.

Ransomware holds you hostage. Another type of malware you want to avoid is ransomware, a threat that can ruin your computer and cost you hundreds of dollars. This is frequently directed at large organizations with hundreds of computers, but ransomware can also be aimed at individuals.

Ransomware freezes your computer so you can't access anything. In effect, the computer is rendered inoperable. Once a ransomware attack has taken place there will be a pop-up message on your computer to alert you to what has happened. This will also contain details about how you can unlock your device, usually by sending a payment to obtain a digital key.

The payment for a ransomware demand is often requested in the Bitcoin digital currency, which seems in keeping with the digital nature of the crime being committed. Frequently the key does not exist, and the payment is never seen again.

To avoid a ransomware attack, use anti-virus software that includes ransomware protection. But if you do suffer this type of attack, try the following steps:

- Do not pay any money. Even if you do make some form of payment, there is no guarantee that your computer will be released from the ransomware.

- Try rolling back your computer to a previous state, before it was infected with the ransomware. Not all ransomware attacks will allow this but, if it is possible, it can be done on a Windows desktop computer or laptop using Settings > Update & Security > Recovery. Click on the *Get started* button below the *Go back to the previous version of Windows 10* heading. On a Mac using macOS, use the *Time Machine* backup app to go back to a previous version.

- Take your computer to a recognized software security expert. Search online to find one in your area. As long as your files and system are backed up you should not lose any valuable documents.

Remove sneaky spyware from your computer

All forms of malicious software are nasty, but spyware is particularly devious. It infects your computer and then looks through all the information there. Whatever it finds it then reports back to the spyware's author. Companies can track your every move online, then build a profile of you to sell to advertisers.

The information spyware finds can include details in files and folders. It can also include things like keystrokes used on websites, so the spyware can recognize login details and passwords. This type of spyware activity is known as keylogging.

Luckily, help is at hand when it comes to removing sneaky spyware with a range of apps designed for this task. The large anti-virus companies all have products designed to remove spyware. It may be included in a comprehensive package for a range of malicious software. Here are some choices to look at.

- Kaspersky at *kaspersky.com*

- McAfee at *mcafee.com*

- Norton at *norton.com*

- PCProtect at *pcprotect.com*

- TotalAV at *totalav.com*

Don't let scammers catch you in their 'phishing' net

One of the most common forms of scams aimed at computer users is known as phishing. This is a relatively simple form of cybercrime as it does not require a complicated virus or spyware.

Instead, phishing involves asking people for their sensitive financial information, such as bank account details and login details for online accounts. Why on earth would anyone willingly hand that information over? The phishing request is usually made through an official-looking, albeit fake, email. Phishing emails can pretend to come from some of the following organizations:

- Banks, with a message saying your account has been suspended.

- Courier services, with a message saying there is a problem with a delivery they have for you.

- A cloud service, such as iCloud or Dropbox, with a message saying your account has been locked. This type of message can also be from any organization where users have online accounts.

Included in the phishing email are details of what the problem is and how it can be remedied. Unfortunately, the "remedy" usually involves clicking on a link, which takes you to a page where you have to enter financial details to fix the problem.

Needless to say, this does not fix the problem (since there wasn't one) but instead provides the phishers with your crucial financial details.

Phishing emails can seem intimidating, and it can be tempting to perform the required action. However, the golden rule is that you should not click on any links in an email you have doubts about. Instead, take a few minutes to try and discover if the email is legitimate. Here are some steps you can take.

Check whether you have an account with the organization mentioned in the email. Millions of phishing emails are sent every day, in the hope that users will have the service or account mentioned in the email. Whenever you get a suspicious looking email, take some time to check whether it is relevant to you or not. If it is, examine the email further to find out if it is genuine.

Inspect the actual address of the email. Phishing emails are usually disguised to show the name of the company they are claiming to be from. However, the email address at the top may be very different and bear little resemblance to the actual company.

Click or tap (or right-click, depending on the device being used) on the name of the email sender to view the full email address.

Note the language, spelling, and grammar in the email. If there are numerous spelling or grammar errors this could be a sign the email is not genuine.

Search the web to see if other people have received the same phishing email. The online community is excellent for keeping on top of online scams, and other people will undoubtedly have received the same phishing emails as you and posted warnings about them.

Look up the company's actual website online. Look on the web rather than through any links in the phishing email to see if the named company has indeed reported any problems.

Staying secure

Check the U.S. government website at *us-cert.gov/report-phishing* for up-to-date information about phishing and options for reporting phishing emails.

Another tool in the fight against phishing attacks and misin-formation on the web are scam-reporting websites. These are dedicated to reporting on a comprehensive range of email scams and also fake news reports that are making the rounds. Two sites to look at are Scambusters at *scambusters.org* and Snopes at *snopes.com*.

Simple steps to fight fraud, scams, and ID theft

Fight back against common source of identity theft

Numerous perils in the online world can result in you being scammed, conned, or worst of all, having your identity stolen and used for criminal purposes. However, one of the most common sources of identity theft has nothing to do with the online world, at least not initially. It involves the old-fashioned crime of bag, wallet, or purse snatching.

A new study has found that computer fraud is only 12% of theft cases. Surprisingly, traditional ways are more common. Once a criminal grabs your purse, they have access to details from your driver's license, bank cards, credit cards, social security number, and any other personal items you carry with you. With this type of information, identity theft criminals could build up a comprehensive profile of you and start impersonating you.

Another similar form of identity theft is known as "shoulder surfing," where criminals simply look over your shoulder when you complete sensitive documents or use your bank/credit cards.

But you can fight back. Here are some steps to take to protect the physical security of your sensitive documents when you are away from home.

- Take as few valuable items as possible with you when you go out. Only take what you need. The fewer items you have, the less you have to worry about and protect.

- Keep bags closed. An open bag is an inviting sight for any criminal, particularly if they have their mind set on identity theft.

- Hold your bag or purse in front of you, ideally with at least one arm over it. If it is behind you, you won't be aware what is happening to it.

- Don't keep your wallet in a back pocket. It could fall out or easily be taken by a criminal. Don't keep your smartphone in a back pocket either.

- Don't put yourself in danger if someone tries to take your bag, wallet, or purse, and threatens violence. If this happens, hand over the item, and report the matter to the police immediately.

7 tips to create strong and secure passwords

Creating and remembering passwords for computing devices and online accounts is one of the least enjoyable aspects of the digital world. Add to this the issue of keeping them all safe and secure, and it begins to feel like a real chore.

But help is at hand for creating, managing, and securing your passwords. The first step is to create passwords that are as strong as possible, and ensure they don't fall into the wrong hands. Just remember these tips.

Protect your password on a "need to know basis." Unless you have a very good reason, never share a password with anyone, even family members. Once a password is known to more than one person it can potentially be shared to a much wider audience.

Aim for variety. Make passwords a minimum of eight characters long, preferably more, and use a combination of uppercase and lowercase letters, numbers, and symbols.

Avoid the temptation to choose simple passwords. You may think a simple password is too obvious to guess. Think again. Two of the first options hackers will try are 123456 or PASSWORD. Both are still two of the most common passwords in use.

Don't use easily obtained details. Hackers and identity theft criminals work at obtaining as much information about people as possible. Therefore you should avoid passwords that contain details they could have obtained elsewhere, such as birth dates, pets' names, and favorite sports teams.

Try picking words at random. This can be done from a book or a newspaper. Once you have selected words in this way, ensure that they are used with uppercase and lowercase letters and interspersed with numbers and symbols.

Use different passwords for all your online accounts. This may seem like an unnecessary hassle, but it is worth doing. If one online account is hacked, your other ones will still be protected if they have different passwords.

Change your passwords regularly. This is another chore, but it could ultimately contribute to your online security. It is recommended you change passwords every 90 days.

Password managers — an easy 1-stop solution

Remembering a lot of different passwords can be tiresome and at times frustrating. However, it is possible to never forget an online password again. It's safe, secure, and easy. Just use a password manager.

This is an app that can be used on your computer or mobile device, and it will remember all your different passwords. All you need to do is remember one password — the main one for your password manager — and store it in a safe place, such as a home safe.

You can use your password manager to store passwords for online accounts such as online banking, social media accounts, computer login passwords, and any other items that require a password to gain access to them. Password managers will also offer to create secure passwords when you register for a new site that requires login details.

Three password managers to look at are:

- 1Password at *1password.com*.

- Dashlane at *dashlane.com*.

- LastPass at *lastpass.com*.

Password manager apps can also be downloaded from the appropriate app store for a specific device. Look for them in the Microsoft Store, the Apple App Store, or the Google Play Store.

Forgot your password? 3 tips to save your sanity

It's something everyone dreads — forgetting your computer password and getting locked out. Never fear. Follow these three tips and you'll be guaranteed to get out of that jam.

Add a password hint. Some devices and operating systems give you an option to include a password hint when you first set up a password. You should always do this so that you can use the hint if you have forgotten the actual password. Make sure the answer to the hint is something you can remember easily.

Use a password manager. These are not just for online passwords. Any passwords can be stored here and retrieved as required.

Keep your passwords in a secure location. The best option for this is in a home safe, so the passwords are locked away. Don't keep passwords written down and near the device they are related to. The first place anyone will look for a password is under a mouse mat next to a computer.

9 ways to stop ID thieves dead in their tracks

Identity theft criminals thrive on people's personal information, so the safer you keep it the harder it is for them to operate.

- Protect your Social Security number at all costs, as this is one of the most valuable documents you have. Don't carry it around with you unless you have to, and don't write it down on any documents except essential official documents.

- Make sure you shred all hard copy documents that contain any personal details. A micro-shredder is your best option.

- Do not give out any personal information if you are approached with an unsolicited request. This could be a request in an email, a phone call from someone pretending to be from your bank, or a text message. If in doubt, don't reply.

- One indication of identity theft can be strange transactions on your bank or credit card statements. Keep an eye on these, and contact your bank if you think anything is suspicious.

- If you will be away from home for a period of time, ask someone to collect your mail, rather than leaving it, potentially, for identity theft criminals.

- Use secure passwords on all of your online accounts, and use anti-virus software and a firewall on your computer to keep the information held on it as secure as possible.

- If you are getting rid of a desktop computer, laptop, tablet, or smartphone, make sure it has been reset to its original factory condition to wipe all of the data from it.

- Store any items with sensitive details, such as important documents, in a secure place, preferably in a home safe.

- Check out the government website *usa.gov/identity-theft* for a wealth of information about dealing with identity theft.

Staying secure

One of the best ways to detect identity theft is to check your credit score regularly with a credit reporting website. These give you a free assessment of your credit rating. If you make a habit of it, you can tell if there are any unexplained changes that could indicate identity theft.

Three credit reporting websites to look at are Equifax at *equifax.com*, Experian at *experian.com*, and TransUnion at *transunion.com*. If you think your identity has been compromised, it is possible to put a freeze on your credit reports so no one else can access them.

Report ID theft ASAP for best results

No one likes to think about being a victim of identity theft. But you can't put your head in the sand and presume it will not happen to you.

Keep an eye on all of your personal information and, if you think you may have been a victim of identity theft, act immediately. You should take the following steps as soon as possible.

- Contact your local police and report your concerns. This is important in terms of trying to catch the identity theft criminals, but it will also provide an official date of when you reported the potential crime. That will lessen any responsibility that could be attached to you.

- Report the issue to the Federal Trade Commission (FTC) using their website at *identitytheft.gov*. They have a range of options relating to identity theft and can issue you an identity theft report and, if needed, a recovery plan.

5 myths about computer security and identity theft

You may be confused by all the different information and advice you get about identity theft. Learn the truth to protect your sensitive information.

It won't happen to me. Identity theft can happen to anyone, and the more complacent you are about it, the more likely it is to happen to you.

It's just a financial crime. While financial gain is the major reason behind identity theft, it can also be used by criminals to get jobs fraudulently, obtain medical treatment, or even evade prosecution for a crime.

Identity theft will be obvious immediately. You may think your anti-virus software will warn you of any breaches, but you can't count on it. Criminals are adept at covering their tracks, and they may wait several months until they deploy some of the elements of identity theft. Therefore it is important to regularly check all your online accounts and credit score.

The crime only occurs online. Identity theft criminals frequently operate by stealing bags, wallets, and purses to find information. They also go through trash and take unattended mail that may be lying outside a house.

You will be fully reimbursed if you are a victim of identity theft. In a lot of cases, this will be true. However, if it is deemed that you are in some way responsible for the identity theft, such as leaving an important document lying around in public, or revealing sensitive information online, then you may be liable for some of the costs.

Caution

No one likes to be scammed or ripped off, and this seems particularly unfair when you are trying to do a good thing and donate to charity. Unfortunately, a lot of unscrupulous people try and profit illegally from people's generosity.

So with the huge number of charities out there, how do you know the best and safest ones to use? Thankfully, help is at hand. A number of free websites check out charities for you and provide all the information you need to be confident about donating.

Get the real scoop on any charity so you don't get taken when you give. Have a look at Charity Watch at *charity-watch.org*, and Charity Navigator at *charitynavigator.org* to make sure your money really is going to a good cause.

---

3 simple ways to protect your privacy online

Whenever you're online, you leave a digital footprint of data. How this data is collected and used is a major consideration for all computer users, since no one likes to think of it being used in ways it shouldn't. Here are three important steps you can take to protect your privacy in the digital world.

Read the terms and conditions. When you download a new app or update an item such as the device's operating system, you'll frequently see a page of terms and conditions in relation to using the item.

It is common for people to accept this without reading it properly. However, it is worth taking some time to look at this page, so you can see any details about how your private data is going to be used.

Check the privacy settings on your devices. Get to know the Privacy settings for your devices so you can take control of how your data is used. For Windows, look in Settings > Privacy; for macOS, look in System Preferences > Privacy; for iPadOS/iOS, look in Settings > Security & Privacy; and for Android, look in Settings > Security & location.

Check the privacy settings on your web browser. One of the main issues about privacy concerns online activities. These can be controlled and managed to a certain degree with settings in individual browsers.

- For the Edge browser on a Windows 10 device, look in Menu > Settings > Privacy & security.

- For the Safari browser on a macOS device, look in Safari > Preferences from the Safari menu bar, and click on the Privacy tab. For the Safari browser on an iPadOS/iOS device, look in Settings > Safari, and select the options under the Privacy & Security heading. (This is in the Settings app, since settings cannot be accessed directly from the browser itself.)

- For the Chrome browser on an Android device, look in Menu > Settings > Privacy from within the browser itself.

Common email scams and cons to look out for

The type and number of email scams and cons is developing constantly. You've heard about phishing, but that's not the only type of email scam you need to worry about. Be on the lookout for these as well.

Current events scams. During the COVID-19 pandemic, people endured a range of email scams for fake cures and false warnings. This can happen whenever there is a major national or international incident, so beware of any emails relating to a current crisis.

Money awaiting collection. The classic one for this relates to the Nigerian prince who has a large sum of money waiting for anyone who is willing to try and help him get it out of the country — for a fee of course.

Charity donations. Some scam emails relate to charity appeals, but the money goes straight into the scammers' pockets.

Stock market scams. Emails promoting miracle products on the stock market are usually what they seem — too good to be true.

You don't have to worry about getting hooked by scams and computer viruses over email as long as you follow a couple of very simple rules.

- Don't open any attachments in emails from senders you don't recognize. This is one of the most common ways viruses enter computing devices or criminals get hold of your personal details.

- Never click on links in suspicious looking emails. They are designed to either trick you into giving away sensitive financial details or infect your device with a virus. If you avoid unknown links in emails you can help stop thieves from stealing your identity as well as prevent destructive viruses.

Caution

You know how important your Social Security number is. So do scammers. And they will go to considerable lengths to obtain it. Here are three scams that have hackers running to the bank with your Social Security money.

- Phone scams, where the scammers claim to be from Social Security and state that your benefits will stop unless you provide certain information, including your Social Security number.

- Email (or text) scams (phishing) asking for the same details as a phone scam.

- Mail scams, where you are sent a flyer offering additional Social Security services, such as a security check, if you fill in and return the attached form, which includes a request for your Social Security number.

Protect yourself and send those scammers scurrying by hanging up on the call, deleting the email, and throwing away the mail flyer. If you are contacted in any of these ways, report the scammers on the Inspector General website at *oig.ssa.gov*.

Top ways to dispose of old devices securely

Computer technology moves so quickly that new devices are always available, making it highly tempting to upgrade. While this is sometimes a good option, you should also consider keeping your existing devices if they still do the job you want them to.

When you do decide to upgrade, it's important to figure out what to do with the device you're replacing. Before you do anything, make sure you've wiped your private information off the device. See the next story *Delete doesn't always do it — how to wipe private info off your computer for good* for tips on how to do this. Then consider one of these ideas.

Sell it. Computing equipment can find a good home on a shopping website such as eBay. Even if you don't receive a huge amount of money for it, at least it will be taken off your hands. There are also a number of websites where you can trade in computing equipment. Two to look at are Wirefly at *wireflytradeins.cexchange.com* and Nextworth at *nextworth.com*.

Give it to family and friends. Grandma won't mind that your iPad is a few years old. She'll still be able to find her friends on Facebook and send emails to her grandkids.

Recycle it. One of the most environmentally friendly options is to use a company that will refurbish computing equipment and then sell it to someone else. Look at the Environmental Expert website at *environmental-expert.com*, and search for "computer recycling" to find the nearest company in your area.

Donate it to charity. Old computing equipment is gratefully received by some charity organizations, particularly those that use it for training adults and young people in need. One organization to try is the National Cristina Foundation at *cristina.org*.

Delete doesn't always do it — how to wipe private info off your computer for good

Getting rid of files from a desktop computer or laptop is not always as straightforward as you may think. It is not just a question of deleting it with the delete key. This is particularly important if you are disposing of a device and want to make sure no one else can access any of its contents. Take these steps to make sure that when it's gone, it's really gone.

Delete it permanently. When you delete something from a desktop computer or laptop, this only places a file into the Recycle Bin, or the Trash on a Mac. To get rid of it permanently, right-click on the Recycle Bin icon, which should be on the Desktop, and click on the *Empty Recycle Bin* option (Finder menu > Empty Trash, on a Mac).

For Windows, to bypass the Recycle Bin altogether, select the item in the File Explorer, and press Shift+Delete. Click *Yes* in the dialog box to remove the item permanently.

Use an app. You can also use apps to make sure deleted items stay deleted. These are known as file shredders, and they permanently delete any files and folders that are selected.

File shredder apps are designed for desktop computers and laptops, and they are generally downloaded from their own websites. Some file shredders to look at are Alternate File Shredder at *alternate-tools.com*, File Shredder at *fileshredder.org*, Ccleaner (Windows only), at *ccleaner.com*, and TuneUpMyMac (macOS only) at *tuneupmymac.com*.

Reset your device. Even when something has been deleted permanently from a hard drive, it can still sometimes be retrieved by specialist software recovery companies. This is why hard drives should be wiped clean before devices are disposed of. Resetting the device is a way to wipe the hard drive and return it to its original factory settings.

- On a Windows desktop computer or laptop this can be done in Settings > Update & Security > Recovery. Click on the *Get started* button under the *Reset this PC* heading. Click on the *Remove everything* button to remove all of your personal files, apps, and settings.

- For a Mac using macOS, shut down the Mac and then turn it on again. As it starts up, hold down the Command+R buttons until the Apple logo appears on the screen. The macOS Utilities window is displayed. Click on the *Disk Utility* option, and click on the *Continue* button. Click on the Mac hard drive, usually named *Macintosh HD*, and click on the *Erase* button. Keep the default options in the next window, and click on the *Erase* button to remove all of the files, photos, passwords, and anything else you have created on your Mac.

- Tablets and smartphones can also be reset to their factory condition from within the device's Settings app.

Caution

If you are resetting a device, make sure you have backed up all the content you want to keep, either to an external device, such as an external hard drive, or an online cloud service, or both.

Quick change guarantees online safety for grandchildren

If you're planning to give your grandchildren access to any of your devices, it's important they are kept safe and can only access appropriate types of content. The best way to ensure this is to communicate with the children and their parents.

Find out what types of content they are allowed to access in terms of websites, apps, and age-restricted content, and then apply the appropriate settings on your devices. Also, explain to the children what you have done and why you have done it, so they understand they are in a controlled and safe environment.

All platforms have their own options for setting restrictions for children.

For Windows 10 devices. You can set up a separate account for a child and then apply specific restrictions. To do this, access Settings

> Accounts, and click on the *Family & other users* option in the left-hand panel. Click on the *Add someone* button, and select to *Add a member* (which can be a child).

Create the new account, select the person in the main *Family & other users* window, and click on the *Manage family settings online* option. The online options enable you to manage a child's account for a variety of activities including screen time, controlling apps and games, and content restrictions.

For Macs with macOS. To set up a child's account, access System Preferences > Users & Groups. Click on the padlock icon to unlock it, and enter your login password to enable a new user to be added. Click on the + button to add a new user.

Enter the details for the user, and click on the *Create User* button. Once this has been done, access the new account and select System Preferences > Screen Time. Select the Screen Time options for applying restrictions as for an iPad/iPhone below.

For an iPad or iPhone. A separate account for children cannot be set up using iPadOS or iOS, but Screen Time restrictions can be applied for a child. To do this, access Settings > Screen Time, and tap on the *Turn On Screen Time* button.

Tap on the *This is My Child's iPad/iPhone* button, and set options for *Downtime*, for when the device cannot be used; *App Limits*, for time limits on how long certain apps can be used; and *Content & Privacy*, for restricting certain types of content that can be accessed.

For Android devices. New accounts can be added to Android devices with restricted access applied when the account is created. You can also use parental controls apps. In the Google Play Store, enter "parental controls apps" into the Google Play search box, and select one of the suggested apps.

Shop from the comfort of your own home

8 tips for safer online shopping

The appeal of shopping online is clear — there's a huge range of sites and products, and you can do everything from the comfort of your own home. But there are some issues you should keep in mind before you start. Here are eight things you need to do to make sure you stay safe from crooks and identity thieves, especially if you use your credit card.

- Before you give out your credit card number `https://fca.com` online, look for this. Be sure the website address starts with "https," as this indicates it is a secure site. (Click or tap in the address bar to see the full website address.)

- You can also look for a locked padlock icon in the `🔒 fca.com` address bar as this contains details about the site's security. For web browsers on a desktop computer or a laptop, click on the padlock icon to see security details for the site.

- If you access an online retailer from a Wi-Fi hotspot in a public place, never pay with plastic — your debit or credit card — as it could cost you your life savings. Wi-Fi hotspots are not secure, particularly if you are making financial transactions. It may seem like a good idea to do a bit of online shopping while you relax in a coffee shop, but please don't risk it.

- Be wary of special offers in emails. Check the email address to make sure it's really from the retailer it claims to be. Fraudsters create fake emails with special offers claiming to be from online retailers in the hope of obtaining bank and credit card details once the recipient clicks on the link in the email. Check on the retailer's website to see if the offer is listed there.

- Keep your anti-virus and firewall software up to date. This is important, as online shopping involves giving out sensitive financial details such as your debit or credit card details.

- Find a regular selection of online retailers and keep to these as much as possible. This way, your debit and credit card details will be distributed to fewer websites.

- Some online criminals create fake shopping sites, and anything you spend on them goes straight into their pockets. One way to avoid this is to look for "https" and the lock icon in the web address, as above. Another option is to check the full website address. Sometimes website addresses are abbreviated in a browser address bar to just the name of the company. Click, or tap, in the address bar to view the full website address for the page you are viewing. If it's a fake site the address will look different from what you may be expecting.

- Create an email address, other than the one you have for family and friends, just for online shopping. Take advantage of a web-based service, such as Gmail, and use this whenever you register for a new online shopping site. Any emails from the retailer, or anyone else who obtains these details, will go to your shopping email address, rather than your personal one.

Confirm your choice with product reviews

One of the issues with online shopping is that you cannot try products before you buy them. That's where online shopping reviews come in handy.

These can be an invaluable source of information about an item. But watch out. Even though it is illegal, some companies populate their sites with fake reviews to make their products look more popular. Take these steps to try and ensure you are getting genuine information.

- Look for reviews that seem to stand out from the rest in terms of the language used, to try and identify fake ones. Also, look for reviews that seem very similar. In some instances, automated systems (bots) are used to generate large numbers of positive reviews.

- On a lot of sites, it is possible to ask a question relating to a review. This is a good way to find out a bit more detail about an item.

- Check out the less positive reviews of a product too, as this can sometimes give a more honest account of an item. But bear in mind that some people post negative reviews for malicious reasons. If there appears to be a small number of highly negative reviews amongst hundreds of positive ones, they can probably be disregarded.

Staying secure

Free Wi-Fi in hotels is a great thing. But you need to exercise caution when you use it. It's an insecure method of connecting to the internet, meaning it could easily be hacked by criminals in the vicinity.

So one thing you should never do in a hotel room is any type of online transaction, including shopping, where you have to enter financial details. As you are happily shopping away, someone in the room next door could be stealing your debit or credit card details, giving them access to a spending spree of their own, at your expense.

If they get enough of your account details, it could cost you your life savings. Don't take the chance. Save your shopping for your secure Wi-Fi at home.

Ready to buy a computer? 5 things to think about first

Computing devices are an excellent option for online shopping, but check this list before you spend a dime.

Identify what you need it for. Work out what you want to do with your computer, and then look for one that matches these requirements.

New or refurbished? Although it is always tempting to go for a new, shiny device, have a look at used or refurbished ones, too. You may just find a bargain.

Pay attention to screen size. Find a device that is large enough for tasks such as video chatting and watching movies and TV shows, but small enough to still be portable.

Look at peripherals. Check how many slots there are for items such as attaching USB devices. The more slots the better.

Check battery life. For mobile devices, check the battery life for performing tasks when it is not plugged into the main power, and also how long it takes to recharge.

Secret word that can save you money

If you're looking for a computer, tablet, cellphone — even an appliance — one word can save you money and help you find a bargain. That word is "refurbished."

A lot of companies offer refurbished desktop computers, laptops, tablets, cellphones, and printers on their websites. Some also offer trade-ins on older models.

Look at the websites for the following companies, and use the Search box for "Refurbished," "Trade in," or "Trade up." Some of these programs are offered periodically, so check back with the websites if you don't see one currently available.

- Acer at *acer.com*

- Apple at *apple.com*

- Dell at *dell.com*

- Hewlett Packard at *hp.com* (specializes in refurbished printers)

Companies specializing in electronics also offer refurbished computers. Two to look at are:

- TigerDirect at *tigerdirect.com*.

- Newegg at *newegg.com*.

Caution

Be a little extra careful when buying refurbished computer equipment. Check that it has been wiped clean of any previous content, make sure the specifications meet your needs, look for a warranty, and verify the returns policy.

Compare before you buy for the best deals

When shopping in traditional stores, it's common to compare the price of the same item in different retailers. You can do this in the online world, too, and it's even easier. Just log in to a website that performs the comparisons for you.

These websites check the prices of a wide range of items on different sites, and then provide links to the sites from which you want to buy the item. Some price comparison sites to look at are:

- Pricegrabber at *pricegrabber.com*.

- Shopping.com at *shopping.com*.

- Shopzilla at *shopzilla.com*.

- Become at *become.com*.

Money-saver

Everyone likes a bargain, and with computing equipment it is possible to predict when there will be price cuts, simply by waiting until the latest model of a device is released. New models of desktop computers, laptops, tablets, and smart-phones are released every year, resulting in the older products being sold at lower prices.

If you time it right, you can get a relatively new device for a bargain and never have to pay full price. Look for the release of new products, and as soon as they hit the market, check out the manufacturer's website to see if they have special offers on the older products.

Even if a device is the previous year's model it will still have a good specification and be able to fulfill all of your comput-ing needs.

Hone your buying and selling skills on eBay

eBay is an example of a website that has expanded considerably from its original concept. The site started out as an auction web-site, where users could list items for sale, and other people bid on them for the duration of the auction.

While this is still a major part of eBay, it now also contains a range of online retailers who sell their products for a set price.

It is free to create an eBay account at *ebay.com*, and it can be used by people who want to set up their own online business, or those who want to sell secondhand items in the home, like an online yard sale.

As with any website that is involved with financial transactions, there are some areas to consider when buying or selling on eBay.

Ready to clean out your home? Here's what you need to know if you want to sell your items on eBay.

- You'll pay a small fee to list items for sale (usually a flat, fixed fee).

- There is a 10% fee on the selling price of items, paid by the seller.

- You'll need to provide a comprehensive and honest description of the item, along with good quality photos.

- Set realistic delivery charges. In general, it is best to set the delivery charge at the correct amount for the item, or slightly higher, to cover your costs. Also, include the cost of any packaging that you have to use. If in doubt about how much it will cost to post an item, have it weighed first.

- Never send the item until you have received payment from the buyer.

See a few things you'd love to own? Here are some things to consider when buying items on eBay.

- When you find something you want, search eBay for similar items to get an idea of a fair price.

- Look at the delivery charges. If they seem very high, this could be to compensate for a low selling price for an item.

- Check the feedback of a seller before you buy anything from them. If there is anything that makes you feel uneasy, look for another seller.

- Give your own feedback once you have bought something. Be honest and concise with your feedback so it can help other buyers.

- When buying something in an auction, set a top price that you are willing to pay, and try not to go over it. It can be easy to get carried away in an eBay auction and pay far more than you intended.

- Use the *Buy It Now* option in an auction if you want to buy something at a fixed price.

- "Winning" an auction is only really a success if you cannot find the item for cheaper somewhere else. In addition to checking eBay, look for the same item on other online retail websites.

Buyers and sellers can communicate via messages on eBay. However, never give out any personal or financial details if requested to do so in this way.

If there is any kind of problem with a transaction on eBay, report it in the eBay Resolution Center or, as a last resort, report it to the Federal Trade Commission at *ftc.gov*.

Never pay full price again

The online world is a great place to find a range of money-off deals and bargains if you know where to look. One super site for checking out all of the discounts available to you in your area is Flipp at *flipp.com*, or the Flipp app. Use it to find all the local offers and circulars for stores near you simply by entering your location into the website or the app.

Check out these other options, and you'll never have to pay full price again, for just about anything you can imagine.

- Hip2Save app, or the website at *hip2save.com*

- Slickdeals app, or the website at *slickdeals.net*

- RetailMeNot app, or the website at *retailmenot.com*

- DealNews app, or the website at *dealnews.com*

- The website at *dealhunting.com*, for up to 80 percent off a huge range of items.

Money-saver

Several websites and their companion apps can be used to obtain a range of money-saving options. These include cash back on items in traditional stores and online, paper coupons, digital coupons, and coupon codes. Some to look at are:

- Coupons.com at *coupons.com*.

- CouponCabin at *couponcabin.com*.

- Coupon Craze at *couponcraze.com*.

- CouponAlbum at *couponalbum.com*.

- Rakuten (Ebates) at *rakuten.com*.

Change your receipts into gold

You should always save your receipt when you buy something online. (It should be emailed to you.) This is in case there is a problem with the product and you want to return it.

But did you know you can make money from your hard copy receipts, too? You can get an app that scans your receipts, which are converted into reward points that can be redeemed with participating stores. Some receipt apps also offer cash back.

Have a look at the Fetch Rewards app and the Receipt Hog app. Some receipt apps ask you to take part in market research in order to get the full range of rewards.

How to make easy-peasy returns

Before you buy anything online, make sure you read the website's returns policy. Details of the returns policy are frequently accessed from a link at the bottom of the retailer's website. Some of the items it should include are:

- What is the time limit for returning items? It can help determine how long you keep an item to see if you like it.

- Who pays the postage for returns? This can be an important factor, particularly for heavy items.

- Do you need a reason for returning an item, or can it be sent back unconditionally?

- Are there restrictions in terms of items that cannot be returned?

- What form of refund do you receive? Is it a full cash refund or store credit?

Look for online retailers who provide return labels that can be printed from their site. These can be used with the original packaging, or your own, and will also include the postage if this is part of the returns policy.

Once you have printed the return label and attached it to the parcel, all you have to do is drop it off at the post office.

Hungry? There's an app for that

One growth area in the online world is food delivery. Dozens of companies will now deliver a wide range of food directly to your front door. You can also order food from fast food outlets and local restaurants.

Check out these food delivery apps for both iPadOS/iOS and Android.

- Delivery
- DoorDash
- Eat 24
- GrubHub
- Uber Eats

Get your package delivered in the blink of an eye

It may seem like science fiction, but having shopping items delivered by drone is now a very real prospect. Drones are referred to as Unmanned Aircraft Vehicles (UAV), and the Federal Aviation Administration now allows companies to apply for certificates so they can use drones commercially for civil projects.

Amazon has been one of the first to jump on this, and they are now developing their drone delivery service, known as Prime Air. Although it is not yet in operation it has considerable implications for consumers.

Speed. Drone delivery could transform the speed at which goods are delivered. The stated aim of Prime Air is to get packages of up to 5 pounds to consumers in 30 minutes or less. This means your online purchases will be similar to those you make in brick-and-mortar stores, since you'll get them almost immediately.

Accessibility. One of the issues with drone delivery is that the drone must have a means of delivering the package. Inaccessible households could cause issues, although technology is being developed so the drones can use as many locations as possible.

Consumer rights. Since this is still a developing area, it is hard to say how consumer rights will be impacted. But there will definitely be a change to an organization's terms and conditions if they are flying drones to deliver packages. It will pay to read these changes closely when they occur.

High-tech ways to manage your money

Speed up your household accounts with Quicken

Doing the household accounts and balancing the home budget is not the most glamorous of activities. However, keeping a check on income and expenditures will ultimately save you money. If you need some help, you'll find that Quicken is one of the most comprehensive household budget products available.

Quicken is designed to be used primarily on Windows or Mac desktop computers or laptops. But once you have the program, you can find companion apps to use with iPadOS/iOS and Android devices. To obtain Quicken:

1. Access the Quicken website at *quicken.com*.

2. Click on *Quicken for Windows* or *Quicken for Mac* on the home page.

3. Quicken offers a 30-day trial so you can decide if you want to buy it. This is in the form of a 30-day money-back guarantee.

4. Select one of the options for using Quicken, and click on the *Buy Now* button.

5. Create an account with Quicken with an email address and password. These will be your account login details.

Ins and outs of the Quicken program

Quicken operates by linking to your existing financial accounts and then managing your finances based on this information. To link an existing account to Quicken:

1. Open Quicken, and click on the + button on the home page.

2. Enter the details of the account to be linked to Quicken. (The account has to be with a bank which supports the Quicken software.)

3. Once the account has been linked, Quicken will automatically assign categories for your spending, such as Groceries, so that you can see at a glance where your money is going.

4. When an account is being viewed, use these buttons on the top toolbar to access different functions for working with the account.

5. The details of the account are listed in the left-hand panel of the account window. This includes categories for Cash Account, Savings, Credit Card, and Rental Property.

Entering expenditures. To keep an eye on your expenditures you just have to link your bills to an account in Quicken. To do this:

1. Click on the *Bills* tab on the top toolbar within an account.

2. Select the bill provider to show how this bill will affect your overall expenditures.

Balancing the budget. To ensure that your income and expenditures are as balanced as possible:

1. Select the *Planning* tab on the account home page, and click on the *Budgets* button on the toolbar below the Planning tab.

2. Click on the *Budget Actions* button, and select *Create new budget*.

3. Enter a name for the budget, and click on the *OK* button.

4. The budget will be created based on your income and expenditures.

Staying secure

Click on the *Reports* tab in Quicken to view various options for reporting on your finances. This includes an option to view a credit report, which is always worth doing to see what rating you have, and also to ensure there is no unusual activity.

Check your credit rating regularly to make sure it does not change dramatically, which could be a sign of illegal activity connected to your finances.

You can also do this through the website AnnualCreditReport at *annualcreditreport.com*. It provides a wealth of information about how to get free reports, make freezes, set fraud alerts, find your credit score, correct wrong information, and more.

Click on the *Frequently asked questions* button on the home page (or from the menu button on a smartphone) to find out everything you need to know.

Finances on the go. The desktop computer or laptop version of Quicken can also be used with a companion mobile app, to view your financial information when you are away from home. To use this:

1. In the standard version of Quicken, click on the *Mobile & Web* tab on the top toolbar.

2. Click on the *Get Started* button.

3. Select the accounts you want to use on the companion Quicken app, and click on the *Done* button.

4. Download the *Quicken* app from either the Apple App Store or the Google Play Store.

5. Once you have logged in with your Quicken account details, you will be able to see the account information that has been synced from the desktop version.

9 useful apps to manage your budget

You'll find a wide variety of budgeting apps available, and they all provide similar options in terms of managing household accounts. Some can also be linked to any online bank accounts you have, so these can be monitored and included in your overall money management.

Most household budget apps have a free version, but if you want to expand the app's functions, you'll pay a fee. Here are nine helpful apps to look at — all available on iPadOS/iOS and Android.

- Emma
- Goodbudget
- Spendee
- Wallet
- Yolt
- Fudget
- Money Dashboard
- Spending Tracker
- YNAB (You Need A Budget)

Money-saver

If you are looking to make some extra money in retirement, you can put your passions to work and get paid for enjoying your hobbies. Here are three options to consider.

- Sell products online with an auction site such as eBay.
- Teach your skills for a fee using video chatting, or in person.
- Find a part-time job in your field of expertise/interest, using the web to search for options in your area.

How technology can help with estate planning

One vital area of household planning that is sometimes overlooked is estate planning. When looking into creating your will you should consider one option seriously if you want to prevent the lawyers from siphoning off your hard-earned estate. That's to write the will yourself.

It's possible to create a do-it-yourself will that holds up in court. It's perfectly feasible and will save you a boatload of money. And you can use technology to help you.

Just search for "free will templates" on the web, and use a free template to create your will. (You'll also see a lot of advice about completing the process.)

But don't skip this next step. Once you have created your will, get a pro-bono lawyer to review it, and check that it is legally binding.

And don't forget about your digital estate. In addition to your financial affairs, it's important to think about your online accounts, such as online banking. But avoid putting passwords and usernames for online accounts in your will. It becomes a public document after your death so anyone can get hold of the information in it.

To ensure your heirs don't lose valuable assets, create one simple list that includes financial and online accounts, usernames, and passwords.

Store this list in a safe place, such as a home safe, and let your executor and/or spouse know its location. Your heirs will thank you for taking these important steps.

Money-saver

If you're a fan of store loyalty cards, you can download an app to keep them all in one place. Then simply show your card on your smartphone when you're in the store. That way you won't ever miss any bargains. Three to have a look at are Reward Cards, Stocard, and VirtualCards.

Get the benefits you deserve — for free

No one likes paying taxes, but when you do, it's nice to think you'll get something back. The good news is you can. The taxes you paid get you free info and assistance with retirement, Social Security, taxes, prescriptions, and veterans' benefits.

This can all be done from the website *benefitscheckup.org*. It is run by the National Council on Aging (NCOA) and is a treasure trove of information just for seniors about benefits programs throughout the United States.

To find out what specific benefits are available in your area, enter your zip code into the box on the home page, and click or tap on the *Get Started* button. There is also an online Live Chat option that can be used for queries and information.

After looking through all the great information on this site, you may start to think your taxes have been a good investment for retirement after all.

Money-saver

A lot of products you buy will come with a warranty to protect the consumer from defects in the product for a period of time. Retailers and manufacturers offer warranties for differing lengths of time, but did you know you can extend a warranty for free? It's a secret, money-saving tip many people don't know about.

If you buy something with a credit card, just ask your credit card company if they will extend the manufacturer's warranty. You can also ask the retailer when you buy a product, as some are flexible about extending warranties.

Check out the Federal Trade Commission's website at *consumer.ftc.gov/articles/0252-warranties* for more details about your warranty rights.

Protect your money when banking online

Online banking gives you great flexibility in terms of conducting financial activities. However, with this comes the inevitable risk of scam artists trying to steal your money or your financial details. Here are some things to be aware of when you sign up for online financial services.

Be cautious with all aspects of online banking. If something does not feel right when performing any kind of transaction, stop and cancel anything you have done.

Don't feel rushed or intimidated when using any aspect of online banking. This is particularly true if you are contacted and asked for any of your bank details. It could be a fraudster trying to get you to divulge sensitive information about your online banking activities.

In many cases, these scams operate by pressuring people into thinking they have to make a quick decision to stop something bad happening to their account. In reality, the reverse is true so, if in doubt, ask for more time to think about it.

Contact your bank if you think you've been approached by a scammer. If you're not sure a call or email is legitimate, contact your bank directly and tell them the details. If it was a genuine email or call they will be able to verify it.

Use a strong password for any online financial accounts you have. Also use two-factor authentication if they offer it. See *7 tips to create strong and secure passwords* in the chapter *Simple steps to fight fraud, scams, and ID theft* for help in creating the perfect password.

Check your bank's policy on fraud. Make sure your bank or financial institution has a guarantee against any fraud you may be a victim of as a result of online banking. Read this guarantee carefully. You'll want to know the circumstances in which you will receive a full refund if you are a victim of an online fraud.

In most cases you should get back 100% of your money, but check for any situations in which you would be liable for some of the costs. Details should be on the bank's website.

Do not access your online bank account in public areas. This includes places where people can physically see your login details or access them through a Wi-Fi hotspot. Also, make sure that you log out as soon as you have finished an online banking session.

Secret shortcuts to customer service

You know how frustrating it is to call a customer service department. All those buttons to press and automated messages to tediously work your way through. How would you like to speak to a real person and bypass endless button pushing?

Thankfully, it is still possible to get the human touch with almost every customer service call you make. Just check out the GetHuman website at *gethuman.com*.

Simply type a company name into the Search box on the home page to find the customer service details for the company. This includes the current wait time for a call, a skip waiting on hold option, and an option to chat with an expert.

Money-saver

So you want to get a better rate on your cable, phone, and internet? Where do you call? It's not the customer service department.

Instead, try the cancellation department. Companies hate their customers leaving and may be so eager for you to stay that they offer you a better deal than your existing one.

Hold your ground if the first offer is not to your liking. But don't push it too far and insist on something unrealistic, or they may just say "so long."

Cut the chaos — organize your life with helpful apps

Get productive with word processing

Word processing may not seem like the most glamorous computing task, particularly when you have options like watching movies or video chatting, but it remains one of the most popular activities on computing devices.

Word processing has evolved over the years, and a lot more of it is now done on mobile apps rather than a desktop computer. But it is still a vital option for anything from writing a letter to compiling a family history. You have numerous options for word processing, both paid and free. Here are some to check out.

Word. Word is a very powerful and sophisticated app that can produce documents to a high standard. For anyone doing a lot of word processing work, Word should certainly be considered, even though there is a fee for using it.

Pages. This is the Apple word processing app for users of macOS or iPadOS/iOS. It can be downloaded for free from the App Store. It is a full-featured word processing solution, and there are options for exporting Pages documents into other formats, including Word.

Google Docs. This free online word processing app can be accessed at *docs.google.com* if you have a Google Account. It is an excellent option as you can create and edit documents online and also with the Google Docs app. You'll find a range of attractive and easy-to-use templates to help you get started with your documents.

Apache OpenOffice Writer. This free word processing app has grown out of the highly successful OpenOffice suite of productivity apps. While it no longer enjoys the popularity that it once did, it is still an excellent word processing option. It is part of a suite of apps that also contains a spreadsheet and a presentation app.

LibreOffice Writer. Similar to Apache OpenOffice Writer, this is another free word processing app that more than holds its own with some of its better known competitors. It is part of a suite of apps that also contains a spreadsheet and a presentation app.

Most word processing apps come in a suite of apps, which include options for creating spreadsheets and presentations. Microsoft, Apple, and Google all have their own productivity suite of apps.

- Microsoft uses Excel and Powerpoint, for spreadsheets and presentations respectively, in the Microsoft Office suite.

- Apple uses Numbers for spreadsheets and Keynote for presentations.

- Google uses Sheets for spreadsheets and Slides for presentations.

Mobile planning apps assist on the run

Planning apps are widely used on mobile devices and are an excellent option for keeping everything organized on your tablet or smartphone. Some to look at are:

- Any.do. A list-making app that also includes a calendar for keeping everything up to date.

- Daily Planner - Habit Tracker. Keep track of your daily tasks and activities.

- Evernote. A comprehensive note-taking app.

- Planner Pro - Daily Calendar. Your very own personal organizer.

- Todoist. A powerful list-making and organization app.

- Wunderlist. Ideal for creating and sharing lists and tasks.

Money-saver

You do not have to buy an expensive suite of productivity apps such as Microsoft Office when there are powerful word processing and spreadsheet apps you can use for free. Look for suites that contain at least a word processor, a spreadsheet, and a presentation option.

Another useful feature is a PDF editor. Some free suites to look at are OfficeSuite, ONLYOFFICE, Polaris, and SmartOffice.

Use OneNote to save time with small docs

Notes apps are an excellent option for documents with smaller amounts of text than created in a word processing app. You can download Notes apps from your device's app store, and you'll also find some pre-installed on different devices.

The default notes app on Windows 10 devices is OneNote. Notes created here can also be used with the cloud service OneDrive. To use OneNote:

1. Click on this icon on the Windows Start menu to open *OneNote*.

2. The top toolbar provides the functionality for OneNote.

3. Click on the *Home* tab to access formatting options, such as text formatting, lists, and paragraph styles.

4. Click on the *Insert* tab to insert additional content into a note, including a table, a file from your computer, a photo, web link, or an audio file.

5. Click on the *Draw* tab to draw freehand content into a note.

6. Click on the *View* tab to select viewing options for the notebook area.

A *closer* look

Productivity and planning apps are a great way to keep all your organizational activities in a digital format. If you feel like you're surrounded by an ever-increasing amount of paper, the digital world can help. Try these three ways to get rid of the piles of paper in your life.

- Use a scanner to scan paper documents and then get rid of them once you have them in digital form.

- Keep more items on your smartphone, such as online receipts, notes, and lists.

- Ask companies to send online bills rather than hard copy ones. Most organizations now have an option for paperless billing, which can usually be found on their website.

Easy way to always have your notes with you

On macOS and iPadOS/iOS devices, notes are created with the Notes app. This is an iCloud app, so as long as Notes is turned On for iCloud (Settings > Apple ID > iCloud > Notes), notes created on one device will automatically be saved in iCloud and available on your other Apple devices. To create notes with the Notes app:

1. Tap on the *Notes* app to open it.

2. Tap on this button to create a new note.

3. Tap in the text area of a new note to access the keyboard. Start writing the note.

4. Tap on this button to delete the current note.

5. Tap on this button to share a note (via social media apps, Mail, Messages, and other messaging apps that you have on your device), or copy or print a note.

6. Tap on this button to invite people to view and edit a note.

To apply a range of formatting options to a note:

1. Double-tap on a piece of text to select it.

2. Drag the selection handles to expand the text selection.

3. Select one of the formatting options that appear above the selection.

4. Tap on this button to create a checklist from the selected text.

5. Checkboxes are added to the list. (These are the round buttons to the left-hand side of the text.) Tap on a checkbox to show that an item, or a task, has been completed.

6. Tap on this icon on the bottom toolbar, and tap on the *Take Photo or Video* button to take a photo or video to add to the note. Or tap on the *Photo Library* button to add a photo or video from the photo library on your device.

Android devices 'Keep' your notes organized

Several notes apps can be used on Android devices. One excellent option is the Google Keep Notes app. If this is not already pre-installed on an Android device, you can download it from the Google Play Store.

Google Keep offers a range of formatting options for creating notes, after which they are placed on a noticeboard, displaying all of your notes. To use Google Keep Notes:

1. Tap on the *Keep Notes* app to open it.

2. Tap on this button to create a new note.

3. Enter content for the note. Tap on this button to access options for adding checkboxes, photos, or a voice recording.

4. Tap on this icon to pin a note to the top of the noticeboard.

5. Tap on this icon to add a reminder for the note, which will be displayed as an alert at the appropriate date and time.

6. The most recent note is added at the top of the noticeboard. If it has been pinned as in Step 4, it will remain at the top of the noticeboard.

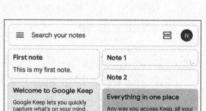

7. Swipe a note away from the noticeboard to remove it.

8. Go to the website at *keep.google.com* to access notes from any online device once you have logged in with your Google Account details.

┌─ **A closer look** ──────────────────────────────┐

Two other important organization apps are Contacts and
Calendar. The Contacts app acts as an address book. People
you add here will appear as prompts when you enter names
for sending an email or a text message.

A Calendar app can be used to add events, and you will be
prompted when the event is due. Windows, macOS,
iPadOS/iOS, and Android devices all have their own default
Contacts and Calendar apps. You can also download others
from the relevant app store for your device.

└──┘

Reminder apps — better than a string around your finger

Even with the best organization apps it is easy to forget things.
This is where reminder apps come into play.

Reminders can be added for hours, days, weeks, months, or even
years in advance, and you will receive an alert when the reminder is
due. Reminders can be used for all kinds of tasks.

- reminders for important medication

- reminders for regular meetings with family or friends, such as
  a weekly club

- reminders to phone a family member at a certain time every week

- reminders for birthdays and anniversaries

Apple devices (macOS, iPadOS, and iOS) all have a pre-installed
Reminders app. If you use iCloud, reminders you create will be
available on any other Apple device with the same Apple ID.

On a Windows desktop computer or laptop, the search box to the
right of the Start button can be used to create reminders. Android
devices can download reminder apps from the Google Play Store.

Entertainment magic — stream movies, music, and more

Enjoy recreation and relaxation at your fingertips

Streaming has become a firmly established option for listening to music and watching TV shows and movies on computer devices. Streaming does not download any content onto your device. It enables you to listen to music, or watch TV shows or movies, by providing the requested content over the internet from the streaming company's server.

When the streaming ends, the content is no longer available on your device, although you can always stream it again. You'll need a Wi-Fi internet connection to use a streaming service.

Why would you want to stream? Check out some of the advantages.

Huge amounts of content. Streaming services gather content from a range of different places, so you should always be able to find something you want to watch or listen to.

Take it on the go. If you are away from home, you can log in to your streaming account, and watch, or listen, on a device such as a tablet or your laptop.

Watch ad-free. Streaming services don't usually have ads interrupting their shows, although with some companies you may have to pay more for the ad-free option.

Protect the grandchildren with kid-friendly viewing. Streaming services have a range of options for protecting younger viewers, from kid-zones to parental controls.

Access original high-quality shows. Some streaming services invest millions of dollars in creating their own movies and TV shows, which are often of a very high standard.

Once you start looking, you may get overwhelmed by all the streaming services available. The main thing to decide is whether you want to pay for a subscription or get content for free.

Many services offer different content, and several of them offer a mix of the available options. The types of content available on streaming services for movies and TV shows include:

- Original content. Some of the larger streaming services are able to create their own original content. Subscription services including Netflix, Amazon Prime Video, Apple TV+, and Disney+ all create their own original content.

- Licensed content. This is content that streaming services can show for free. It can cover a significant number of movies and TV shows. The larger the library of free content, the more attractive the streaming service is to potential users.

- Paid-for content. This is content that the streaming service does not have a license to show for free. For instance, on Amazon Prime Video you may access one movie that is free to view, and then choose another that you'll have to pay to rent or own.

- Aggregated content. Streaming services that do not produce their own content operate by offering the content from other services, and this is one way to get access to a wide range of streaming options from a single service.

The larger streaming services usually offer a combination of original content, free content, and paid-for content.

A *closer* look

Streaming services for movies and TV shows are usually accessed by one of three methods:

- using a box, which connects to your television with a cable.

- using a stick which is inserted into the back of your television, usually into an HDMI slot.

- using an app on a desktop computer, a laptop, a tablet or a smartphone.

Some services offer options for using either a box or a stick for accessing content via a TV.

---

3 smart ways to cut your cable costs

Cable services have been a popular way to watch TV for many years. Cable companies have also been able to offer additional packages, such as cellphone services, so you can get different options from the same company.

This is now being challenged by online streaming services, which are becoming much more prominent. But cable is still a useful option, particularly if you watch a lot of live sports or you do not have a good internet connection.

If you want to stick with cable, here are the top things you can do to save money on your cable and cellphone charges.

Unbundle multiple services. If you get your TV, internet, and cellphone contract through the same provider, it could be financially beneficial to look for different companies for each service. Just asking to do this may get you a better offer.

Contact the cancellation department and say you want to leave. By doing this you may find that a much better offer materializes remarkably quickly.

Read your contract carefully. Understand what is, and isn't, allowed with your contract. Once you have a good understanding about this, you will be in a much stronger position to negotiate a better deal.

The world is yours with a streaming stick

You can watch just about any movie and TV show available, or listen to any kind of music, from the comfort of your living room. One little box, or stick, will open the world to you.

Roku is just one of many hardware options you can choose for streaming. Others include the Amazon Fire TV, Apple TV, and Google Chromecast. To get started, you buy the required device to provide the streaming service.

Traditionally, this has been a box which connects to your TV with an HDMI cable, but many people prefer a stick, which plugs into the HDMI slot in the back of your TV. You'll find them on Amazon from $29.99 upwards, depending on the type of device.

Once you have bought your Roku device, link it to your Wi-Fi router by following the instructions on your TV. After that you can create a Roku account, and then you are all ready to start streaming movies and TV shows.

There is no charge for setting up a Roku account, which allows you to connect to the vast range of content it offers. A lot of it is free, and you can also subscribe to services such as Netflix, or rent or buy movies and TV shows.

6 top services for movies and TV shows

Movie and TV lovers are extremely well catered to in the streaming world. Here are some of the top services you'll want to check out if you're willing to pay a monthly fee.

Netflix. This is the world's largest streaming service, with over 183 million subscribers worldwide. In addition to a large library of free movies and TV shows, Netflix also has a considerable catalog of original material, and this remains one of the big attractions for subscribers.

Amazon Prime Video. If you have an Amazon Prime membership you can also access the Prime Video service. This has a range of original Amazon content and also a large library of movies and TV shows, some of which are free, and some which have to be paid for.

Apple TV+. The Apple TV service offers movies and TV shows that can be bought or rented. The Apple TV+ option is a subscription service that uses original material created by Apple. It can be accessed through the Apple TV app by tapping on the Try It Free button. There is a seven-day free trial of Apple TV+.

Disney+. Focusing on content from The Walt Disney Studios and Walt Disney Television, Disney+ can offer some of the best-known, and well-liked, movies and TV content, including content from not only Disney, but also Pixar, Marvel, Stars Wars, and National Geographic.

Hulu. Another major streaming service that has a wide range of content from different outlets. One of the features of Hulu that sets it apart from some other streaming services is its extensive live TV streaming service, where TV shows are streamed in real-time. This is particularly popular for live sporting events.

Sling TV. This is another option for watching live TV streaming.

Money-saver

You may be trying to decide whether to give up your cable and try streaming. Go ahead and cancel. You can watch your favorite shows for free instead.

Netflix may steal the spotlight, but don't worry, you don't have to subscribe to the major providers and pay an arm and a leg. There are plenty of free streaming services out there. The range may not be as great as for the paid services, but it is still reasonably extensive.

Two services to look at are Crackle at *crackle.com* and Popcornflix at *popcornflix.com*. You can also check out free trials the paid services offer. Just remember to cancel at the end of the free-trial period if you don't want to continue, or you'll be charged.

Take your music wherever you go

If you have a passion for music, you'll love the music streaming services with their vast libraries of music. They operate in a similar way to streaming services for movies and TV shows — you sign up for a streaming service and then access the musical content you want.

It will be streamed over a compatible device, and the good news is that music streaming can be used on desktop computers, laptops, tablets, and smartphones. Some streaming services are free, but you will probably have to put up with ads being played in between the music you want to hear.

Most paid-for options offer a free trial, with additional options for creating a family account so that several family members can have access to the same service.

Some of the main music streaming services include:

Spotify. This is one of the most popular music streaming services, and it is independent of the major technology companies. There is a three-month free trial for Spotify, after which a monthly fee applies. For this you get unlimited ad-free music from the huge Spotify catalog. There are also options for *Family* and *Student* plans.

Apple Music. This is Apple's subscription streaming music service that can be accessed from the Music app on devices using macOS, iPadOS, and iOS. There is a three-month free trial for Apple Music, and then you can choose a subscription option from *Individual, Family,* or *Student.* To start using Apple Music, click or tap on the *For You* button on the bottom toolbar of the Music app.

Google Play Music/YouTube Music Premium. During 2020 the Google Play Music service moved to YouTube Music. This consists of a free version — YouTube Music — which contains ads, and the paid-for subscription version, YouTube Music Premium.

Amazon Music Unlimited. This is Amazon's music subscription service. Amazon Music is a free service that is provided with an Amazon Prime subscription. The Amazon Music Unlimited option is an additional, paid-for, service which provides access to over 60 million songs.

Pandora. This is another independent streaming service. Its specialty is giving users the means to create playlists (stations) based on a range of criteria and types of music. Pandora also offers a significant selection of podcasts.

Choose the best device for your e-books

Digital technology works well when it presents an additional option for performing an existing task rather than replacing it altogether. This has been the case with e-books and e-book readers (e-readers).

E-books are digitized versions of hard-copy titles, and they can be read on dedicated e-readers and also on tablets, desktop computers, and laptops — even smartphones. E-books have not replaced their hard-copy cousins, largely because people still like the feel of paper when they read a book.

However, e-books fulfill a very useful purpose, especially if you don't want to fill up your luggage with a lot of books when you're heading out on vacation.

Here are your best device options for reading e-books.

- Dedicated e-readers, such as the Amazon Kindle or the Kobo Aura. These are designed specifically for the task of reading e-books, and use a range of technologies to create the most paper-like viewing experience.

- Tablets with an e-book app, such as the Books app on iPad or the Google Play Books app on an Android tablet. Both of these apps also provide access to their respective stores for buying and downloading more e-books.

Caution

It's important to try many digital devices out first so you get a good idea how they feel in your hands, much like you might test out a new car. This is particularly true of an e-book reader, since you will stare at it for long periods of time.

Make sure it feels comfortable in your hands, and check the screen and its lighting to see whether it strains your eyes. A tablet is a little different since it will be used for a range of tasks, but if possible, test it with the relevant app anyway.

A stand for your e-book reader or tablet is also a good option, so you don't always have to physically hold the device.

Download digital books in a snap

You'll access your e-books from an online bookstore and download them onto your device. Unlike movies, TV shows, and music, they are stored on your device, rather than being streamed over the web.

You may have to pay for most of your e-books, but you'll find a considerable number of free titles, too. You can also look for free samples, usually consisting of one or two chapters, that you can download to see if you like a particular book. Here are your main options for acquiring e-books.

Amazon Kindle Store. Since Amazon began as an online book-seller, it is understandable that it also has a major presence in the e-book market. Through the use of its own Kindle e-reader, Amazon has built up a large library of e-books, accessed through the Kindle Store on the Amazon website.

There is also a Kindle Unlimited option, which is a monthly subscription service that provides access to over a million e-books as well as magazines and audiobooks.

Apple Books Store. This can be accessed from the Books app, and downloaded items can be read on macOS, iPadOS, or iOS devices. The Books app is where e-books are stored and read once they have been downloaded from the Books Store.

Google Play Store. For Android users, the Play Books app operates in a similar way to the Books app on an Apple device. Content is accessed and downloaded using the app, and the items can then be read on the app.

Kobo Store. You can use this with a Kobo e-reader, such as the Kobo Aura, and download content from the Kobo Store at *kobo.com*. Titles from the Kobo website can also be accessed from the Kobo Books app. You have over 6 million Kobo titles to choose from, and also a range of audiobooks.

eBooks.com. This is an independent e-book store and has over a million unique titles. Their e-books can be read on a variety of devices.

Most major bookstores also have e-books on their websites.

Helpful hints make e-reading a breeze

Whatever method you use for accessing and reading e-books, you'll find the process for reading them is similar.

1. Tap on the e-book in your e-reader's library, or within the appropriate app on a tablet or smartphone, such as the Books app or the Play Books app.

2. Swipe left and right on the screen to move between pages. Or tap on the left-hand or right-hand side of a page to move in that direction.

3. Tap in the middle of the page to access the reading controls.

4. Tap in the top right-hand corner to bookmark a page.

5. Tap on this button to access the table of contents and any bookmarks or notes that have been added. ☰

6. Tap on this button to select options such as text size, screen brightness, and screen background color.

7. Drag on the slider at the bottom of the page to move through the book.

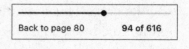

Back to page 80   94 of 616

8. Press and hold on a word to select it and activate options, such as looking up a definition of the word.

Special website provides free e-books galore

Looking for more free books? You can't do any better than Project Gutenberg, found at the website *gutenberg.org*.

Named after one of the first pioneers of printed books, it has over 60,000 free titles. You'll find numerous classic titles, such as *The Adventures of Tom Sawyer* by Mark Twain and *Oliver Twist* by Charles Dickens.

You can download and read these books on any e-reader and also online on the Project Gutenberg website. And you don't even need to register.

Project Gutenberg titles are free because their copyright has expired. That means every year more titles become eligible to be included in this tremendous free catalog.

Powerful tech tools put health care at your fingertips

The 21st-century way to track your health

Technology has always been a natural fit with health and fitness, and in the digital age it is becoming an integral part of people's daily lives. With mobile devices like smartphones and smartwatches accompanying you wherever you go, it is much easier to constantly monitor exercise, diet, and health factors such as heart rate.

Smartphones. Through the use of apps, smartphones can monitor your health and fitness activities throughout the day, and also at night while you sleep. You can download health and fitness apps from your smartphone's app store, but check first to see if any are pre-installed on your device. The iPhone has the Health app, and Android smartphones can use the Google Fit app.

Smartwatches/fitness trackers. These devices are worn on your wrist and have significant levels of computing power. Part of their job is to monitor your health and fitness. One advantage of smartwatches and fitness trackers is that they contain sensors, so they can monitor areas such as heart rate and, in some instances, heart condition.

The world of apps has embraced the area of health and fitness, so you'll find apps that can monitor everything from how far you walk to your daily calorie intake. Here are some ways apps can be used to monitor — and boost — your health and fitness.

- Fitness tracking apps can keep a record of a specific activity, such as how far you have walked during a timed period.

- Diet and calorie apps can provide you with healthy eating plans and also keep a record of your calorie intake and exercise.

- Workout apps supply a range of workouts that you follow through videos and animations. Find your favorite — they cover everything from aerobic exercise and weight lifting to yoga and Pilates.

Make tracking easy with your smartphone

Since you will probably have your smartphone with you most of the time, it's ideal for tracking your health and fitness.

Both iPhones and Android smartphones have pre-installed health apps (Health app for the iPhone, and the Google Fit app for Android smartphones). They can be used for a range of tasks, from counting the number of daily steps taken to viewing details about your heart rate.

In addition to the pre-installed health apps on the iPhone and Android smartphones, hundreds more health and fitness apps can be downloaded to help you keep a daily record of all your activities. Look in the Health & Fitness category in the Apple App Store or the Google Play Store.

Apple Watch — it's not just for telling time

The Apple Watch is a marvel of modern technology. It does all the normal things a watch can do, but when you link it with your iPhone, it can do so much more. The latest version, the Apple Watch 5, can be used for a significant range of health options.

The device works closely with the *Health* app on your iPhone. Data collected on the Apple Watch is fed back to the Health app, where you can analyze it in greater detail, using graphs and charts. The information is also stored on the Health app so you can look back on it over a period of time. Here are some of the things the Apple Watch can do.

Keep an eye on your heart rate. The *Heart* app can display your heart rate using the sensors on the back of the Apple Watch. If the app detects an unusually high or low heart rate, it can send you an alert.

You can set this up on the linked iPhone by opening the *Watch* app and selecting My Watch > Heart > High (Low) Rate. Set a high, or low, rate and if your heart rate goes above (or below) this, you will receive an appropriate notification on your Apple Watch.

Identify possible problems. Not only can the Apple Watch (version 4 and later) monitor your heart rate, it can also identify potential problems. This is done by creating an electrocardiogram (ECG), which records your heart's electrical signals. That provides important medical information relating to the performance of your heart. See *Monitor your heart with your watch* for more details.

Track your workouts. The *Workout* app can be used to record details of workouts for a range of different activities. The app records the type of workout, the duration of the activity, the number of calories burned, and average heart rate during the activity.

Set daily targets for moving, exercising, and standing. Use the *Activity* app to record your activity during the day. It will even give you reminders to stand every hour, to ensure you are not sitting for too long during the day.

Detect falls. The sophisticated sensors in the Apple Watch can detect when a hard fall has occurred. If this happens, an alert will appear asking if you are OK or if you want to phone the emergency services by tapping on the *Emergency SOS* button.

This action will also alert your emergency contacts, which are added to the Health app on your iPhone. If an emergency SOS call is made, they will be contacted and sent your location. If you are unresponsive for 60 seconds, an emergency call will be made automatically.

Monitor noise. External noise can have a detrimental impact on your hearing if it is too loud or too constant. The *Noise* app on the Apple Watch can be used to detect when noises are over a certain level of decibels, so you can move away from the noise or use earplugs to lessen its impact.

Help you de-stress. For something you do all the time, the benefits of breathing are often underestimated. The *Breathe* app on the Apple Watch can be used to concentrate on your breathing, to help you relax, and take some of the stress out of the day.

A closer look

In addition to the Apple Watch, numerous other smart-watches and fitness bands are available to help track your health and fitness. Here are a few to look at.

- Fitbit Charge
- Garmin Vivoactive
- Withings Steel
- Fitbit Flex
- TomTom Spark

Monitor your heart with your watch

The Apple Watch is so sophisticated that it can take an ECG of your heart. This is done with the ECG app on the Apple Watch, the sensors on the back of the watch, and electrodes in the Digital Crown, which is similar to the winder on a regular watch. The ECG app can be set up from the Health app on an iPhone.

1. Open the Health app and, if the setup does not start automatically, tap on the *Browse* tab on the bottom toolbar.

2. Select Heart > Electrocardiograms (ECG) > Set Up ECG App.

3. To use the ECG app, tap on the *ECG* app on the Apple Watch, and hold your finger on the Digital Crown, shown here, to generate an ECG in only 30 seconds. This can be used to show if you have atrial fibrillation, which is a serious type of irregular heart rhythm.

Caution ─────────────────────────────

The ECG option on the Apple Watch is not a way to check for heart attacks. Any irregular results from the ECG should be shared with your doctor immediately.

The Apple Watch should be considered a companion health device. It should not be used instead of professional advice from your doctor.

If you use the health features on the Apple Watch, it is a good idea to discuss it with your doctor, so you can get the most benefits out of its sophisticated technology.

Apple Health app provides a wealth of information

The Apple Health app is one of the pre-installed apps on the iPhone. It is not included on the iPad. It can monitor a range of health activities and also link to an Apple Watch to share information that has been collected. To use the Apple Health app:

1. Tap on this icon to open the *Health* app.

2. Tap on the *Browse* button on the bottom toolbar.

3. Tap on one of the main categories to view its details, such as *Activity*.

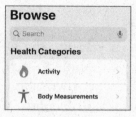

4. Items are listed within each category. Tap on an item to view more details about it, such as *Steps*.

5. The details that are displayed are those collated by the app. Tap on the *Add Data* button to add more details manually.

6. Tap on the *Summary* button on the bottom toolbar to view details of the most commonly performed health activities.

7. Tap on an activity to view additional details about it.

8. Tap on the *Edit* button on the Summary home page.

9. Tap on the items you want to appear on the Summary page. Items with a solid star next to them will appear on the Summary page.

10. Tap on the *Done* button.

'Smart' way to access your doctor

The Apple Watch is the most comprehensive smartwatch in terms of joined-up health monitoring. One of its features is to link to health providers so you can share your health information digitally.

The health provider has to sign up for this service, so ask your doctor if it's something they are involved in. In some cases, health information from an Apple Watch can be sent directly to your health provider, and your doctor can then act accordingly. This is done through the Health app on your iPhone.

It is also possible to link to participating health providers to view your medical records via the Health app and see when they are updated. To do this:

1. Open the *Health* app on your iPhone.

2. Tap on the *Summary* button on the bottom toolbar.

3. Swipe up the page until you get to the *Access Your Records* section.

4. Tap on the *Get Started* button.

5. Participating health providers will be listed. If yours is on the list, you will be able to link to them so you can access your records. You have to create an account to do this, and enable Location Services for the Health app on your iPhone.

Staying secure

While one of the many functions of a smartphone is to help with your health and fitness, it can also help keep you safe and secure by storing important numbers. Here are seven numbers to always keep in your smartphone for your safety — and none of them are for friends or family.

Your doctor should be No. 1. Then include the insurance companies for all your insurance policies, a local locksmith, a reliable towing company, your own home telephone number, free directory assistance, and the emergency numbers for your bank and credit cards in case they are lost or stolen.

Google Fit app — Android's health care solution

The Google Fit app is the health app for Android smartphones and tablets. On some devices it will be pre-installed. If it is not, download the app from the Google Play Store. To get started with the Google Fit app:

1. Tap on this icon to open the *Fit* app.

2. During the initial setup of the Fit app, you can specify certain health and fitness goals, such as a target number of steps to reach each day.

3. On the Fit home page, tap on the *Profile* button on the bottom toolbar.

4. Enter personal details so the Fit app can assess your activities accordingly.

5. Tap on the *Home* button on the bottom toolbar to view a summary of your activities.

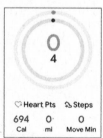

6. Tap on a category on the home page to view details about it.

7. Tap on the + button on the home page to add a new category.

8. Tap on the item to enter details for it, or to start doing it, such as *Track workout.*

A closer look

The Fit app can be used on an Android tablet or smartphone. However, it is more effective on a smartphone, since this is easier to carry with you if you want to track an activity, such as going for a walk.

Connect to emergency services in an instant

An iPhone can be used to make calls to emergency services without having to use the Phone app. To do this:

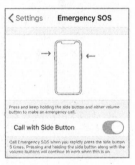

1. Access Settings > Emergency SOS.

2. Drag the *Call with Side Button* option to On.

3. Once the Call with Side Button option has been turned On, the emergency call can be made by pressing the On/Off button five times in quick succession.

4. An emergency call can also be made by holding down the On/Off button and either of the volume buttons, to access the screen for turning off the iPhone. From this screen, tap on the *Emergency SOS* button.

The Apple Health app can also be used to display your important medical information in case of an emergency. To do this:

1. Open the Health app, and tap on the *Summary* button on the bottom toolbar.

2. Swipe up the page and, in the *Set Up Your Medical ID* section, tap on the *Get Started* button.

3. Enter details of any medical conditions as required. These will be displayed on the Lock screen in the event of an emergency.

4. Swipe up the page and, under the *Emergency Contacts* heading, tap on the *add emergency contact* button. Enter the details for one or more emergency contacts. Your emergency contacts will be notified if you make an emergency SOS call, and your location will also be sent to them.

5. Tap on the *Done* button in the top right-hand corner to finish setting up your Medical ID.

A closer look

It's not always possible to get to your doctor in person. If you find yourself in that situation, try the website HealthTap at *healthtap.com*. This is a valuable online resource with over 100,000 doctors available to give free medical advice. Unfortunately it can take up to 24 to 48 hours for them to get back to you. You can opt for a paid version that should produce faster results. However, if it is a serious medical emergency, always go to your local hospital.

---

10 apps to improve your health and well-being

The Apple App Store and the Google Play Store both have a dedicated category for Health and Fitness. Many of these apps help make exercise less daunting, and help you get started and stay motivated.

MyFitnessPal. This app keeps track of your diet and counts your calorie intake. It can be used to scan barcodes for foods so you get the exact dietary information about everything you eat. The app can also be used to set specific dietary goals and monitor your exercise.

Calory. This is an app for counting calories and keeping track of your weekly, monthly, and yearly progress. If you enter your weight, height, and daily activity level into the app, it will calculate a suggested daily calorie intake, which you can then monitor with the app.

MealPrepPro. Keeping up a regular healthy diet can feel like hard work at times, but help is on hand with this meal planning app. The app provides healthy meal plans that are personalized to your own requirements.

Once you have entered the required details, the app will provide the ingredients for the meal plan and details of the recipes to make. Each recipe has an accompanying video to follow. The MealPrepPro app requires a monthly or annual subscription, but there is a seven-day free trial.

Seven – Quick At Home Workouts. As the name suggests, this app provides exercise workouts that can be done in the home in just seven minutes. The workouts include stretching and aerobic exercise. There are several different exercises within the seven minute period, and each one is accompanied by a video that can be paused, so you can do all the exercises at your own pace.

5 Minute Home Workout. If you feel like something a bit shorter than the seven minute workout, try the five minute one instead.

Beginner's Workout. If you are looking for an exercise app that does not seem too intimidating, this could be the one for you. Designed with seniors in mind, the app offers daily workouts of up to 20 minutes. The workouts do not require any special equipment and can be done in your own home. The free version of the app offers one routine for each level of activity.

Yoga: Down Dog. Yoga is one of the best forms of exercise, and it is excellent for both strength and flexibility. This app provides a different yoga practice each time you use the app, and there are over 60,000 different variations that can be used.

5 Minute Pilates. Another recommended form of exercise for flexibility is Pilates. This app provides quick and regular workouts at home that can be done on a mat or even just a soft floor.

Reflectly — Self-care journal. This is a self-help app where you can write down your thoughts and feelings. The app will prompt you for more information, depending on what you have written.

Pillow Automatic Sleep Tracker. This app can improve your sleeping patterns by monitoring your sleep cycles throughout the night. You can use it on an Apple Watch or on a smartphone placed near your pillow. The app can also play an alarm at the point when you are in the lightest stage of sleep, so that you wake up more refreshed.

Money-saver

Would you like to get prescription eyeglasses for as low as $8? It's perfectly possible to get them wherever you live just by shopping on these websites. Try *voogueme.com*, *goggles4U.com*, and *zennioptical.com*.

Stay up to date on health breakthroughs

Interested in exploring the latest health breakthroughs? Growing numbers of seniors do it online. No doctor's fees, no newsletter subscriptions, no waiting — just the facts, all for free, at these bona fide websites. Here are the best, most reliable, sites to search.

- Centers for Disease Control and Prevention at *cdc.gov*

- Consumer Medical at *consumermedical.com*

- Consumer Medication Safety at *consumermedsafety.org*

- Drugs.com at *drugs.com*

- MedicineNet at *medicinenet.com*

- U.S. National Library of Medicine at *nlm.nih.gov*

- USA Gov Health Information at *usa.gov/health-resources*

- WebMD at *webmd.com*

2 fun ways apps get you moving

Staying healthy and fit can sometimes be a tough task. Let technology help by motivating you throughout the day.

Boost your health in just two minutes. How would you like to see impressive health benefits just by doing something for two minutes every hour? It seems hard to believe but it's true.

Simply stand up and walk around for a couple of minutes if you have been sitting down for a long time. That gets your heart pumping and your muscles working, which goes a long way toward keeping you healthy.

Smartwatches have a function that will remind you to stand up if they recognize you've been sitting for nearly an hour. Once you have done your two minutes of standing and moving, the smartwatch will notify you with a congratulatory message.

If you own a Fitbit, it will also remind you to move each hour, usually for a particular number of steps.

Get rewarded for your efforts. Staying motivated when following an exercise program or trying to lose weight can be the hardest part, particularly over a long period of time. But health and fitness apps can offer encouragement in this area, too.

Once targets have been set within the app, you will be presented with a reward every time a target is met. Admittedly, these are just in the form of virtual rewards, such as a trophy or a gold star, but it can still provide the motivation to keep going.

┌─ **A *closer* look** ────────────────────────────────

Uncover little-known secrets doctors never tell you by doing
this one thing. Check out the website ProPublica at
projects.propublica.org/vital-signs to view data relating to
how medicine is really practiced across the United States.

Are you being overcharged for your health services? This site
will let you know. It can tell you how much health care
providers get paid for their services, and how much drug and
device companies pay the doctors.

If you need to find a surgeon, you can look up the surgical
performance of medical professionals. Another option is
SurgeonRatings at the website *checkbook.org/surgeonratings/*.

└──────────────────────────────────────

Unravel the secrets of Social Security and Medicare with your computer

Trying to navigate through the options, services, and benefits available from Social Security and Medicare can, at times, feel like you
are working your way through an endless maze. Thankfully, various
websites can provide a way through the maze and offer advice
about what you're entitled to. Three to have a look at are:

- Social Security Administration at ssa.gov. Not only does this
  site contain all the information you need to know about
  Social Security, you can also create a *mySocial Security*
  account, where you can see estimates of your Social Security
  benefits based on your earnings.

- Medicare at *medicare.gov*. The official government website for
  Medicare where you can find out information about costs,
  search for care providers, and find out what is covered for
  you, and what is not.

- MyMedicare at *mymedicare.gov*. This is where you can create your own account on the Medicare website, so you can get information directly related to your own situation.

Money-saver

By law, you're entitled to a "benefits checkup." It's free (you've already paid for it with your taxes) and it will tell you all of the benefits your tax dollars entitle you to — discounts on prescriptions, rent, food, utilities, even taxes.

Check it out at the website *benefitscheckup.org*. Enter your zip code into the Search box on the home page to find benefits programs in your area. Click on the *Find My Benefits* tab on the top toolbar to access a questionnaire, which will be used to assess the benefits you're eligible for.

---

1 simple step to low cost — or free — prescriptions

Free prescription drugs sound too good to be true, but you can do just one simple thing and get free, or at least greatly reduced, medications.

Join a Patient Assistance Program (PAP), and you may be able to get prescriptions at a fraction of their original price, or for free, depending on your circumstances. These are programs run by pharmaceutical companies, aimed at helping people who can't afford the full price of prescriptions.

Four websites to look at for more information about PAP, and for applying for cheaper prescriptions, are:

- GoodRx at *goodrx.com*.

- Medicine Assistance Tool at *medicineassistancetool.org*.

- Needymeds at *needymeds.org*.

- RxAssist at *rxassist.org*.

High-tech help for better sleep

For something that takes up approximately a third of everyone's lives, sleep is an activity that is sometimes underestimated in terms of people's overall health and well-being.

However, the benefits and importance of sleep are now becoming more widely recognized. Here are some things to consider in relation to sleep, and how technology can help you improve it.

- Everyone has their own sleep cycle. This is known as the circadian rhythm.

- Experts recommend that everyone get between seven to nine hours sleep a night.

- If you miss out on sleep, it is not possible to "catch up" by sleeping longer the next night.

- Getting a good night's sleep on a regular basis can help combat disease, improve your mental health, enhance your appearance, and aid your diet.

- You can use apps on tablets and smartphones to help you get to sleep by playing a range of soothing sounds, such as rainfall or waves.

- Apps on tablets and smartphones can also be used to monitor your sleep, as can smartwatches. This includes the amount of sleep you have each night as well as the type and quality of sleep.

Savvy travel — your online guide to cheap escapes

Where to get the best travel deals and trip advice

Part of the fun of a vacation, whether it's at home or overseas, is in the planning. And the web has made planning the ultimate trip even easier. It can help you find the best deals in airfares, car rentals, accommodation, and entertainment — especially if you're over 50 and want to find the very lowest rates.

Travel websites are a great way to look at a huge range of deals and offers. You can find the cheapest airfares online without making dozens of calls or going to all the websites of the individual companies. Check out these websites to get the best deal in town.

- Cheap Caribbean at *cheapcaribbean.com*

- Expedia at *expedia.com*

- Goibibo at *goibibo.com*

- Kayak at *kayak.com*

- Orbitz at *orbitz.com*

- Priceline at *priceline.com*

- Skyscanner at *skyscanner.net*

- Travelocity at *travelocity.com*

- TravelZoo at *travelzoo.com*

The web puts the world at your fingertips and helps you to get a jump on planning your next trip. Need some help deciding where to go? These websites offer general travel advice for seniors.

- Frommers.com — look at *frommers.com/slideshows/848278-best-vacation-ideas-and-destinations-for-seniors*

- Money.com — look at the travel section at *money.com/section/travel*

- Smarter Travel at *smartertravel.com*

- Stridetravel at *stridetravel.com*

- Trips to Discover at *tripstodiscover.com*

Cool apps to help with vacation planning

Both the Apple App Store and the Google Play Store have a Travel category, which contain apps that can be used for almost every aspect of your vacation, including these areas.

Getting packed. These apps can be used to create packing lists, and you can check off items as they are safely packed away. Better still, you can keep lists for specific locations or activities so you will know what to take for every vacation.

Planning your time. Being organized on vacation can make all the difference, particularly if you have limited time available. Apps for planning your itinerary are an excellent option, so you can keep notes of all the things you want to do. However, don't plan things too rigidly — leave some time for being spontaneous.

City guides. Every self-respecting city around the world has its own app for guiding visitors around. This will usually include advice on accommodations, getting around, eating out, sights to see, and local customs.

Getting around. If you want more detailed information for getting around a city than provided by a city guide app, you can also use transit apps for major cities around the world, covering the main forms of transport.

Vacation dilemma — which devices to take?

Packing for a vacation is definitely not the most fun part of it. Let's face it, deciding what to pack can be a chore. Now that you're tech savvy, you have another consideration — which digital devices do you take?

It's better to take the minimum that you need, since the more you have, the more you have to look after. Unless you have good reasons to take extra devices, your travel tech should consist of:

- a smartphone. This can be used for communication with family and friends back home, via text, phone, or video chatting. It is also useful for finding your way around with a maps app, and for taking photos with a camera app.

- a tablet. This can be used to view photos that you have taken, read e-books, and have video chats with the folks back home on a larger screen.

If you want to stick to the bare minimum, a smartphone should perform all the digital tasks required on vacation — although reading e-books can be a bit frustrating with the smaller screen.

Staying secure

Tablets and smartphones are valuable anywhere, but in certain locations they may be viewed as particularly lucrative items to steal. It is therefore important that you keep them out of sight as much as possible to avoid putting yourself in danger of being robbed or attacked.

---

10 travel apps to help you on your way

Everyone will have their favorite travel apps, depending on their destinations and activities. Here are some that should help cover every aspect of your vacation.

App in the Air. A comprehensive app for organizing all your flight requirements. It can store your itineraries and boarding passes, and alert you in real time about your check-in times. It can also find recommended places to eat and free Wi-Fi hotspots at your selected airport.

Flightradar24. Track flights from around the world in real time. You can follow incoming or outgoing flights, so you always know when you need to be at the airport for a flight.

GetPacked (iPadOS/iOS), or PackKing (Android). Two apps that can help you get organized before you leave. You can create packing lists for certain locations or activities, so you have them available if you make the same type of trip again.

iTranslate Translator. One of the numerous translations apps that are available. This one provides translations in over 100 languages, with male or female voices, and includes a dictionary and a phrase book.

Rome2rio: Trip Planner. An app that provides all your required travel options for a selected destination, covering accommodation, bookings you have made, and transit options.

TripAdvisor. One of the most popular travel apps, providing reviews for hotels, restaurants, and excursions for locations around the world.

TripIt. A popular and effective app for managing your vacation. Once you have booked a vacation online, send all the details to the app, and these will be included with your vacation itinerary. All the details about your flights, accommodation, car rental, and excursions will be available in one place.

Visited: Map where I've been. Keep track of places you have visited by marking them on a map with this app.

World Explorer. For finding out about your next vacation destination, this app has thousands of articles, suggestions, and recommendations for locations around the world.

XE Currency. This app can be used to convert currencies from around the globe, so you will always know how far your vacation money will go.

Staying secure

Most airlines now have an option for downloading your boarding pass to your smartphone when you check in online. You can either get a PDF document emailed to your smartphone, or download the pass to an app that stores it on your phone.

Since you can't take a flight without your boarding pass, it's good to have a backup to the hard copy version right there on your smartphone. You'll never have to worry about losing it again.

On an iPhone, you can use the Wallet app to store your boarding pass. On an Android smartphone, the Google Pay app can be used. In case of any technological malfunctions, it is best to take both the digital version of your boarding pass and a hard copy.

Pros and cons of using travel reviews

It is always useful to get other people's views on something you are going to do, whether it is buying a new car or going on vacation. The travel industry has embraced the online world when it comes to reviewing almost every aspect of a vacation.

The largest review site is TripAdvisor, as an app or at *tripadvisor.com*. It has over 700 million reviews of hotels, restaurants, cafes, excursions, and activities from around the world. You can search for specific names or locations from the TripAdvisor home page, and it provides a wealth of travel information.

In addition to TripAdvisor, some other travel review sites to look at include:

- Google at *google.com*. The old favorite Google also includes travel reviews in the wide range of services it can provide. Enter a search term such as "restaurants in Hawaii" or "hotels in Florida" and Google will show the results and reviews of selected items. You'll also see links to results from other travel review sites, such as TripAdvisor.

- Facebook at *facebook.com*. Not just for communicating with family and friends, Facebook also has an extensive review network, where users can Recommend, or Not Recommend, locations and businesses.

- Yelp at *yelp.com*. Originally just a restaurant review site, Yelp has now expanded reviews on local services and nightlife.

Websites for specific vacation services, such as hotels, also have extensive reviews of the options on their sites. Three to have a look at are *booking.com, hotels.com*, and *trivago.com*.

As helpful as review sites are, they do have their downsides. Here are some things to think about as you browse through.

Everyone reads the same reviews. Travel review sites seem to have shrunk the globe considerably, to the point where a lot of people only go to places mentioned on these sites. Many of these are excellent, but it is worth remembering that if you go somewhere that is mentioned on a review site, you can guarantee that other people will have the same idea, too.

You need to use more than one travel review site. This will give you a wider view of a particular establishment or activity. You can also consult hard-copy guidebooks but, by their very nature, they are more likely to be out of date than an online review site, which can be updated on a daily basis.

Don't become tied to review sites, or even guidebooks. Some of your best experiences may occur when you branch out on your own and trust your instincts. Traveling is sometimes about experiencing the unexpected, so ditch the review sites for at least a few of the options on your vacation.

Worldwide Wi-Fi hotspots — a lifeline for travelers

Travelers have begun to take internet access via Wi-Fi for granted and expect it wherever they go. Thankfully, these expectations are increasingly being met, as the options for connecting to Wi-Fi worldwide are growing every day.

Wi-Fi via national chains. Many national chains have free Wi-Fi access in their outlets around the country, and also around the world. If you are away from home and unable to find a Wi-Fi connection, try some of the following national chains.

- Apple Store
- Dunkin' Donuts
- McDonald's
- Starbucks
- Buffalo Wild Wings
- Marriott Hotels
- Panera Bread
- Whole Foods

Free Wi-Fi networks. A growing number of cities around the world are offering Wi-Fi networks covering areas within the city, not just individual Wi-Fi hotspots in restaurants or coffee shops.

These networks include a range of outdoor spaces, such as parks and, in some cases, even subway stations.

Wi-Fi networks such as these operate in a similar way to Wi-Fi hotspots. You connect with the network name and a password, and then you can use free Wi-Fi for as long as you are in range of the network.

Some of the cities around the world that are leading the way with free Wi-Fi networks include Barcelona, Boston, Hong Kong, New York, Osaka, Paris, San Francisco, Seoul, and Tel Aviv.

Apps for finding hotspots. Finding Wi-Fi hotspots when on vacation can be a bit hit and miss. However, a number of apps can take the guesswork out of finding hotspots, as they identify all of the available ones wherever you are in the world. Some to look at are:

- Boingo Wi-Finder (iPadOS/iOS and Android).

- Free WiFi App: WiFi map, passwords, hotspots (Android).

- Find Wi-Fi — Automatically Connect to Free Wi-Fi (Android).

- Instabridge (iPadOS/iOS and Android).

- Shaw Go WiFi Finder, covering Western Canada (iPadOS/iOS and Android).

- WiFi Around — Nearby Hotspots (iPadOS/iOS).

- Wi-Fi Finder — Connect Internet (iPadOS/iOS).

- WiFi Finder + Map (iPadOS/iOS).

- WiFi Map (iPadOS/iOS and Android).

- WiFi: WiFi map and passwords (Android).

Easily navigate around your destination

It has never been easier to research vacation destinations around the world. Not only can you find out a wealth of information about them on the web, it is also possible to navigate around them before you even get there.

This can be done with a maps app such as Google Maps or Apple's Maps app. With either of these at your fingertips, you can check out the layout of a destination and also locate restaurants and tourist attractions.

To do this using the Google Maps app, which can also be downloaded to an iPad/iPhone or an Android device:

1. Tap on *Google Maps* app to open it.

2. The Search box is located in the top left-hand corner.

3. Enter a location into the Search box. This can be a city, a street name, a zip code, a tourist feature (such as the Golden Gate Bridge), or even a restaurant. Tap on one of the search results.

4. The location is displayed on a map, as shown here.

5. To the left of the map is an information panel that provides general information about the location.

6. Tap on this button in the top right-hand corner to access the options for viewing the map.

7. In the *Map type* section, select an option for viewing the map from *Default, Satellite,* or *Terrain.*

8. In the *Map details* section, select items that will appear as an overlay on the map, from *Transit, Traffic, Biking* and *3D.*

A closer look

If you want to take your travel research a step further, use the Google Street View app to journey virtually through a location. This is displayed at street level, and you can navigate through the streets using the on-screen arrows.

6 top tips to stay healthy while you travel

When you're on vacation, you certainly don't want to waste time being sick in bed. Here are some steps you can take beforehand to help ensure you stay as healthy as possible.

Research your destination online. Find out as much as possible about where you are going. This will not only help you appreciate it more when you get there, it can be invaluable in pointing out potential health hazards. This is especially true if you'll need vaccinations or if the region has particular health concerns.

The web is ideal for finding out all the best health information for your destination. However, if you find any health warnings on the web for a certain country or area, make sure you double-check it with at least one other reliable source.

Check whether the water is safe to drink. While you're doing your research online, this is another thing to look into. If you use a travel agent, you can ask them about the water in your intended destination. If in doubt, drink bottled water.

Consult with your doctor. If you are in doubt about any health issues related to your vacation, ask your doctor for advice. Also, if you take any regular medication, make sure that you have enough for the trip.

Create reminders for medication. Use a reminders app or a calendar app to create reminders for any regular medication you have to take (and any other health issues for your trip).

Set up your smartwatch to check your heart rate. You may think you're just fine to walk all over the city, but knowing your heart rate throughout the day will help make sure you don't over-exert yourself.

Take advantage of health-related apps. Download these helpful apps to make your vacation even better.

- A water tracker app can help make sure you drink enough water throughout the day, particularly in warmer locations, to avoid dehydration.

- Use a relaxation app to help you get to sleep, which could be harder if you are in a different environment.

- A health app, or a pedometer app, will count the number of steps you take to ensure you are keeping fit on your vacation.

- Use a yoga or Pilates app to stretch and relax after a long day of sightseeing.

3 smart ways to keep your vacation photos safe

Keeping your vacation photos safe is an important part of your digital organization while away. No one wants to lose weeks of vacation photos before you even get home. Here are some steps to take to ensure it doesn't happen.

Back up photos to the cloud. For iPadOS/iOS devices, use iCloud to back up your photos while on vacation. For Android, use Google Drive. Also, third-party options such as Dropbox can be used from any device.

Back up photos to an external device. If you only have mobile devices, such as a tablet and a smartphone, it may be possible to use a USB adapter to connect a flash drive to the device, and copy your photos here. However, this is only compatible with some models, so check your device's specifications first.

Email photos to yourself. To ensure that your photos are not just saved on your tablet or smartphone, or in the cloud, you can also email them to yourself.

This will keep them in your Inbox until you want to access and download them. Emailing is best for a small number of photos, such as your favorite ones from your vacation.

Simplify your life with a digital assistant

3 special helpers make your life easier

Smart speakers and their digital voice assistants are becoming increasingly popular in the home. Simply ask them a question or give them a command, and they will do your bidding. No more searching online for current weather conditions or the hours of your favorite restaurant.

And they can do so much more. They set reminders, play music, tune in to radio stations, provide a daily news update, connect to a smart TV to control your programs, control smart home devices such as lighting and heating, and even enable online shopping just with voice commands.

You can even add skills and actions to make them more productive, similar to downloading new apps to your tablet or smartphone.

The major technology companies have recognized the benefits of smart speakers in the home. The three main digital voice assistants, and their related smart speakers, are produced by three of the technology giants — Amazon, Google, and Apple. Here's what you need to know.

Alexa. Amazon's digital voice assistant is used with the Echo range of smart speakers, which come in various sizes and can perform different tasks. For instance, the Echo Show has a screen that can be used to make video calls, and also view movies and TV shows from a streaming service such as Amazon Prime Video or Netflix.

Google Assistant. This is Google's digital voice assistant that is used with the Google Home smart speaker. In addition to the standard model, there is also a Google Home Mini version, so the system can be used in different rooms around the home.

Siri. Apple's digital voice assistant operates with the HomePod smart speaker. This is the most expensive of the three smart speakers and, like the other two, has excellent sound quality.

A closer look

Like any digital device, smart speakers sometimes do not behave the way they should. The two main issues that can occur are problems with the Wi-Fi connection to your home network and sound issues.

For Wi-Fi connection problems, check in the Settings section of the smart speaker's companion app, which is used to set up the smart speaker. If the Wi-Fi connection is not working, try moving the smart speaker closer to the Wi-Fi router, or reset the Wi-Fi connection in the smart speaker's app.

For sound issues, make sure the volume on the smart speaker is turned up, and check the sound settings in the smart speaker's companion app.

Set up your smart speaker in 4 simple steps

Setting up a smart speaker and its digital voice assistant is usually done with an app on a tablet or smartphone. This will enable the digital voice assistant to connect to your home Wi-Fi network, so that it can then access all the required content from its linked service, such as Amazon, Google, or Apple.

The Google and Apple digital voice assistants usually have the relevant apps, Google Assistant and Home, pre-installed on their respective tablets and smartphones. The Amazon Alexa app has to be downloaded to a tablet or smartphone from either the Apple App Store or the Google Play Store.

The general process for setting up a digital voice assistant is:

1. Open the relevant app on a tablet or smartphone, and access the Settings option.

2. Select the device to be set up.

3. Select the Wi-Fi network for the digital voice assistant to connect to.

4. You will be notified if the setup has been successful, at which point the digital voice assistant should be ready to use.

Apps — the best way to manage your home assistant

Digital voice assistants can be set up and controlled via their companion apps. The apps can be used on a range of devices to manage digital voice assistants.

The companion apps for the different digital voice assistants are:

*   Amazon Alexa app for Alexa on the Amazon Echo smart speaker. This can be used on iPadOS/iOS and Android mobile devices. You can use the app to set up and apply settings to Alexa and also add skills that expand its functionality.

*   The Google Assistant app for the Google Assistant on the Google Home smart speaker. You can use it on iPadOS/iOS and Android mobile devices to connect to a Google Home device and apply settings for it.

*   The Apple Home app for Siri on the HomePod smart speaker. This is only available on iPadOS/iOS mobile

devices, and is designed specifically to control smart home devices using Siri. For general setup options for Siri, the Settings app can be used on an iPad/iPhone (Settings > Siri & Search).

How to wake up your sleeping device

Smart speakers are always listening, waiting for an appropriate instruction, so they can provide a response. You need to speak a specific word or phrase so the smart speaker knows when to react. This is known as the "wake word," and different devices have their own options.

- For Alexa on an Echo smart speaker, the wake word is "Alexa." This can be changed in the Settings of the Amazon Alexa app. To do this, open the Amazon Alexa app, and tap on the menu button in the top left-hand corner. Select *Device Settings*, and select the device for which you want to change the wake word. Tap on the *Wake Word* button, and select a new wake word as required.

- For the Google Assistant on a Google Home smart speaker, the wake word is "Hey Google" or "OK Google."

- For Siri on the Apple HomePod smart speaker, the wake word is "Hey Siri."

Staying secure

Since smart speakers are always listening for their wake word, it is possible they can be activated without your knowledge. There have been instances of smart speakers recording conversations without anyone being aware of it as well as other stories that spark concern. These are rare occurrences, but it's important to remember that smart speakers are "always on" and could be recording anything you say.

---

11 fun questions put your digital friend to the test

Smart speakers really are quite intelligent, and they can answer a wide range of questions. Here are some helpful, and even fun, questions you might want to ask. Remember to start each one with the wake word of your particular voice assistant.

"What's the news today?" This can be in the form of a news briefing, using several different news outlets. You can specify which outlets you want to receive your news from, and also the order in which it is given. So you could have reports from a couple of news services and a sports update as well.

"What's the capital of India?" Digital voice assistants are excellent for answering a range of factual questions.

"What will the weather be like next week?" Weather forecasts are a particularly strong point for digital voice assistants, and they can give you the weather conditions from around the world.

"How far is 15 miles in kilometers?" Conversions can be handled with ease by digital voice assistants, whether it is distances, temperatures, weights, or currencies.

"What movies are playing near me?" As long as you have entered your location into the digital voice assistant's settings, it can provide you with local information for items such as movie theaters and restaurants.

"How do you say 'Good morning' in Spanish?" Digital voice assistants are excellent at linguistics and are able to translate over 100 languages.

"Find me a burrito recipe." Looking for inspiration in the kitchen? Just ask your digital voice assistant for suggestions and recipes.

"What is 47 multiplied by 33?" Never reach for a calculator again. Just use your digital voice assistant's math skills. That skill alone makes it worth its weight in gold.

"What do you look like?" Digital voice assistants can answer some surreal or philosophical questions, but the answers may not always provide intellectual insight.

"Tell me a joke." Digital voice assistants can be used to tell jokes, although the quality is perhaps questionable.

"Can you sing me a song?" Digital voice assistants can also sing songs that they have made up, but their singing is often on a level with their joke telling.

A closer look

You may be surprised at how human your digital voice assistant appears sometimes. When you ask it a question, it will tell you if it can't understand what you're saying and, in some cases, ask you to repeat it.

Smart speaker — a powerful ally when you're home alone

If you had a smart speaker during the COVID-19 pandemic that started in 2020, you had the very latest health information right at your fingertips.

During the coronavirus outbreak, smart speakers were constantly updated with news and advice about the issues surrounding the pandemic, such as health information and news relating to the situation.

All you had to do was say "[Wake word], tell me the latest COVID-19 news" or "[Wake word], give me the most up-to-date health advice on COVID-19."

During any national or international event, the smart speaker's manufacturer will provide this type of information. It is an excellent way to keep up to date with significant events, especially if you're confined to your home for an extended period of time, for any reason.

Smart speakers are great companions as they do not need any physical interaction and can keep you informed and entertained with news, sports updates, music, audiobooks, jokes, general knowledge facts, and much more.

Expand your digital assistant's knowledge and skills

Alexa and the Google Assistant come with a lot of knowledge already pre-installed. In reality this comes from the databases of their respective companies, Amazon and Google. However, it is possible to expand the knowledge of Alexa or the Google Assistant.

This is done through the use of skills (Alexa), or actions (Google Assistant), which is the equivalent of downloading a new app to your tablet or smartphone to increase its functionality.

Skills with Alexa. The tasks that Alexa can perform are provided through skills. Some skills are already pre-installed for Alexa, like the time and date, while others, such as relaxation sounds, can be added. To add more skills for use with Alexa:

1. Open the *Amazon Alexa* app, and tap on the menu button.

2. Tap on the *Skills & Games* button.

3. The Skills & Games home page is where you can view available skills and then download them for use with Alexa. Tap on the *Discover* tab to view the latest recommended skills.

4. Tap on a skill in the Discover window, or search for one using the *Categories* tab, or tap on the magnifying glass icon in the top right-hand corner of the window to search for skills using keywords.

5. For the selected skill, tap on the *Enable To Use* button above a description of the skill.

6. The skill is added to the *Your Skills* window of the Skills & Games section. The number of currently enabled skills is also displayed.

7. To disable a skill, access the *Your Skills* window, select the skill, and tap on the *Disable Skill* button. Skills can be enabled again, using the same process that was used to enable them initially.

Actions with Google Assistant. As with Alexa, the Google Assistant can perform an impressive range of tasks with the Google Home smart speaker. However, it is possible to expand the Assistant's functionality through the use of actions, which is the equivalent of adding skills to Alexa.

There are over a million actions that can be added for the Google Assistant from the Google Assistant app. To do this:

1. Open the *Google Assistant* app, and tap on this icon on the bottom toolbar.

2. Suggested actions are listed, as shown.

3. Tap on an item to view its details.

4. Tap on the *Try It* button to activate the action.

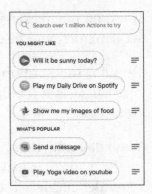

A closer look

Apple's Siri does not have additional skills or actions that can be added in the same way as for Alexa and the Google Assistant. However, apps that are designed to work with Siri can be downloaded from the Apple App Store to provide extra functions.

Never forget to take your meds ever again

Do you need to be reminded to take your medication or pay your monthly bills? Ask your favorite assistant for help. Your digital voice assistant can set a reminder to make an announcement at a specific time, thus relieving you of the burden of trying to remember everything.

You can set up reminders using a voice command to Alexa, Google Assistant, or Siri, but you may want to create them using the companion apps (for Alexa and Google Assistant), so you can see the details of the reminder. This is usually done in the app's Settings, where the time and date can be set for the reminder.

Using reminders on a smart speaker is a useful way to make sure you never miss a range of activities that you do daily, through the week, on the weekends, or weekly. Here are some areas where you can set reminders and free up your mind for more enjoyable pursuits.

Regular medication. If you have to take any medication on a regular basis, set a reminder accordingly, for either a daily item or a weekly one.

Weekday activities. For something that you have to do every weekday, such as picking up your grandkids from school, set a reminder and it will be announced Monday to Friday.

Paying weekly or monthly bills. If you have any bills that need to be paid regularly, a reminder can be added for them.

Social activities. Want to make sure you don't miss your weekly bridge game? If you have a regular social event, it can be added as a reminder for the appropriate time.

Keeping in touch. If you call a family member or friend on a regular basis, a reminder can be a good way to ensure you never forget phoning at a specific time. This is particularly useful if the other person lives in a different time zone.

Let your home assistant bring music to your ears

Smart speakers contain high quality speakers and are ideal for playing music around the home. You have several music options to choose from.

- Listen for free to music that is available through your digital voice assistant's connected music library, such as Amazon Music for Alexa, and Google Play Music/YouTube Music for the Google Assistant.

- Listen to radio stations.

- Subscribe to music streaming services such as Amazon Music Unlimited or Spotify Premium. There is also a free version of Spotify, which includes advertisements.

When playing music, Alexa, Google Assistant, and Siri can perform a range of tasks. Simply tell them what you want them to do.

- "[Wake word], play [album] by [artist]."

- "[Wake word], play next/previous song" (if an album is being played).

- "[Wake word], play [song name] by [artist]."

- "[Wake word], pause/stop song."

- "[Wake word], play songs with cars in the title."

- "[Wake word], volume up one."

Special features make it easy to keep in touch

Another advantage of a smart speaker is that you can use it to communicate with your family and others in a variety of ways.

- Talk to family members throughout your home. If you have more than one smart speaker, you can send messages between them, just like having an intercom system. No more shouting from one floor to the other.

- Send text messages. If one of your contacts has a cellphone number included, you can send them a text message by saying, "[Wake word], text Brad and say 'Hi Brad.'"

- Send messages to a companion app. Messages can also be sent from the smart speaker to its companion app, and vice versa.

- Make phone calls. As with text messages, voice calls can be made to anyone with a cellphone number in the smart speaker's contacts. For example, you can say "[Wake word], call Ann." The smart speaker will repeat the request to confirm you are calling the right person in your contacts, and then make the call. You'll use the smart speaker to conduct the conversation, so remember that anyone nearby can hear what you're saying. Obviously, this is not the best option if you want to talk privately.

A closer look

If you want to use your speaker to chat, you need to activate the communication function in its companion app. For instance, for Alexa, look for the *Communicate* button on the bottom toolbar in the Amazon Alexa app. This is where you can specify and manage your communication options.

Simplify your shopping with Alexa

Once you get computer savvy, you may do a lot of shopping online. Amazon makes it even easier for you by programming its Echo smart speaker to allow voice purchasing. After you set it up, you simply ask Alexa to make your purchases for you.

The Google Home smart speaker can also be used for voice shopping, from Google Express or Walmart.

To shop with Alexa, enable 1-Click purchasing for your Amazon account on the Amazon website. Then set up the Amazon Alexa app to enable voice purchasing.

1. Open the *Amazon Alexa* app, and tap on the menu button.

2. Tap on the *Things to Try* button.

3. Tap on the *Shopping* button.

4. Details about using voice shopping are displayed. Tap on the *Enable Voice Shopping* button.

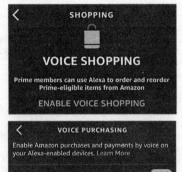

5. Drag the *Purchase by voice* button On to enable voice shopping, provided 1-Click purchasing has also been activated for your account on the Amazon website.

6. Once Alexa has been set up for voice shopping, you can start making purchases on Amazon using voice commands. Simply say, "Alexa, buy now" after Alexa has reviewed the request.

If you're not sure about it, you can check out the item on the Amazon website before you buy it. When you ask for a specific item, Alexa will repeat the details and place the item in your Amazon Basket. You can review the details on the website and then choose whether to buy it.

After you place your order you can check your Amazon Orders History page to verify that it went through.

Staying secure

If you have activated voice shopping for Alexa, it is a good idea to have some form of security to prevent anyone making unwanted purchases using voice purchasing with your Amazon account. One option is to create a four-digit voice code that has to be entered whenever a purchase is made. This can be added on the same page you enable voice shopping in the Amazon Alexa app.

Go hands-free with smart home devices

Create a smart home — it's easier than you think

The concept of the smart home — one in which some of the electronic devices are controlled via voice controls, apps, or accessed remotely — is not a science fiction vision of the future. It is very much part of the here and now, and a realistic, affordable option.

For a smart home to work to its full potential, you need a number of elements in place.

- Smart home devices, including lighting, heating, and security.

- Apps on tablets and smartphones, and online access. These can be used to manage and control smart home devices.

- Smart speakers and digital voice assistants for controlling smart home devices with voice commands.

It is not essential for smart homes to use all three of these elements. For example, you can operate your smart home devices without a smart speaker. But to get the complete experience, it is worth having them all.

The good news about setting up and using smart home devices is that it is easier than you think. You don't need a lot of technical knowledge, and once you are up and running, you may wonder how you ever lived without them.

Lighting. Smart lighting systems, including smart light bulbs, and a bridge that connects to your Wi-Fi router, are a great way to get started with a smart home. Individual lights can be controlled around the home with an app, a smart speaker, or a remote control.

Groups of lights can also be used to create artistic effects, known as scenes. Smart lighting apps contain a range of settings that can give you maximum control and flexibility over your lighting system.

Heating. A smart heating system can be controlled through an app or a smart speaker so you can turn it on and off, set the temperature, and create a timed schedule.

Smart heating systems can also be used to determine whether anyone is at home, and regulate the temperature accordingly. That's a great way to save money on your heating bills.

Security. You can install extensive smart security systems, using external cameras and alarms, and control them via an app or a smart speaker.

In addition to security cameras, smart locks can add more security to your home. They can be activated by key cards, key fobs, apps, smart speakers, time limited PIN codes, and even remotely.

Drapes and blinds. Drapes and blinds can be controlled using an app, or a voice command to a smart speaker, providing they have an electronic mechanism to open and close them.

Plugs and sockets. You can install individual smart plugs throughout your home, so you can turn your devices on and off without having to physically press a switch.

Amazing apps put you in control

It's remarkable to think you can control your home with the touch of a button. And you don't even have to be there to do it. It's all thanks to amazing apps. Here are some things to know about smart home apps.

- Smart home devices usually have their own branded companion apps that can be used to control them. For example, the Philips Hue smart lighting app is used with the Hue smart lighting system.

- Generic apps can be used to control multiple devices. These are not linked to a specific product and can control a range of smart home devices, such as lighting, heating, and plugs, rather than just one individual item.

- Apps can be downloaded from the Apple App Store and the Google Play Store, and can be used on most tablets and smartphones to control smart home devices.

- You can use the apps to control your smart home devices when you are at home, and also remotely when you are away from home — even out of the country.

- Apps can perform standard actions such as turning devices on or off, and they can also perform more complicated tasks, such as creating a routine to apply a number of actions to the device in sequence.

Staying secure

Digital technology delivers a great many benefits, and sometimes it even provides some unexpected bonuses. During the COVID-19 pandemic, one of the ways the disease spread was through infected surfaces, including light switches and plugs.

Since the smart home can remove the need for physically turning devices on and off, it means the risk of touching infected items is greatly reduced. Just another way technology can help your overall health and well-being.

Follow these steps to make setup a snap

The operation of smart home devices is generally similar for different types of devices, although some require extra hardware for them to operate. The general process for setting up a smart device in the home is as follows.

1. Physically install the device. For example, fit a smart light bulb into a light fitting, plug a smart plug into a power socket, or install a smart thermostat for smart heating. You may want an electrician to help with the last one.

2. Download the relevant app for the smart device. Apps can be downloaded to tablets and smartphones from the Apple App Store (for iPadOS/iOS devices) or the Google Play Store (for Android devices).

3. Install a bridge to your Wi-Fi router. This only applies to some smart home devices, such as lighting systems. If a bridge is used, it acts as the connection between the smart home device and the router and provides a greater range of functionality. Some devices can communicate directly with their companion app or a smart speaker via your Wi-Fi router without the need for a separate bridge.

4. To use a smart home device with a smart speaker as well as an app, enable the required skill/action for your smart speaker.

5. Turn on the smart home device if it has not already been turned on in Step 1.

6. Open the device's app. Initially, you may have to set up an account for the app, using an email address and password. This will enable you to control the device remotely when you are away from home.

7. The device has to be added to the app so the app can communicate with it and control it. Tap on the *Add device* option (or similar) to add a new device.

8. Select the device to be added, and complete the setup process for the device. This will include linking it to your home Wi-Fi router, so the app and the device can communicate with each other.

9. Once the device has been set up, you will then be able to control it through the app, or by using a smart speaker. This includes turning it on or off and setting timed schedules for the device.

A closer look

Smart lighting is one of the most accessible and affordable options for adding smart devices to your home. It can be set up in minutes, does not need an electrician (or any electrical knowledge), and creates a dramatic impact once it is up and running. Smart lighting also works impressively with smart speakers.

The best news about a smart lighting system is that all the components can be linked to existing elements in your home, and there is no need to alter any current equipment.

Save energy — and money — with smart heating

Smart heating systems let you control your central heating with a wireless smart thermostat that you manage through a related app or with a smart speaker. You can also control temperature remotely, so you always have the ability to monitor and manage your heating.

A smart thermostat is connected to your home Wi-Fi and can be used to control and manage your heating in a number of different ways.

- Turn your heating on or off, either through an app or a smart speaker, using a command such as, "[Wake word], turn heating on/off."

- Set the heat to a specific temperature.

- Create a schedule for your heating to come on or go off at specific times. This can be as many times as you like during the day.

- Turn your heating on or off remotely (using the app).

- Use an economy setting so you can keep your heat on without wasting unnecessary energy.

- Apply a frost setting when you are away from home if you are worried about freezing pipes.

The elements of a smart heating system include:

- a heat link thermostat that connects to the central heating system. The heating system is then left on, and the heat link thermostat takes instructions from the smart thermostat. A heat link thermostat should be fitted by a qualified installer.

- a smart thermostat (also known as a learning thermostat), which communicates with the heat link thermostat connected to the central heating system. The smart thermostat is able to monitor room temperatures and adjust them accordingly. The smart thermostat can be placed anywhere in the home.

A companion app is required to set up and manage a smart heating system. These can be downloaded to a tablet or a smartphone from the Apple App Store or the Google Play Store.

Secure your house with high-tech wizardry

Security is a major issue for any homeowner as it is important to know that your home is as secure as possible. You'll be amazed at the options you have with a smart home system. Here's what you can expect.

Security cameras. In addition to burglar alarms and security lights, you can install smart security cameras that you can monitor on your tablet or smartphone to keep an eye on your home even when you're away.

- Internal security cameras. Indoor smart cameras can be used to monitor individual rooms in the home.

- External security cameras. Cameras can be affixed around the exterior of your home so they can video anything that takes place. These are usually fixed in one spot and offer a single view. It is worth getting as high a quality camera as possible as this will ensure a better picture quality, and images will be clearer. Also, it is important to use cameras that can capture images in the dark, using infrared or a night-vision equivalent.

Security systems. Some manufacturers provide full smart alarm systems that can be controlled through an app on your tablet or smartphone. Some of the elements of these include:

- Wall-mounted alarm. This is what goes off if unexpected activity is detected by the alarm sensors in the home. The alarm will flash and emit a sound when it is activated.

- Smart alarm app. This is the companion app for the smart alarm system. Once it has been downloaded to your tablet or smartphone it can be used to arm and disarm the alarm system. The app can also be used to configure the alarm to your own requirements, and it will receive alerts if any suspicious activity is detected.

- Manual control unit. This is located within the home and is used to manually arm and disarm the alarm, and apply settings.

- Internal door and window sensors. These are used to determine if doors and windows have been opened while the alarm is armed. If this happens, the wall-mounted alarm will be activated, and an appropriate alert will be sent to the app on your tablet or smartphone.

- Internal motion sensors. These are used to detect movement in the home while the alarm is armed. If this happens, the wall-mounted alarm will be activated, and an appropriate alert will be sent to the app on your tablet or smartphone.

Video doorbells. These not only give you peace of mind in terms of viewing who is at your door, they also enable you to talk to people while they wait to come in. Here's what you get.

- Physical doorbell. This is affixed at a convenient position at the front or back door. It contains a standard doorbell and also a video camera that records visitors once they have pressed the bell.

- Companion app. This is used to view the video feed from the doorbell. You can also use it to speak to people who are waiting at the door. They should be able to communicate with you too, using the internal microphone in the doorbell.

Let technology help keep your home tidy

Within the world of smart home technology, you can even find automated devices that will help you with your chores. These include robotic vacuum cleaners. Once you set them up, you can leave them to do the hard work, while you spend your time doing something more enjoyable.

Robotic vacuum cleaners are now widely available and, although they are generally still more expensive than their manual counterparts, they are an effective and efficient way to keep your home clean. You'll find a range of options in terms of price and function. Here are some things to look at to help you choose.

Navigation. Your home is full of objects of different shapes and sizes, so you want a robotic vacuum cleaner that can navigate around them effectively. It does this with either cameras or sensors, or both, to identify any objects to be avoided. When robotic vacuum cleaners identify an obstacle, they will either navigate around it or move off in another direction to avoid it.

Mobility. The majority of robotic vacuum cleaners use wheels to move around. Another option is to use tank-type tracks that can move over uneven surfaces and bumps. This option provides greater functionality than for devices using wheels, although they may not maneuver as well. Unfortunately, they usually draw the line at navigating up and down stairs.

Cleaning. Look for a robotic vacuum cleaner with brushes that extend along the width of the device, so it can clean edges as it moves over them. The height of the device is also important. You want it to be low enough to clean underneath furniture if possible. Measure the gaps between various pieces of furniture and the floor, and compare these with the device's height.

Charging. Robotic cleaners usually need to use a base station to charge their battery. This is plugged into an electrical socket and then placed on the floor so the device can return to it automatically when it recognizes its power is running down. When looking for a robotic vacuum cleaner, check the runtime — how long the device can operate without the need to recharge.

Index